SECOND EDITION

Systemic Coaching and Constellations

The principles, practices and application for individuals, teams and groups

John Whittington

KoganPage

LONDON · PHILADELPHIA · NEW DELHI

First published in Great Britain and the United States in 2012 by Kogan Page Limited
Second edition 2016

2nd Floor, 45 Gee Street	1518 Walnut Street, Suite 1100	4737/23 Ansari Road
London EC1V 3RS	Philadelphia PA 19102	Daryaganj
United Kingdom	USA	New Delhi 110002
www.koganpage.com		India

© John Whittington, 2012, 2016

The right of John Whittington to be identified as the author of this work has been asserted by him in accordance with the Copyright, Designs and Patents Act 1988.

ISBN   978 0 7494 7549 9
E-ISBN   978 0 7494 7550 5

British Library Cataloguing-in-Publication Data

A CIP record for this book is available from the British Library

Library of Congress Cataloging-in-Publication Data

Names: Whittington, John, 1958- author.
Title: Systemic coaching and constellations : the principles, practices and
   application for individuals, teams and groups / John Whittington.
Description: Second edition. | London ; Philadelphia : Kogan Page, 2016. |
   Includes index.
Identifiers: LCCN 2015040200| ISBN 9780749475499 | ISBN 9780749475505 (ebk)
Subjects: LCSH: Employees--Coaching of. | Executive coaching.
Classification: LCC HF5549.5.C53 W486 2016 | DDC 658.3/124--dc23 LC record available at
http://lccn.loc.gov/2015040200

Typeset by Graphicraft Limited, Hong Kong
Print production managed by Jellyfish
Printed and bound in Great Britain by Ashford Colour Press Ltd

CONTENTS

PART THREE   Application 155

ACKNOWLEDGEMENTS

I'd like to thank all those who have guided, supported and encouraged my journey into and through this approach to working with relationship systems. Firstly Judith Hemming, who shared many insights and fresh ways of seeing systems that changed my work and life, and continue to resource me many years later. Richard Wallstein and Jutta ten Herkel, consistent in their challenges for my truth in every encounter, walked alongside as I began to facilitate. Ty Francis, who did so much to pioneer this approach in organizational life in the UK, created a safe space to learn and teach. Vivian Broughton, Gaye Donaldson, Terry Ingham and Sue Abbotson shared their energy and perspectives generously, each adding to the richness of my journey.

Nicola Dunn, who can disentangle system dynamics with a few well-chosen words and respectfully reveal hidden loyalties in personal and business systems, continues to share her insights generously. Her reading and critique of the penultimate draft of the new chapter on 'Belonging' in this second edition added important nuances and additional levels of clarity.

Many other individuals have shared their perspectives through their writing. These first- and second-generation facilitators and authors include Hunter Beaumont, Gunthard Weber, Bertold Ulsamer, Albrecht Mahr, Franz Rupert, Gary Stuart, Dan Booth-Cohen, John Payne, Klaus Horn, Regine Brick, Marcus Speh Birkenkrahe and Daan van Kampenhout. With thanks to you all for your wise words.

Some time after a training in family constellations and my journey into coaching and then systemic coaching, Jan Jacob Stam emerged as a teacher with a particular focus on organizational systems. Thank you for your inspiring, co-creative approach and your encouragement of me as a writer and teacher.

All of us were inspired by the work and teachings of originator Bert Hellinger, without whom none of this would be. His extraordinary synthesis of philosophies and methods, combined with his unique insights into the human condition and relationship systems in life and at work, have left us with a robust methodology and a breadth and depth of insights that resource and sustain systems. Because of Bert and then many others who developed this work in organizational and other contexts, thousands of individuals, families, teams and other systems now flourish.

Janet, Lynn, Paul, thank you for allowing me to facilitate family and personal issues workshops with you for several years. That experience led to such deep learning about family systems and continues to nourish my teaching and facilitation in the world of leadership and team coaching.

I would not have so much experience in this work without my clients, with whom I have learnt so much about leadership, organizational vitality and the application of this way of working in many different contexts, industries and locations. Thank you all for so willingly venturing into the system and the unknown in search of systemic solutions.

This book emerged naturally out of the trainings that I'm privileged to facilitate. I continue to learn from the searching questions coming from such a rich and wide range of experienced coaches. I don't always have all the answers, but know I can rely on the stance and methodology of systemic constellations to reveal them.

Thank you to Roman who originally invited me to take the trainings into the Czech Republic. Working with you, Dana and interpreter and now co-facilitator Pavel is always such a pleasure. Dariusz, who invited me to facilitate the training in Warsaw and subsequently translated and published this book in the Polish market, I thank you for the first invitation and the many that followed. Agnieszka interprets with such speed and calm clarity, adding depth to the work. My thanks to Janet who invited me to travel to Seattle to facilitate the trainings there and to many other hosts from St Petersburg to Milan and from Glasgow to Toronto; thank you for inviting and hosting in such welcoming ways.

A community of professional practice and learning has grown out of the trainings and I know that the next generation of facilitators, teachers and writers is now emerging. That is a delight and the numbers grow, slowly, all the time. The world and the world of coaching will benefit greatly from your expression and application of this profound and yet very practical way of working with individuals, teams and whole systems.

This book would not have begun or been completed without the support of Jo Howard, who enthusiastically introduced me to the publishers. My thanks go to the Kogan Page team for their support through the publishing process and their invitation to create this second edition. My thanks to David Clutterbuck, who enthusiastically agreed to write a Foreword to the first edition, and to Chris Dalton, who agreed to introduce this one.

I'd like to thank my support team of Sue and Steve, who, through their patient administration of all I do in my work as a coach and facilitator, create the space for me to think, write and teach. Thanks to my sons Sean and Ollie for their understanding and patience while I write, and my partner Loretta for her quiet wisdom, insightful observations and love throughout.

Since the first edition of this book my mother, aged 93, died peacefully in her sleep. I thank her and my father, now 93 himself, for the life they so lovingly gave me. I dedicate this book to them.

FOREWORD TO THE
SECOND EDITION

If you want to learn how to untie knots among the interconnected threads of personal, professional or organizational systems, then you've come to the right place.

I know from both my personal experience and professional practice that systemic constellations are an extremely powerful and effective way of resolving inertia and embedded patterns. A willingness simply to stand in the truth of a relationship system is perhaps all you need to get started in this field. But that's saying a lot, because it asks you to trust that the process itself will guide you from what is to what could be.

Although the principles and practices of working with systemic constellations are simple and intuitive, becoming a facilitator is also a personal journey. For this reason, having the right guide for that journey is essential. Bring your own interest and curiosity and let it meet the experience, humility and systemic perspective that John Whittington brings to his work, and you have all the necessary ingredients.

Anyone who has already tried this work will appreciate that the process of facilitating a constellation is by its nature challenging to capture in words. Like the systems they represent, constellations are experiential, embodied and personal. In his writing John has managed to tread the delicate line between showing and telling with both precision and clarity.

Having the first edition to hand while I work with management teams, MBA students and individuals has helped me maintain awareness, focus and balance. It has also given me the courage to trust that a system is the best explanation of itself. This has been proved for me time and again, in different contexts and across different cultures.

John has prompted a generation of practitioners to focus their efforts into the heart of the system, beyond the individual or team in front of them. The system itself becomes the client and that's a subtle but important shift of focus.

An intelligent, enquiring and vibrant community of professional practice is now emerging and this book offers to support that constellation as it takes the work even further into the world of coaching and organizational development.

Chris Dalton
Associate Professor of Management Learning,
Henley Business School

PREFACE TO THE SECOND EDITION

Over recent years the words 'system' and 'systemic' have entered the vocabulary of all of us who watch the news. People talk about 'systemic failure', 'systemic risk' and 'systemic health problems'. People say that there are challenges 'in the system' and talk of all kinds of things being 'systemic'.

In the world of coaching and organizational development this has resulted in some useful understanding but also some confusion. Some get the words 'system' and 'systemic' mixed up with ideas about coaching teams and groups. However, truly systemic coaching is coaching that prioritizes the system, whether that is in one-to-one coaching, team development or group work.

When I teach and write about systems and 'systemic coaching' I'm sharing an understanding of what sustains and limits relationship systems. The hidden organizing principles of systems that impact us all as individuals, whether alone or when we gather with others in groups and teams.

So 'systemic coaching' is coaching that prioritizes the system and is informed by an understanding of the organizing principles of systems. This information and perspective is embodied in the inner attitude or 'stance' of the coach and shared through the application of systemic questions, interventions and constellations. The stance and methodology can be applied in all supervision contexts, individual coaching and leadership development, team and group coaching as well as large group interventions, organizational design and development.

If that sounds unlikely I encourage you to read the case studies written by those who have trained in this work. There you will see the range of application from individual leadership development to team coaching and supervision in multiple contexts.

In general my students are braver and more imaginative than I am, and it's their work that is so worth reading if you want to understand how this approach can reach into and support client systems. There are more still on the Coaching Constellations website so you have lots of different contexts to browse.

In the first edition I made only a passing reference to the importance and impact of the deep human need to belong. An understanding of this need is one of the distinctive characteristics of this kind of coaching and supports the shift from linear interventions and goals to systemic interventions and embodied solutions.

It's a pleasure to include a new chapter on this subject (Chapter 3) and when you feel ready, I encourage you to explore this and the dynamics around belonging in more detail, if you want to deepen your understanding of systems, your personal journey and professional practice.

I enjoy sharing systemic coaching and constellations because it opens such a rich, safe and profound space in individuals and groups. Constellation after constellation opens like a flower, revealing deep and settling truths beyond all the stories and judgements. The extraordinary process of representative perception in workshops and one-to-one settings remains hard to fully explain but is a process that I know I can rely on completely. Every time, all the time, it works and delivers.

I also enjoy sharing this because working completely blind with no information – often with people who have no previous experience of constellations or what's meant by 'systemic' – is a wonderful way to practice letting go of my naturally sceptical mind. Exploring, testing, teaching and learning at the same time.

The pleasure of supporting others, coaches and clients alike, in dethroning their rational minds and surrendering their authority to the authority of the system is one I feel privileged to have on a regular basis.

It's also such a pleasure to see coaches bring their way of working alongside this way, integrating both, whether it's TA, psychometrics, psychodynamics, Gestalt, Spiral Dynamics, goal-orientated or values-based coaching. The systemic coaching approach supports, challenges and yet nourishes others, rather than competing with them. It adds something, another dimension, with great respect for what is also already present.

I knew I had to write the original book, published in 2012, for myself, to clarify and expand my thinking. I have to write to find out what's true, to find out what I think, what I really feel. It's a private process, one that distils, orders and settles my thoughts and feelings. It's also a somatic experience which generates feelings of complete stuckness and total release and flow. Anyone who has facilitated a constellation will know that feeling.

The fact that so many people read the first edition and that there was demand for a second was an unexpected but welcome outcome, all the more so as I had never published before. So, even though I sometimes have to pretend that I'm still writing privately to find and express my truth, thank you for being there, wherever you are and in whatever systems you belong.

Jean Malaquais put it well when he said: 'The only time I know that something is true is the moment I discover it in the act of writing.'

So thank you for reading this, the second edition of my first book. It expresses what I, my clients and students experience as true.

I hope you find it useful and resourcing for you, your life and work.

CASE STUDY CREDITS

This book includes contributions from coaches, my peers and students from across the world, as well as a selection of my own work. Each brings to life the application of the principles and practices in different contexts. With many thanks to all coaches and their clients who so willingly shared.

In order of appearance the case studies contributed by others are:

Looking for leadership
Coach: John Whittington, London, UK
Client: A change management consultant
198

Past, present, future
Coach/facilitator: John Whittington, London, UK
Client: The boards of the EMCC and the ICF
201

Talk Talk
Workshop facilitator: Maggie Rose, Executive Coach, Southampton, UK
Client: TalkTalk Telecom Group plc, one of the UK's leading broadband, landline, TV and mobile providers
205

Finding authority
Coach: Sarah Cornally, executive coach, Sydney, Australia
Client: Anonymous
217

Be useful, not helpful
Facilitator: Jane Cox, coaching supervisor, Ipswich, UK
Supervisee: Kirsty an internal coach and senior manager within a local government authority.
224

A line of men
Coach: David Presswell, executive coach and team facilitator, London, UK
Client: Michael
263

The heart of the matter
Coach: John Whittington, London, UK
Client: A writer
266

The flow of love
Coach: Wendy Bedborough, London, UK
Client: Anna
268

~

Workshop and studio photography by Tony Harris

~

Illustrations by Joan Scarrott

Orientation
A guide for your journey

The most effective way to understand constellations is to experience them. This makes the process of writing, and indeed reading, about systemic coaching and constellations rather counter-intuitive! They are something to experience, not just to read about.

This has led to a book in which I have tried to maintain a similar path through the principles and practices to that in teaching and when facilitating, where following the energy, the invisible air currents and interests of the group, leads to a deep learning. With this in mind I've included many of the questions that are often asked in workshops and trainings in two Q&A sections.

Case studies – the work in action – are also a central part of this book and will, I hope, support each reader to find their own way into this way of working. They come from my own work but also from my peers and students around the world, each bringing their own facilitation style and approach, each at different stages of their own professional journeys. They will give a flavour of application, one that you will also need to taste for yourself through direct experience.

Alongside the Q&As and case studies are a selection of practical exercises you can try yourself and then, as understanding and confidence grow, start applying with your clients, in one-to-one and group settings. Finally I have attempted to highlight key points in the grey boxes throughout the text. I hope that the combination of different styles and formats will assist you find your own way into this book and this approach to coaching.

From my own experience I know that the learning journey of systemic coaching and constellations can seem very straightforward and then suddenly beyond your understanding or imagination. This can lead to a sense that you are juggling with wet soap: one minute you have it in your hands, the next it's slipping through. This approach to coaching emerges in you over time, almost unnoticed, as you experience, as you train and as you practice, until, after some time it makes sense at every level: head, heart and body. You will know it without fully knowing how you know it and be able to facilitate deep shifts in understanding, alignment and behaviour using the principles and practices built on inner wisdom you didn't know you could access but always knew you had.

The methodology offers a perspective from which to work, from which to listen, from which to respond. This book offers several examples of integration alongside other ways of thinking and working as a coach. There are many more and I trust you will explore them as you bring all that you already have, all that you already trust, together with this way of thinking and working, in service of your clients. Give everything that you bring, everything that you are a place. When combined with this approach you will have something that allows you to face into a very wide range of challenges. In life and at work.

In this second edition you have access to a new Chapter 3, in which you can immerse yourself in the meaning and impact of a human need we all share – to belong. Belonging and the loyalties that emerge from it are one of the most potent influences on life and work so whether you coach private individuals or large teams in global corporates you will recognize the dynamics that emerge as a result.

If, after reading about this particular way of working with issues whose roots rest in the system you would like to learn more, then explore the website links in the Appendix where there are connections, in one or two steps, to every other author and systemic facilitator of every kind, across the world. It's a vibrant and inclusive community of practitioners. The links include some to facilitators who specialize in structural and other forms of constellations which, for the sake of clarity, I have not attempted to include in this introductory book.

There are multiple contexts and contextual layers in organizational systems that one book cannot cover. There are many developments of the approach across multiple applications. This book, especially when combined with experiential training, will be enough to get you started; but it will never be everything. That will come through experience, further learning through reading, practice and application, until the approach feels like your own and you can relax into your 'not knowing' and the process, trusting it completely.

Like you perhaps I'm just a coach. Not an academic, not a trained teacher or experienced writer. I'm simply sharing an approach to coaching, passing on what has been passed so generously to me, because it's transformed my understanding of life and work, and because it feels true. True for me but also all my clients no matter their background, gender, personality, skills, psychological profile or role.

The combination of reading, experiential learning and practice will enable you to support your clients to travel into new territory, unimagined insights and enduring resolutions.

You and your clients will also soon start to enjoy another way of being. And doing.

Enjoy the journey, with them.

PART ONE
Principles

The universal language of systems

01

In all chaos there is a cosmos
In all disorder a secret order.
CARL JUNG

There are many kinds of coach. Some work one-to-one, while others work as facilitators, working almost exclusively with teams and groups. Some set goals; others use a psychodynamic or psychometric framework. Some use models that support the growth of emotional intelligence, team function and leadership presence. Whatever kind of coach you are and whatever your preferred approach, you are just as likely to come across systemic issues as any other. The dynamics that surface in systems and present themselves as 'difficult behaviours', 'dysfunctional teams', 'stuckness', 'repeating patterns', 'conflict' and 'difficulty in occupying role' are familiar to all coaches. When these dynamics are an expression of something in the system as they very often are, then only a systemic approach will have an enduring effect.

Whatever your background, orientation or context, this approach – the systemic coaching stance and the principles and practices described in this book – offers an opportunity to illuminate, clarify and resolve system dynamics while also integrating your own particular style and orientation. This is an approach underpinned by universal principles that maintain system coherence. And we all work, no matter in which context, in and with systems, whether we are aware of it or not.

> In the sometimes apparently chaotic dynamics of our client's world, the quiet but persistent voice of the system can often get lost, misinterpreted and misnamed.

The universal language of systems is one that we all know, but most of us have forgotten how to speak. This approach gives the systems we belong to and work with a voice.

The order of things

Some simple truths, common to all human relationship systems, underpin this approach. These were expressed by originator Bert Hellinger as 'natural orders' and were discovered through a great deal of experimentation and observation. The reason it took him years to develop the methodology of constellations within family and then organizational systems is that he wasn't looking to create a new theory. He was looking, searching, for something more essential. He was searching for what is. What he found and uncovered were timeless truths that underpin human relationship systems.

The insights and understanding that inform this way of working were discovered, not dreamt up by the rational mind. When you've experienced them you almost immediately 'know' them, as truths, at a deep level. This experience leads to an understanding of these 'natural orders', 'organizing principles' or 'forces' that sustain systems. That's why this approach is referred to as profound and phenomenological, the investigation of truths through experience. At first the truths seem to be our own, personal truths. Constellations show them to be universal to the human experience.

Many people, on first approaching this way of working, do so with a degree of scepticism, the author included. Where is the evidence? What research has been done into these claims about ordering forces? Why would dynamics discovered in family systems have any relevance in business, organizations and executive coaching?

These are important and valid questions which have a place in the evolution of this work. Without these questions there may be a danger of this approach looking like some sort of 'belief system' or series of 'rules' that mustn't be broken. With the questions comes a continuous commitment to searching, to exploration, to experience. A search for the consistent truths of the human experience in life and at work.

It's interesting to observe how people who've just experienced a constellation about their own issue ask no questions about 'how it works'. They are too occupied with a new sense of spaciousness and resolution around the issue or question they had previously struggled with. A theoretical model or a leap of faith is not required to validate the experience. Those would add a layer of complexity and rational thinking that is simply not required and would diminish the simple power of a direct experience of system dynamics, hidden connections and resources.

The principles that underpin this approach are, just like the issues it's so effective at tackling, invisible yet tangible in their effect. Identification and understanding of them is based on close observation, experience and testing that leads to insight and resolution.

> What emerges is an understanding of the interconnected nature of everything and everyone in systems. Changing something in one part of the system has an effect on the rest. We knew that already, but this approach explains why and then shows how to work with the resulting dynamics.

The immutable natural orders, the forces that appear to govern systems, seem to be protecting them in an attempt to achieve coherence and flow. These are forces that many individuals, teams and whole organizations continue to work within, without conscious awareness. As a result individuals, teams and businesses are unwittingly caught up in the dynamics that ignoring or disregarding the organizing forces create. These dynamics are manifest as inertia, difficulty with leadership, lack of role clarity, high staff turnover, conflict and other challenging symptoms and behaviours. These are signs of system issues and, through a systemic lens, they offer a window into the underlying forces at play.

Constellation workshops, the environment in which this work was developed, offer a visceral experience of these hidden organizing forces; an opportunity to stand, literally, in the invisible forces and feel their effects. Surprisingly, the experience transfers with ease and impact into a one-to-one coaching relationship and process where objects, not people, are used to represent the various elements of the system.

Whether in a workshop, team application or working one-to-one, constellations are underpinned by the same principles and practices as are described throughout this book and in every workshop and training environment. It isn't the setting in which a constellation takes place that makes it a constellation; it's the systemic perspective and attitude of the coach or facilitator. This comes from an understanding of the underlying organizing forces in systems, the way of accessing them and knowing when a constellation may be the appropriate intervention.

More on all that soon, but first let's broaden out the view and look at coaching from the systems perspective.

From individual and team to system

There are many ways of supporting professional development, resolving leadership challenges and illuminating organizational complexity. There are multiple theories and models available to leaders, coaches and organizational consultants. Each of these perspectives and sources of guidance can and do play a useful role. They each have a place.

In the human and organizational development aspect of business leadership it's incumbent on leaders to ensure that they are creating and modelling strong interpersonal relationships and building high-functioning teams throughout the business. That people find their voice and learn to influence others in effective and motivating ways. That skills such as delegation and assertiveness are learnt and developed to support high performance across the business. That emotional intelligence and leadership, aligned with who you are as well as what you do, is encouraged. Self-awareness increases and self-management may often follow.

After all, business performance improves when you do. Unless you build a good understanding of yourself, your natural strengths and blind spots, it's hard to exert your influence. Building higher self-awareness and emotional intelligence so you can respond to different situations and influence others through a range of styles is an essential ingredient of successful leadership and is especially important in the knowledge and service economy, where clients are buying people and high-performing teams, not products. But that alone – interpersonal, professional and leadership development – is not always enough. Something else is required in addition.

Working at the level of the individual is essential for clarifying and resourcing, but unless a wider perspective – a view of the whole system and the field of information available within and between systems – is also included, crucial information may be missed that can build enduring organizational health and resolve complex or apparently intractable issues. However well an individual performs and aligns themselves with their values, motivations and goals, the hidden forces that act in organizational systems will affect and often compromise their individual skills, talent and performance.

> *There's so much talk about the system. And so little understanding.*
> Robert Pirsig, *Zen and the Art of Motorcycle Maintenance*

Working only at the level of the individual means you may be able to remove the symptom but the dynamic, if it belongs at the level of the system, will simply re-emerge and be expressed through someone or something else. The system doesn't care who or what it entangles; it must try to achieve coherence.

System dynamics don't respond to assessments of personality type, objective-setting or a new strategic plan. Systems are not affected by the team profile or whether there's a particular conflict model being applied. System dynamics are beyond rational intervention and require something else. They need to be addressed by systemic interventions.

A business or 'organizational system' can be looked at as a continuously changing mass of relationships, hierarchies, loyalties and motivations. Like a cloud it hangs in delicate balance, with each part connected to and influencing each other part. When all of the elements have their place, are free to move and play their part, systemic coherence can be achieved.

Organizational health

The concept of organizational health has interested me for a long time, at first as a semi-conscious search for an authentic framework that went beyond empty talk of 'behaviours in alignment with our values', values often dictated by senior management. When I came across this approach to systems I started to get a sense of potential for something more, something deeper than shared understandings of somebody else's values, something beyond the development of individual emotional intelligence and leadership development, something that could perhaps lead to whole system health and coherence.

With a systems perspective and understanding it becomes clear where some of the complex dynamics that emerge in organizational and business systems come from. Systemic constellations, systemic consulting and systemic coaching have a role to play in clarifying, illuminating and resolving these invisible dynamics. They allow a different, broader landscape to be seen and worked with. They enlarge the problem context and allow new sources of resource and resolution into the field of view.

Let's take a minute to step back from coaching and constellating and look at this broader picture of organizational health.

> *Unfortunately, given the linear thinking that predominates in most organizations, interventions usually focus on symptomatic quick fixes, not underlying causes. This results in only temporary relief and it tends to create still more pressures later on for further, low-leverage interventions.*
>
> Peter Senge

An organization is a body of people with a shared intention who are working together to create something that is greater than that which would be possible alone. An organization really is an attempt to create a whole that is quite literally greater than the sum of the parts. It's a system. It can be for commercial ends or not-for-profit – the dynamics that arise are common to all human systems, whether in the public or private sector.

Some organizations have many thousands of employees. A few – technology companies, national health systems and some international retailers for example – have over a million employees in one vast interconnected system. These are huge and complex systems of men and women. And each interacts with many other systems – overlapping and interacting with contractor systems, suppliers and of course customers.

In addition there are many hundreds of thousands of businesses that are smaller than 10 people – and many of them are very successful and profitable. Increasingly these small systems, led by visionary entrepreneurs, are growing and competing with very large systems. They often become large systems themselves. But size doesn't matter; the dynamics can occur between two people or between 200,000.

So, what do we mean by organizational health in systems?

> Organizational or system health is a sense of vitality in both the human and commercial dimensions of a business, and is predicated on a number of things being aligned; on a number of natural forces being acknowledged and attended to. These systemic influences and forces make themselves known, make themselves felt, in a number of unusual but strangely familiar ways.

When people leave an organizational system 'under a cloud', when their contribution to the organization and the length of time they made that contribution for is not fully recognized and acknowledged, it has a long-term effect on the people that remain. When people leave in a difficult way or when the truth about their leaving is hidden, they are 'remembered' in a particular way – a way that entangles those that remain in the system. One of the great myths in business and certain kinds of leadership is that you can simply remove people from a system and then forget about them. Time and again we see how that has exactly the opposite effect that we imagine or hope it may have.

A system is not the sum of the parts but a product of their interactions.
Russ Ackoff

On the other hand, individuals often join a business with an inner sense of superiority due to their long experience, their expertise, or the way they were recruited into the job. People who arrive with only a sense of their own worth and what they can give to the system, will often be experienced by those they are trying to lead as disrespectful and self-serving. These are often very experienced and talented people. They rarely intend to cause a disturbance in the system – after all, they left somewhere else to join and want to apply their experience and expertise. But if they have inadvertently arrived in a role without inwardly holding a sense of respect for those who have worked in and contributed to this system before them, including the previous role-holder, they will struggle to gain the respect of those they expect to follow them.

These brief examples of system forces at work shine a different light on organizational life, developmental and team coaching, and organizational consulting. Many businesses lose their competitive advantage or suffer crippling inertia because of these hidden dynamics working through the system.

> In a healthy relationship system everyone who has contributed is acknowledged and the history of the system is spoken about, including all the difficulties. Everything has a place. Roles are created in conscious connection with the purpose of the whole system. There is a balance between what each individual and team gives and what they receive. Everyone feels safe and able to relax into their own authority and apply it, willingly, for the good of the system.

Organizational system health can be felt at an individual, team and whole company level. It's tangible. Leaders feel empowered, respected and useful. Each person in the organization knows that they are occupying a respected role that has its place, a secure and trusted place, in the system.

In a system with high levels of organizational health, staff turnover is low and motivation is high. There are no secrets, no shame about difficult events in the past, and nobody who has made a contribution to the system is forgotten or excluded. People want to stay and make a full contribution because they know that they're doing something that will be valued and have an impact as part of a whole – a whole that can achieve things that are more than the sum of its parts.

The part can never be well unless the whole is well.

Plato

But when health is absent, so are the people. Individuals who are unsure of their place, their role or their level of responsibility in the system cannot be fully present and so don't bring their talents and experience fully to the business. They withhold something, unconsciously resisting a fuller contribution. Trust, loyalty and motivation are missing or unreliable.

When individuals and teams find themselves entangled with system dynamics they get drawn towards behaviours, attitudes and levels of performance that complicate things for them and the business around them. Individuals represent the stance and opinions of what's missing or has been excluded. Rivalries and recurring patterns that appear to be beyond change emerge. Energy and motivation are inconsistent; insecurity and shame surface. There is distrust and conflict and people experience high levels of stress. The system may grow but it becomes more difficult to work in and more people experience difficulty in their role.

Systems operate through self-righting mechanisms that many leaders and followers are unaware of. But they experience the impact of ignoring or violating these immutable and timeless principles, as the system will sacrifice members in order to achieve coherence and completeness.

If organizational systems are to become more healthy, if organizational design, learning and development, coaching and HR are to be more effective, then leaders and those who work alongside them will need to understand and embrace another way of looking at organizations. Not only are we seeing the end of the lone hero leader but also perhaps a change in the focus of coaching that unwittingly supports an individual, non-systemic view. This shift is beginning to happen, slowly, in some industries in some locations. But much of the orientation is still towards the individual and the individual approach; the leader as hero. That approach makes the presumption that one person or team believes they could be 'powerful' enough to change the system. This is where systemic coaching, coaching with the whole system in mind, can add a fresh perspective and real value. It does this by supporting leaders to find and exert a leadership approach that respects the higher authority of the system. This in itself requires an understanding of systems and a certain humility in coach and coachee.

> *Our traditional view of leaders – as special people who set the direction, make the key decisions and energize the troops – is deeply rooted in an individualistic and nonsystemic worldview. So long as such myths prevail, they reinforce a focus on short-term events and charismatic heroes rather than on systemic forces and collective learning.*
>
> Peter Senge

System leadership

It can be useful to think about leadership as a role that is serving a natural system over which the leader has very little control. When leaders see their function as one of service they have begun to reframe the concept of leadership. The idea of servant leadership is not new but, like other elements of this approach, the differences here are subtle yet important. Systemic leadership needs to be alert to the energies across the whole system, working in service of the purpose and coherence of the whole system, rather than purely focusing on the people.

They say that change won't happen unless it's driven by and supported from the top. In fact, change won't happen if the system doesn't require it for its own health or survival.

The behaviours of the individuals and teams are signposts for what is really going on at the level of the system, the level of the organizing forces. Attempts by leaders to ignore or change the ordering forces of systems quickly manifests as inertia, complex leadership challenges, difficulty with the hierarchy, repeating patterns or a feeling of 'stuckness'. Leaders and teams often imagine, for example, that simply having a clear purpose, intention, goal or mission will be enough. However, the system may resist because the purpose or the human dynamics around it are not aligned with the systemic organizing forces.

> One of the reasons there are so many different models, theories and ideas about leadership is that it becomes very complicated if you approach it entirely at the level of the individual or team.

Leaders often believe that if only they can develop sufficient self-awareness to access their natural strengths, work on their blind spots and self-manage, they may be able to surmount any challenge the organization throws at them. The system dynamics remain unaffected by all of this human effort. It's too much for one person, one way of leading, or one model to handle. A systemic perspective, where the unseen psychological and energetic ties are revealed, illuminates an alternative approach that can liberate energy and fresh clarity across complex organizational systems large and small.

The principle of acknowledgement

System-orientated coaching can support the flow of leadership, team and organizational health. It offers a way of identifying the ordering forces and hidden dynamics they create and integrating the understanding into leadership to help keep business aligned, in flow and generative. Understanding and then applying the invisible ordering forces in systems begins with one simple idea: acknowledging what is.

The theme of acknowledgement underpins everything in the principles, practices, attitudes and application of this work. Acknowledgement might seem like a strange or rather simple principle to have in mind when coaching for development, change or organizational health, but the lack of acknowledgement in modern businesses is one of the most common causes of difficulties.

This is not about the simple acknowledgement that things are difficult. It is not, for example, about saying anything like: 'That must be difficult for you'. Those kinds of words may be described or even heard as empathetic but they will be experienced at a deeper level as a judgement, an assumption and one that often weakens the client and risks reattaching them to their story of how things are. Systemic coaching is about strengthening the client and freeing them from their stories. And strength comes from yielding to what is really, essentially true. This is a theme we will return to many times.

When coaching, it's easy and common to focus on outcomes, as if looking only at what *could be* will somehow be enough to move on from what *is*. In this approach, acknowledging what is, and staying with that before moving forward, allows for an illumination and system level resourcing, releasing and resolving to develop. The methodology for doing this surfaces inner pictures, which create the starting point for a developmental, leadership or team journey to begin in a different, often unexpected, place.

Looking at the broader landscape most businesses have fallen on difficult times, let people go, and struggled with competitive pressures, financial challenges or other issues. It's common to try to forget these difficult times when the good times return. This lack of acknowledgement has a negative impact on the system and creates artificial and short-lived levels of motivation and loyalty. Alternatively, when everything is given a place, when difficult events in the company history are acknowledged, when those who have contributed are recognized, then the system can settle and move on.

When something, or very often somebody, is excluded, not given their place and not acknowledged, leaders and followers will experience difficulties.

> **Whatever you try to exclude will always hold a powerful energy that will distract until it is re-included.**

The point about acknowledgement is that leaders and businesses that face into the realities of the present, together with their difficulties and successes in the past, build trust, loyalty and respect. Individuals and teams know they can trust what the company says and their place in the system, free of entanglements in the past.

When starting to work in this way, if that's what you choose to do, remember to start by acknowledging things just as they are, and you will be on your way to developing a fuller understanding and systemic practice. This is because acknowledgement is the key principle and process of systemic coaching and constellations, and often the single most powerful intervention when working with systems. I'd also go further and say that the system itself will not allow you to access or influence it unless you acknowledge what is, just as it is, first. That in itself requires a certain humility and a willingness to step back for a while from solutions, even coaching itself, and the search for objectives and goals.

The first stage of every constellation is designed to support the client to stand in the truth of the current situation, the current reality. To stand in the difficulty, the map of the question, developmental challenge or stuckness. To simply acknowledge what is.

This approach is extended throughout the whole process, as the client is encouraged to face directly into the truths – of the system, the individual or the team – and work with a full understanding of the reality of the situation. This liberates fresh energy and insight and surfaces an openness and coherence in coach, client and the coaching process itself. This in turn leads to fresh levels of contact, enduring developmental journeys and lasting resolutions to complex challenges.

Let's return briefly to the example described before – the natural tendency to express empathy by saying something like: 'That must be difficult for you'. Let's imagine you are working with a senior executive and he or she is struggling to find their place, in their leadership authority. It's an abstract feeling and hard to get a focus on.

In this way of working you can invite your client to set up a physical map of the relationship dynamics using the processes described later in this book. It's immediately clear from this that they are 'looking' at their team but that the team, or at least some of the members of the team, are 'looking' away. Some are even looking out of the system, to something else. This kind of situation is expressed in the first photograph in this book (page 143).

If this were coaching without knowledge of system dynamics or the mapping processes, you might, for example, express empathy, offer help or perhaps encourage the client to set a goal or objective to move forwards out of this situation. You might analyse the team through the use of any number of measurement tools or 360 feedback mechanisms. You might use a psychodynamic or psychometric approach. These can all be useful when working at the level of the individual or team. But systems and system dynamics have no interest in and are not affected by measurement, feedback, goals, psychometrics or empathy. These have no impact on systems and the forces that sustain and balance them.

> *It is hard to think in terms of systems and we eagerly warp our language to protect ourselves from the necessity of doing so.*
>
> Garrett Hardin, Ecologist

In this way of working, this particular approach to dealing with complex systems, the coach acknowledges 'what is' in a particular way. As you'll discover as you read about and experience this approach, this may include inviting your client to say a short phrase or system-orientated 'sentence' out loud. For example, in a one-to-one coaching session you might invite your client to say, in this example situation, something like this as he or she 'looks' at their team from their own place in the map they have created: 'Because you are looking elsewhere, I have no authority here.'

The difference in the kind of verbal acknowledgement we are exploring here is in four areas:

1 This kind of acknowledgement is designed to acknowledge what really is – the truth of the system – without judgement, empathy or partiality. It's not about trying to help resolve it or move away from it.

2 This kind of acknowledgement is spoken from the place in the system in which it belongs.

3 This kind of acknowledgement is designed to support the client to fully stand in the difficulty.

4 This kind of acknowledgement is spoken by the client, not you.

Acknowledgement of this kind brings relief to systems and opens up wider possibilities for leaders, teams and whole organizations.

The hidden forces in systems

In addition to acknowledging what is, and in order to start effecting real change in your coaching clients, you will also need to develop a kind of inner radar for the organizing forces of systems so you can support your clients to see and then acknowledge them too. These organizing forces, rather like those that influence the weather system, are beyond human intervention and exist in order to sustain a dynamic balance in systems. They create invisible fields of influence over everything in their path. Although invisible, you can see their effects. Imagine it like a magnet. You can see the effect it has on the iron filings but you can't see the magnetic field that's at work.

Much coaching, organizational design and organizational development is attempted with either the magnet or the iron filings. Systemic coaching and constellations are working at the level of the invisible field. Understanding and being able to work with this invisible field is important if you want your coaching to effect change in the systems with which you are asked to work.

These forces are as a result of the systemic conscience, the organizing force which attempts to maintain the coherence of the whole system. This idea of 'conscience' is described in detail in Chapter 3. The way I understand and share the organizing forces of systems with students of this work, and very often my clients, is as follows.

TIME

What comes first has a natural precedence over what follows:

- Those who join a system first have precedence over those joining later. Length of service is important in organizational systems.
- Starting with the founders, if their place and contribution is acknowledged by those that follow, the system can create space for new members to join and flourish.

- People who join systems later, especially if they have 'high authority' and experience, need to hold an inner respect for those that came before and what they contributed. What came first made what follows possible.

- When a new leader recognizes that they are in the *last* place, in the context of the natural organizing principle of TIME, it settles the system and allows their authority to manifest and have influence.

- Acknowledging the history is always important in understanding the present and future challenges.

- All patterns repeat themselves until the underlying dynamic is acknowledged and resolved. By understanding the past, their place in it and the impact it's had on the present, leaders, individuals and teams will be able to find their place in the future and change the patterns.

> **All systems will balance out a TIME precedence that has been denied.**

Acknowledging the impact of TIME in organizational systems

We saw earlier how, when a senior executive joins an organizational system and assumes that their experience, personality and knowledge will be enough to support them to find their authority in their new role, they may be disappointed by the response. One of the most common reasons, when all else is well, is a failure to acknowledge what and who came before them; the simple fact that they owe their place to everyone who is in the system already.

This simple truth was first revealed in families and family constellations when it became clear that for an individual to be resourced, to thrive in life, they need to give each person who has contributed to their life a place, to honour them. To honour everyone who contributed to their coming into life, into their family system, for without them they would not be. This is true even if their parents hurt them, tried to exclude them or didn't welcome them when they arrived. They are still the source of their life, still came before them and as such have a place in the order of things. So it is in business. What and who came first came before what and who joined later.

This idea of acknowledging what and who came before them usually comes as quite a shock to executives who feel themselves to be on a 'fast track' to leadership. It's a shock that they are usually very grateful for being given, because it surfaces a humility and sense of place in the larger order of things that everyone recognizes when they experience it. Most leaders actually settle into themselves and their natural authority, as they realize they are not everything, simply a part of a much larger whole that stretches back in time.

In this book you will find several examples of the importance of acknowledging TIME when working from a systems health perspective. You will also soon be able to include it in your framework when facilitating constellations of your own. To begin with, simply remember that in the future the past is always present.

> *Without the past you can create with your client an idea of how the future might be, you can even create hope for the future. But that is not real systemic change in the client, which is what we imagine you're interested in and what we believe coaching is all about.*
>
> *The person in the present is their past. And if you do not know about their past and understand as much as you can about the whole person then you won't know what it is you're trying to change. If you do not know where 'here' is it is pretty unlikely that you will get 'there'.*
>
> Paul and Virginia Brown, *Neuropsychology for Coaches*

At this stage it may be useful to consider some exercises that you can apply in one-to-one or team coaching situations. Like all the exercises in this book, you should try these on yourself and with others in trainings and peer groups before facilitating with your clients.

TIME: An exercise for use in one-to-one coaching

If you're working with an individual who has recently joined an organization or team, invite them to set up the key elements of the system using objects on the tabletop or floor markers. (This phrase 'set up' means to choose representative objects for each of the key elements in the system and place them in relationship to each other using your 'felt sense' rather than your rational mind. It is in this way that a true inner picture emerges and reveals the underlying relationship structures.) They should set them up as if on a clock face in order of belonging to the system, starting with the first element (founder, founding idea or product, or first team member, for example) at 12 o'clock.

It doesn't matter if they don't know the precise order in which others joined but, as they build up a visual image according to the order of time in this system, they will see something of who and what came before them and that they are in the last place. Few words are required; the insights and understanding usually flow naturally and you'll see a new level of awareness and an inner shift to a deeper respect for what is in your client.

It's also important for leaders to recognize who preceded them in the same role and to respect their contribution. There are several case studies later in this chapter that will bring this simple idea to life. First, here is an exercise that illuminates this.

TIME: An exercise for use in one-to-one coaching

If you are working with an individual who has recently been moved or promoted into a new role, you can invite them to set up a representative or floor marker for the person who occupied the role before them. You can then ask them to put in a representative for the person before them, the one before them, and so on and so on. Simply standing in front of the previous role holders gives the current role holder a very different perspective on their task and the way that they occupy the role.

Finish this exercise by placing a representative in for the purpose the role is designed to serve. Then explore and discuss how your client can find their place in relationship to the past, to the purpose and to the future.

When thinking about how the organizing principle of TIME may have been ignored or violated in a team you are working with, you can invite the whole team to try this exercise. (This exercise is expanded and developed in Part 3 – Application.)

TIME: An exercise for use in team coaching

If you work with teams and you are working with a team facing change, or dealing with communication issues or conflict, then invite them to stand in a line or semi-circle in order of time – who joined the organization (or the team if appropriate) first, who next, and so on. Invite them to do this in silence, trusting their 'felt sense' of their true order. Then invite them to check the accuracy of their ordering with those adjacent to them. After you've offered each the opportunity to speak from their place, you can invite each to look at those who preceded them and say: 'The work you did before I joined made a space for me. Thank you.'

This simple 'standing in the truth of what is', the organizing principle of TIME, can have a profound effect on team dynamics. It opens a systemic perspective on a team workshop whether or not you stay with systems-oriented interventions.

If appropriate you can also then invite the people who have been acknowledged as belonging for the longest time to look down the line at those who joined recently and say something like: 'Everything we've learnt by being here for longer we will pass on to you gladly, so you can use it for the good of the whole system.'

If you use this exercise at the start of a team day and then refine or agree a team purpose, you can invite the group to resume their 'standing in the order of joining' line at the end of the day. Having written the team purpose on a large piece of paper, place it on the floor and then invite each, starting with the one who joined first, to stand in a place that has meaning for them. This acts as a powerful catalyst for a bigger conversation.

The exercise described above is also very effective when working with teams or groups that are the product of a merger or acquisition. For groups or teams that have previously been rivals or have a degree of competition between them it's very effective to allow them to stand in two circles, representing how they were *before* they came together. This allows each not only to find their order of TIME within themselves but also to make it explicit which system was first. Very often in acquisitions (which themselves are often misnamed as 'mergers') the acquired system is actually the first to exist. When you can let that be seen and acknowledged, then there is likely to be a great deal more respect and clarity within and between each system.

In some cases you may find yourself working with two teams or divisions within the same company who need to work together more closely, though not form one team. For an example of application in this context see the case study on page 205.

There are several more exercises offered later in this book for use in coaching in both one-to-one coaching and with teams.

While developing my skills and experience as a coach I enjoyed working with a number of executive students attending the London Business School MBA programmes in London, Dubai and Hong Kong. The understanding of the importance of TIME proved a useful and illuminating way to settle challenging group dynamics.

The executive students were randomly placed in groups of six and had to complete team tasks, supporting each other in complex challenges against tight time schedules. However, they faced a group with no hierarchy, no assigned leader, nobody in charge. Whilst this aspect forms a key part of the learning, it can also be so alarming to some students that they struggle to function. In my work as a coach I wanted to work in alignment with the Business School's approach but also to experiment with offering an experience that would allow them to have a natural hierarchy in mind when working together. My intention was to allow students to have an embodied experience of 'who came first' in a way that settled their temporary system and resourced them all.

So I invited the student groups, particularly those that were facing difficult group dynamics, to stand up in a semi-circle in order of age. However, they were to do so in silence, without asking each other their date of birth.

I remember one example of the application of this approach very vividly. This particular group were not in real contact with each other, with poor eye contact, no sense of team and a strong feeling of there being a lot of unspoken tension. Inviting them to remain in silence, I asked them to stand in a semi-circle according to age, with the person who felt like the eldest standing at the 12 o'clock position around the table we were gathered around.

They followed the invitation and slowly moved around each other, in silence, until they settled. It seemed to me and to some others that there had been a misunderstanding. The student who appeared, visually, to be the youngest stood at 12 o'clock and the student who certainly appeared to look the oldest stood in the youngest place, at the other end of the semi-circle. Not for the last time on my journey with this approach I began to wonder about system forces and the ability of humans to embody, to feel into, and to trust their 'felt sense.'

I invited each student to share their birthdays, starting with the person who was standing in the position of the oldest. As he did so the others gasped in astonishment. As they took turns to speak, each confirmed that their intuitive sense of where they belonged in the order of TIME was exactly right. The person in the youngest position also confirmed that he was indeed the youngest – aged just 24.

This led to a moving exchange of personal stories, in particular from the oldest student, who was from a part of Africa where respect for age ran deep through their family systems, ancestors and culture. The youngest, who expressed deep relief at 'finding my place' and being recognized for his true place in the order of things, told his story of a traumatic childhood illness that had left him exhausted and with damaged skin, looking much older than his years. The exercise and sharing of simple truths settled and connected the group at a deeper level than any amount of talking or warm-up exercises.

The rest of that session was one of the most productive, lively and yet respectful that I was privileged to facilitate. Each person knew their place and they came together, as a result of making that explicit, into a highly effective temporary team.

In every case where I tried this approach, the students would sit down again with a palpable sense of ease and engagement with something more than simply the course they were studying or the current pressing task. In each case I saw how it allowed for 'bigger conversations' about authority, hierarchy and leadership. When we respect the natural order of TIME it provides a safe and resourcing natural hierarchy into which we can lean and gain strength.

PLACE

Everyone, and everything, has a right to a different but unique and respected place in the system:

- For a system to thrive, everyone and everything that has belonged must be given a place. When a right to a place is denied and people are suddenly or disrespectfully excluded from a system, this creates a strong dynamic as the system attempts to 're-member' what or who has been excluded until they and their contribution have been acknowledged.

- Everyone who has had a place in the system needs to be acknowledged so that they and the system are free to move on and flourish. What you try to exclude or refuse to acknowledge a place for, someone will stay loyal to and secretly follow. The simple awareness of who belongs and who has a right to a place, gives the system freedom to move and to act.

- There is a phenomenon often seen in systemic coaching and constellations called 'the ejector seat syndrome', where occupants of a particular role suffer the same or similar difficulties to the previous person in that role. The role itself seems to be burdened in some way:

- This occurs when someone has left quickly, in a negative way, or the real reasons are not explained, or when the organization doesn't acknowledge that person's contribution to the company.

- Leavers need to be able to vacate the role fully, helping to ensure that the person who steps into that role has the best possible chance of success.

- If the most senior employee, or even founder, refuses or resists, at an unspoken level, to fully occupy their place and their own authority, this causes a difficulty in finding place and authority throughout the system. Leaders must lead.

- Each element, each person and each role has a place in a particular order depending on the system formation and purpose. It's possible to discern which roles are the most important for the vitality and health of the business system and in what order all roles need to be for each system. For example, it is often the case that board or executive roles are seen as equal, but there will be a 'better' and 'worse' place for each role to exist in relation to the other roles and in relation to the rest of the system. This systemic hierarchy is far more powerful and exerts more force on a system than the hierarchy leaders and consultants like to think they can impose.

- Businesses that try to keep facts secret – the bad year, the industrial accident that we don't talk about, the fact that we had to let some

people go a few years back – slow down the system and create a culture of defensiveness and instability.

- Everything has a place. In order to let things go, you must 're-member' them fully first, acknowledging what they were able to contribute. Then they are free to leave.

> **All systems will balance out a right to PLACE that has been denied.**

Acknowledging the impact of PLACE in organizational systems

We will do anything to protect our belonging to the system. Belonging is one of the deepest human needs. We are constantly checking this and asking ourselves: 'Am I in, or am I out?'

In family systems when children try to take care of parental problems there is a sense of confusion and burden. When people try to carry the burden of another, to take their place for them, they inevitably fail and often exhaust themselves, and lose their own place, in trying. Similarly, if someone behaves in an organizational hierarchy as if they were entitled to a different place, a dynamic is set up and causes conflicts. There are vivid examples of this through the book in the case studies, and you will see the dynamic often if you integrate this approach in your work.

Whether working one-to-one or with a team, if you hear of people who have been 'fired' or of difficult events that have been excluded, you can invite your client to identify representatives for those elements and, using the processes described in this book, give them a place. This kind of systemic exercise can have a profoundly aligning effect on an individual, team or whole company.

The following brief exercise is designed to support your client to simply acknowledge what or who has been denied a place and so can be used when this issue surfaces in a coaching conversation. It can also be used if you have a sense that something or someone who has made a contribution is not being talked of or really acknowledged.

PLACE: An exercise for use in one-to-one coaching

Simply invite your client to set up a few representatives for the system as it is, for example divisions or groups of people, products or services. Then invite them to include a representative for the people or events that have been excluded.

If you are working with a team leader, invite them to set up representatives for every member of the team as it is now. Then ask them to add in all previous members of the team and work with each, finding a contribution to acknowledge. Leadership with this more complete picture of the team in mind is experienced in a different way.

As before, you can also add a representative for the team or organizational purpose. This in itself acts as a useful agenda-setting exercise with a team leader, as they look at the relationship between the elements within this system.

Few words are usually required, though if you are working with the most senior individual in the system, or the one with the most responsibility for what's excluded, you can make appropriate systemic interventions as described later in this book.

This brief exercise is one of several system-orientated ones that will beome familiar to you if you decide to include a systems perspective in your coaching.

EXCHANGE

A dynamic balance of giving and receiving is required in systems:

- In all interactions there needs to be a balance of exchange: between employers and employees, and between the organization and its customers and suppliers.

- It's not only about the money. Truly motivating people and meeting their need for exchange is very rarely about giving them more money. In fact that can often have the opposite effect.

- If people feel they've been given too much money they withdraw some of their personal energy from the company and, like a spoilt child, they may become troublesome. The one who receives too much withdraws as they feel unable to repay the debt.

- The most valuable commodity in any exchange at work is usually acknowledgement and feedback. Regular, planned and expertly delivered feedback on performance, combined with progressive developmental support, is key to getting the balance of exchange between employer and employed improved.

- In this way it's possible to see that coaching itself can form an important part of the exchange process in organizational life and leadership.
- Another context in which this organizing principle often becomes evident is in situations of merger or acquisition. The reason that many fail is connected to the lack of balancing of who, what and which organization has given the most. Ambition, greed and artificial evaluations together with hidden information often cause a violation of this principle, and the dynamic expresses itself in behaviours and departures that damage the business.
- These unconscious and invisible levels of exchange are very important in supporting organizational health and allowing the visible and conscious exchange mechanisms of money, cars and health plans to take their place and have their useful effect too.

All systems will balance out an imbalance of EXCHANGE.

We all have an internal balancing sense calibrating the level of giving and receiving in multiple areas of life and work. You can see EXCHANGE at work in intimate relationships. One of the many insights that the first generation of systemic facilitators revealed was that, in an intimate relationship where there is an imbalance of giving and taking, the one who *receives* too much eventually feels burdened and wants to leave the system. To regain their strength and sense of self they may leave to join with another with whom they can grow and give back, or find other ways of balancing the level of exchange.

The very first place we sense this fine inner balance of giving and receiving is when we are young children, within our family system. For love and life to flow in a family, parents give and children receive. This dynamic is often slightly out of balance because parents, through their own wounding or lack of resource, may not be able to offer more than the life they have passed on. If parents could not access or receive from their own parents fully, if there was something missing, then they may look to get this from their children. The children then feel sucked into their parents' lives, so instead of being the frame, the parents become the picture.

In many cases children sense that they haven't received enough from their parents and will often spend the rest of their lives looking to address this imbalance. This, one of the most common sources of addictive behaviours, can be seen as a movement towards the parents, to receive, that was stalled or interrupted. As if frozen in that reach for more, children grow into adults who act that reaching out in life and work. Other reactions may be to close and withdraw, along with attempts to break contact with parents or, equally isolating and painful, become 'bigger than' them and forgive them. To either walk away from or take a superior position in relation to the source of your life and hope to retain a sense of identity or feel resourced is doomed to failure. Yet many people spend years attempting to find ways of achieving this need for balance in giving and receiving, in exchange.

The balance of giving and receiving, so acutely felt in childhood between parents and children, is finely tuned and each generation of a family system tries to adjust and balance it. However when we can simply receive what was available we can live life more fully.

When working with systems, understanding them is, inevitably, easier if you begin to understand your own. So we'll come back to this balance of exchange in families again at the end of this book and explore how you may be able to support yourself, adjust the balance for yourself, resource yourself, and in other ways, in other contexts, your clients.

Our inner sense of exchange is vitally important to us. The really important point about EXCHANGE is that an imbalance creates a much deeper bonding than a balance, which sets people free. And so it is in business and organizational life, at every level and in each exchange. As it is above, so it is below.

Try this next exercise on yourself and then, if and when appropriate, with a client. All coaches are, by definition, in a second, third or fourth career. This exercise can support a deep integration of your past professional expressions of yourself by allowing you to see what has been given and what has been received from each of your key experiences.

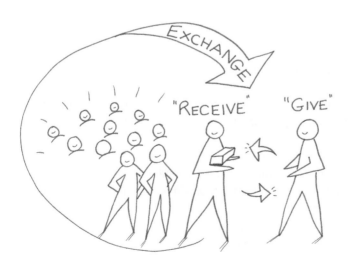

EXCHANGE: An exercise for yourself

Write down the three or four key jobs or careers you've had since leaving school. You can include advanced education (university and beyond) if you like and if this feels important. Write each on a single piece of A4 paper or large Post-it and fix them to a plain wall, about a half a metre apart, in a line and at eye level.

Slowly take your place in front of the educational or professional experience that came first. Stand in front of it, finding just the right distance that embodies what feels like the 'true place', just as it is in your inner picture of the relationship between yourself and this past experience.

As you stand in front of each in turn, notice what feelings, memories and sensations emerge. This in itself is good practice for tuning into your body and standing in relationship to a representative for something – the basic building block of constellations.

As you connect with your truth of each experience begin to experiment with the short sentences that you will be using at other times as a facilitator. In this exercise use words firstly to express what is, 'sentences of truth', that simply name what's true for each experience. Then, when you have acknowledged 'what is' start to explore the balance of giving and taking, the principle of EXCHANGE.

Sentences emerge in the moment, in context and from the visceral sensations of your experience as you stand in front of each representative marker. Follow your own inner truth.

For example, you may find yourself using sentences like these when acknowledging 'what is':

> 'This was painful for me.'
> 'This was a great pleasure for me.'

And you may find yourself using sentences like these when acknowledging a healthy balance of EXCHANGE:

> 'Thank you. I learnt a lot.'
> 'What I learnt here I will keep and use well. Thank you.'
> 'I remember you with great affection. Thank you for everything I gained. I will use it well.'
> 'What I gave you, you can keep.
> What you gave me I will keep, thank you.'

Or you may find yourself using sentences like these when acknowledging an *imbalance* of EXCHANGE:

> *'I stayed too long.'*
> *'It cost me too much to stay. I had to leave you.'*
> *'I'll keep what was useful for me and leave the rest with you.'*
> *'I gave too much. More than I had energy for.'*
> *'I learnt something important here. Thank you.'*

Use these example sentences as a starting point if you need to. They are simply examples of the kind of short form sentences that may emerge as you stand in each place along the line of your life/work journey. You will create your own, what matters is that they are true for you, they separate your responsibility from the responsibility of others, acknowledge the balance of EXCHANGE and support coherence in the system, aligned with the underpinning principles of systems.

Give yourself time, 20 or 30 minutes, as you work along the line, integrating each and acknowledging what's been given and received, what you can keep that resources you, and what you can leave behind with respect. One of the things you may discover is that while the organizing force of EXCHANGE is finely balanced, when you can thank the source for what has been given, you can receive and integrate it more deeply and then leave it behind more completely.

~

If you've done this exercise then you have also had your first experience of the core building blocks of a constellation. Standing in relationship to representatives placed in order of TIME; an embodied sense of a relationship dynamic; movement; words that acknowledge what is; others that articulate the sense of belonging in each system, the sense of PLACE; and others that relax the system and allow for integration. And, if you found yourself bowing your head slightly in thanks or respect as you stood in front of each element, then you've also experienced one of the rituals that allow for an acknowledgement of EXCHANGE and settle systems.

~

So, hidden forces create hidden dynamics and the dynamics cause visible symptoms, often through behaviours. The behaviours with this source are an unconscious attempt to realign with the organizing forces and are symptoms of a system issue. Symptoms are the system's way of showing that something wants to be seen, something is searching for completeness.

The invisible field is being pulled out of alignment and people say that 'the culture is changing around here'.

When there is tension or conflict at a senior level it's often because the natural system hierarchy or need for acknowledgement has not been seen or given a place. Working with system mapping, systemic coaching and constellations, it's possible to identify hidden dynamics that are limiting the flow of leadership and commercial success through the system, as well as find resources and the 'best place' for each role, function, team and person.

Naturally it's important not to use knowledge of these natural ordering forces in a critical manner or to give a client an impression that they have somehow got something 'wrong'. It is not that people act out of alignment with the organizing principles wilfully, but rather because of deep and unconscious loyalties. To be respectful when integrating knowledge of these ancient principles into contemporary coaching processes is essential, as leaders may otherwise reattach to their familiar story and stay stuck.

The organizing principles in action

The organizing forces are the key drivers of healthy systems, and starting to identify when they are in play and when they are being ignored or violated will lead you and your clients to many insights and understandings. As you develop your stance you will soon discover that they 'show up' as you begin to work with clients and you will discover that you 'know' them as they become relevant.

I remember the first time I facilitated using these principles and practices with a team: four leaders who were also the founders of the business. In a mini workshop I tentatively explored the origins of their system – asking each in turn to stand, in order of date of joining. It soon became clear that the person who was leading the business, in the 'first position', was in fact following the energy of another in the group who had created the original momentum for starting and had been feeling rather sidelined. The simple exchange of the phrase 'You came first' brought relief to them both and also to the other two, who, at this stage were just observing.

Next I asked the third founder to stand in a place that made sense at the visceral level. He did, but struggled to find or settle in one place. Inviting the next, the fourth and final founder, to join, it very soon emerged that there had been a fifth member in their original group. Expressing this simple fact, 'forgotten' in all our previous discussions, allowed a bigger conversation to take place. Some frustration and anger was expressed at the contribution the 'missing' founder had made – there was an imbalance of EXCHANGE – however, the acknowledgement of this also settled them.

What became clear was that the third founder had stepped into a system 'ejector seat'. In other words, he was experiencing the negative feelings of isolation and therefore difficulty in performing that the 'missing' founder had not been allowed to express, and so had left in the system when departing.

I worked with the remaining founders to include the contribution the other founder had made. This included an acknowledgement of his powerfully effective contribution to the start-up phase. I offered them sentences of acknowledgement along these lines: 'Thank you for what you were able to contribute at the start. It made a difference and was useful.' They said these and other sentences willingly as they turned to face a chair we had placed in amongst them, a chair that identified the original PLACE of the fifth founder. After this, the man trying to occupy his role felt refreshed, realigned and much more able to make a valued and valuable contribution. He was now able to find his place in the exercise and later the organization, which he had been privately thinking of leaving.

We concluded the exercise with the four remaining founders standing in an arc, facing a flip chart that represented their customer base. Each individual found their PLACE, in the order of TIME and according to their role and function.

Only weeks later, they found a healthy way of resolving the imbalance of exchange with the founder who had left, thanking him for what he had been able to contribute. They still remain in easy contact with him and have been able to find occasional projects on which to collaborate, as well as others on which they compete. Through their professionalism and sheer hard work, and galvanized by the fresh energy this constellation surfaced in them, these four founders went on to become one of the most successful businesses in their sector and thrive today around the world. Their focus on organizational system health has remained with them since that day.

~

This serves as a useful and I hope encouraging example of how all three ordering forces or 'organizing principles' can surface in a simple constellation, and how much can be achieved with relatively little knowledge held within a respectful systems-orientated stance and framework. In this example the order of joining, acknowledging the organizing principle of TIME, was important. So was the balance of EXCHANGE between the founders: who had given what and when. And thirdly PLACE: the impact of excluding somebody who had made a vital contribution in the system and the importance of a certain order, a certain place, within the system. (This useful subtlety within the idea of PLACE, the order of roles in relationship to each other, will emerge again later in this book and in your work.)

~

Knowledge of the ordering forces in systems allows you to develop hypotheses about possible system dynamics. You may or may not then move on to sharing your hypothesis with your client, depending on the context.

This aspect will become clearer as you develop your own practice. One of the ways of sharing the underpinning principles is of course to invite your client to set up a map of the system issue; to map what is. That in turn can lead into a constellation. The gift of the constellation is that it will often show the client where they or others are acting out of system-alignment. It also goes further by showing exactly how the system can be realigned and brought back into balance.

Walking in the field

Tuning into the 'field of information' between the parts of a system, between all the people in a system, is the source of the hidden resources and solutions held within systems. You'll remember the magnet analogy. This invisible element is often referred to as the field. I believe it was Albert Einstein who said: 'The field is the sole governing agency of the particle.' In other words, don't look at the individual alone but look at the invisible forces acting on the individual. Don't just look at the talent and experience in your clients, look at their relationship to everything else that they come from and are connected into. Look at the system. Engage with the system.

One of the ways of looking at and working with coaching clients and organizational health is a systemic constellation. This intervention, this approach, was developed in an attempt to support the growth of individual, leadership and organizational vitality in all kinds of systems, whether private, public or global corporate systems.

> A systemic constellation is designed to restore the integrity of a system, to restore the flow of leadership, of commerce and organizational health.

Facilitating a constellation often feels like walking through a field: a field of information that rewards you and your client with insights and clarity in the most unexpected ways.

It's often a pleasure and a privilege to share this approach with clients, as it changes something at an elemental level about how they approach their particular set of challenges, and indeed the coaching relationship and pro-cess. You'll also find that, once understood, they never forget the underlying principles and can begin to apply them without the need for continuous intervention. This in itself leads to transformational change in relationship systems at work and in life.

I've yet to meet a client, from any walk of life or work, who doesn't under-stand the natural organizing forces in systems, when respectfully explained in the context of a pressing issue. However, they may often say something like: 'I don't *want* that to be true, but I can feel that it absolutely is! Tell me more.' That's the great benefit of this work – it's a sharing of underlying 'principles' that underpin all human experience at work as in life. That is why the insights it offers are consistently welcomed when sensitively and appropriately shared. There are many examples of this throughout this book.

The shift in focus from the individual to the wider system is in itself a systemic intervention, and you will often hear a sigh of relief as clients understand at a deep level that it is not all about them, not all about their IQ, EQ, personality, leadership style and interpersonal skills. There's something else, something universal at play and they can explore that whilst also exploring and developing their self-awareness and interpersonal behavioural change. The individual and the system perspectives are both important but one without the other is missing a part of the whole.

An understanding of the naturally occurring organizing forces that govern and sustain systems will be important as you expand your facilitation of this approach. Working with an understanding of these forces in mind informs the stance and processes that allow this work to deliver the benefits it offers. Even if you never facilitate a full constellation, an understanding of the principles can inform and guide your existing approach to coaching conversations and your preferred frameworks in a way that can enrich and deepen, creating lasting impact.

As you progress in an understanding you'll find that you can weave in and out of the language of systems and systemic constellations, introducing it subtly and in alignment with where your clients are on their journeys. This approach provides a holding framework, not always the picture. And that framework is often enough to make small but important shifts in your language and stance, small shifts that support deep and lasting change in the system.

Back to the start
Origins and definitions

"You can add up the parts
But you won't have the sum
'ANTHEM' BY LEONARD COHEN

Systems and the forces that sustain them

Revealing and resolving unconscious patterns in relational systems can create a significant shift in perceptions, behaviours and actions, and constellations provide a fresh way of doing that. But what do we mean by 'a system', what are the forces that influence it and how do we access and work with the resulting dynamics effectively?

A system can be described as a set of interacting or interdependent entities forming an integrated whole. Systems are often large and complex but we are rarely consciously aware of them. If we refer to them at all we may call them our 'reference system'. We know when we are not aligned with our reference system, but we may not know why, or how to realign. Constellations offer a unique way of doing this, restoring integrity to the whole, allowing life, leadership, teams and whole organizations to flow.

A useful way of thinking about systems is to think of a white fluffy cloud on a spring day. It's an attractive image, but hidden in that cloud are all kinds of movements, interactions and interdependencies. Its very existence hangs in the balance, vulnerable to change caused by air temperature, air movement and human intervention.

A cloud is a natural constellation of water droplets and vapour in a large natural system that is subject to constant change. Each water droplet is connected to several others; each is constantly changing its position in relationship to each other. A change in one part of the cloud affects others. As a light wind picks up, our little cloud gets dispersed and separated, making smaller clouds around it. Some of the water vapour evaporates and disappears. But it remains in the air in a different form, perhaps to reappear later.

This cloud is complicated, and impossible to control. It's vulnerable to a wide range of forces, most of them invisible. The visible forces are relatively easy to predict and respond to. An aeroplane wing sweeps through one side of the cloud but it simply drifts back together again, its shape and form slightly changed but not destroyed. Invisible forces are much harder to predict or react to.

A gust of wind blows our cloud into a very different shape. The sun goes down and the temperature drops. Invisible heat waves rising off the land hundreds of feet below push the cloud up higher and higher until it merges with another and drifts over the horizon. When we look again it's gone, replaced by another huge, dark mass that tumbles over itself in a bid to remain intact whilst being buffeted by rising air and high and changing winds. Lightning streaks through the cloud and it begins to rain. Everything has changed and changes again. And all because the larger system, of which the cloud is a small part, is trying to remain coherent, in a constantly changing dynamic balance.

So it is with organizational systems. Ever changing, full of visible and invisible forces in between the parts, forces that create dynamics and behaviours. Coaching with the whole system in mind, rather than addressing each water droplet, or separate clouds, is systemic coaching. It requires an ability to see and work with the whole, understand the forces that are acting on it, and retain a view of and compassion for it all, just as it is, not just the individual parts.

> *The major problems in the world are the result of the difference between how nature works and the way people think.*
>
> Gregory Bateson

Constellations

A constellation is a practical intervention that can illuminate the invisible and unspoken dynamics behind a relationship difficulty, a stuck issue or a persisting challenge. Constellations provide a way of exploring and clarifying almost any kind of relationship system – between people and teams across and within businesses but also any other kind of relationship from the intra-personal to the abstract.

A constellation creates a three-dimensional spatial model, sometimes described as a 'living map', that can be used in a number of contexts to illuminate new information and liberate fresh resources. The creation of a constellation allows facilitator and client to work at the source, to see patterns, to illuminate and disentangle difficult dynamics, and then find clarity and resolution for a wide range of issues and challenges.

Constellations work because we all carry within us an unconscious inner map of everything and everybody we have been or are in relationship with. The inner image is brought to the surface through a constellation and allows us to explore so that a new image can be internalized and integrated into our life and work.

However, a constellation is more than simply an external expression of a pattern that shows the nature of the underlying relationship structures. A constellation is an event that connects facilitator and client to an invisible field of information in a system and provides a way to realign the elements, giving each a place. By placing the individual in the context of the larger truths of the system they occupy, constellations illuminate new information and fresh insights, restoring clarity and offering coherence. As the hidden loyalties and entanglements are revealed and brought into the consciousness, the system can relax and offer fresh resources to all its members. For this reason constellations affect 'heart and soul' as well as head, and so offer a profound connection to something beyond words. As a result the process and benefits of a constellation remain with the client at an embodied level.

The first stage of a coaching constellation – mapping – can be used early on by coaches, whilst a fuller understanding and practice develops. The hidden depths emerge as your own journey with this methodology evolves and your understanding of the principles and practices develops.

The purpose of a constellation is to restore system coherence so that everyone and everything is given its place and is free to operate at its best, from that place. In the coaching context this means that clients can manifest their experience, talent and skills once the system is brought into alignment and they can find their place.

Systemic coaching

There are many useful models and approaches to coaching and each has a valuable part to play in supporting and developing people and the organizations in which they work. A systemic coach considers personal, leadership, team or whole organization issues in the context of the system in which they belong.

Systemic coaching is that which acknowledges, illuminates and releases the system dynamics so each element can function with ease. It is coaching that prioritizes the system.

Systemic coaching, when informed by a particular stance and the constellation processes, is the basis for resolving systemic issues and is informed by the principles that guide and sustain systems. This is a solutions-orientated approach but solutions are not found in the same way as in other interventions. A relentless search for solution can shipwreck the process of coaching. This approach takes a different path to finding solutions, one that starts by standing in the truth of the system, just as it is.

The workshop experience

Constellations were originally developed in workshop settings to illuminate and resolve complex personal and interpersonal patterns. An understanding and experience of the workshop setting is important before learning about its application in coaching. What follows is a brief generic description that cannot hope to replace the direct experience.

Constellation workshops are generally small with about 20 participants, so there is explanation, demonstration and time for questions throughout the session. The group sits in a circle and, under the guidance of the facilitator, uses the space in the centre to set up each 'living map', each constellation. To begin each piece of work, the person who is bringing an issue briefly describes, to the facilitator, the difficulty or challenge they are facing.

Once there is clarity about the essence of the issue or the change required, the facilitator, if a constellation is appropriate, invites the client (sometimes referred to as the 'issue holder') to select workshop participants to 'represent' each of the core elements in the system being explored. This approach of representation is central to this way of working and is experienced throughout the workshop.

The client is invited to include a representative for themselves in the constellation. Standing behind each representative and allowing the experience of the relationship they are thinking of to occupy them, they place their hands on the representatives' shoulders and guide them, intuitively, to a place that feels true. As a result a pattern is created, an external picture of a largely unconscious inner image.

Think with your whole body.

Taisen Deshimaru

This is the start of a constellation and, even at this early stage, it often reveals fresh insights about the relationship structures in the system being explored. The form of the next stage of the constellation depends on the issue, the representatives' feedback, and the facilitator's observations and interventions. During the constellation the facilitator gathers information and insights from the representatives.

Each person standing in the constellation is asked to report their experience. This experience is informed by a mixture of things including the way in which they were selected and placed into the constellation and their spatial relationship to other representatives. It is also influenced by what they have heard and seen and by the ability of all workshop participants, without previous experience of constellations, to tune into hidden information in that particular relationship system. This phenomenon is called representative perception.

> *Representative perception is responsible for an effect that almost every constellation shows: the representatives are able to make important statements about system dynamics and about information which they have not previously received verbally. This phenomenon is particularly useful if a representative can point to a missing resource or fact which the client had not thought of, but which, when it is mentioned, leads to a realignment and profound change in the client's mental model.*
> Marcus Birkenkrahe, Berlin School of Economics

I spend much of my time facilitating constellations with representatives in workshop settings, with coaches in the trainings looking at their client cases and with leaders in organizations looking at their challenges. In both contexts I'm privileged to witness the phenomenon of representative perception on a daily basis. It's the part of the methodology that is most powerful and most reliable, but also the part that's hard to understand or describe.

As the underlying dynamics gradually become clearer, the facilitator works with the representatives by inviting them to move to different places within the system map and offering them short phrases, or 'sentences of truth'. These are informed by both an understanding of the underlying principles and acknowledgement of what's revealed in order to illuminate, heighten, release or disentangle the limiting dynamics.

The combination of close observation, feedback from the representatives and facilitation brings reconnection and resolution to the constellation. The process and result of a constellation, lasting from a few minutes to over an hour, provides the issue holder with insights, fresh energy, and resources for enduring resolution. They may be invited to stand in the constellation and get a perspective from within their own system.

People sitting in the circle that surrounds the constellation may represent a part of the system or the system boundary. They will often become a rich source of information about the system, often in particular about secrets or excluded and unacknowledged elements.

> *The constellation process opens a door to a hidden dimension of inner images and unspoken statements.*
> Dan Booth-Cohen

The constellation leaves the client with a revised, often completely new, picture of the system dynamics. This picture can be internalized and so acts as a catalyst for a significant change in the way they hold the system and their place within it.

As an observer you may be invited to take part in other people's constellations as a representative or be part of the circle that forms a boundary to the system being illuminated. It's very common that someone else's work will resonate deeply and that through their constellation you will clarify an issue of your own. For this reason the workshops are an engaging and rewarding learning experience for everybody who attends, whether or not they work directly on an issue.

Whoever or whatever someone represents in a workshop, they will have an embodied experience. It may be mild but it is always distinct, discernible and provides information that is used to guide the next steps. On many occasions the experience may be powerfully evocative for the representative. On some occasions the experience will be so powerful that they find it difficult to come out of the feelings and return to themselves.

In these situations the facilitator will carefully and sensitively 'de-role' the individual so they can settle back into themself again. The basis of any de-roling procedure is to return the contents of the representative experience to the system in which it belongs, while also recognizing that some of the information and insights will be of use to the person who represented them. A common form of de-roling is based on a set of words that are designed to achieve this. For example, the person who is struggling to get free of the feelings they had when in the constellation is invited to look at the client or 'issue holder' and say something along these lines: 'I represented someone/something important/powerful in your system. What was mine/ useful for me, I'll keep. The rest I'll leave with you and that system with great respect.'

This approach usually serves to separate out the individual's own experience from the client's system and respectfully returns the energy and potency of each to where they belong. Because some of the information and insights from the representative's experience will have been of great interest to the representative, the workshop experience is often described as just as evocative, illuminating and useful for those who simply 'observe' and represent as for those who bring an issue and become a 'client'.

Workshops are conducted in a safe and respectful environment where confidentiality agreements are usually made verbally between the participants. However, it is also common to work 'blind' where only the client (or 'issue holder') and facilitator know what the issue is and what the people chosen as elements of the system represent. This is an effective way to 'test' the forces that act on systems and the resulting dynamics, and will often result in some very useful understanding emerging amongst the participants and client.

Coaching constellations

Constellations in coaching can be used to diagnose problems, illuminate hidden dynamics and resources, and point towards fresh pictures of resolution. Although a constellation may, from the outside, appear to be simply a spatial representation, constellations add value because they draw out a systemic awareness that is otherwise unavailable to leaders and their coaches or consultants. The purpose of a constellation is to restore the integrity of the whole system, to restore a systemic coherence that supports the flow of leadership through the system. In this way the work also gives coaches, consultants and leaders the ability to get in touch with their own inner coherence and so enhance their own presence and performance.

> A constellation encourages participants to 'get out of their heads' and work from their 'felt sense' – at an intuitive level of 'knowing' that is very different from our normal understanding of knowing.

The largely non-verbal language exchange experienced in a constellation frees leaders, coaches and consultants from their familiar stories and allows a deeper systemic picture to emerge. Standing in the truth of that picture – the first stage of a constellation, and referred to as mapping – is often enough to start to free up fresh energy and allow new possibilities to emerge. Truths, insights, resources and solutions then start to emerge from the knowing field – the source of invisible information that naturally emerges in constellations.

Often, short sentences are offered by the facilitator or coach in constellations. These are designed to name the hidden loyalties and entanglements that exist in systems. Once these are spoken they begin to set the system free by revealing and disentangling what has become entangled or confused. The mix of silence, movements and system-orientated sentences encourages coach and leader alike to become more present and for fresh information and solutions to emerge.

Constellations are unusual in that they allow the client or 'issue holder' to experience themselves as both a participant and an observer at the same time. This is true in both workshop and one-to-one settings. In a workshop the client is most often invited to choose a representative for themselves and in one-to-one coaching a representative object. This is the beginning of the disentanglement process and leads to fresh information and greater clarity. By using representatives and tapping into the representatives' perception, coaches and leaders are given a unique insight into the dynamics of the systems they are exploring. This allows coaches to illuminate fresh information and sources of resolution that were previously unimaginable.

The application of systemic constellations in coaching is the subject of this book. They are underpinned by an understanding of the underlying principles and an inner attitude, a stance, which forms the foundations for this way of working. In a training environment you will hear many descriptions of the features and benefits of the work. The content doesn't differ, but the expression will. Just as you thought you had a complete understanding, you'll discover more, in each and every constellation.

The origins of this approach

The approach was originated in Europe by Bert Hellinger through application within family and then organizational systems. It has now been experienced by many hundreds of thousands of people across the world in personal, organizational, educational and other settings.

Hidden loyalties, identifications and entanglements are often revealed quickly, creating a reputation for getting to the underlying dynamics, freeing up a system and releasing fresh energy that leads to resolution. The combination of stance, principles and the practices have allowed coaches, leaders, teams and whole organizations to disentangle themselves from complex and limiting dynamics, as well as proactively build organizational health and make contact with fresh resources across the system.

Recognition of the importance of understanding systems is not new. After all, it was Aristotle who said: 'The whole is greater than the sum of the parts.' Hellinger's insights and the development of constellations allowed a new level of understanding of ancient truths and a new way of working with them to be applied in contemporary life and work.

In particular he highlighted and articulated a central and vitally important aspect of the human experience whether in relationship to self, another or larger systems like organizations. The importance and impact of the deep, arguably the deepest human need.

To belong.

His focus on the importance of belonging, and his use of the terms 'systemic guilt' and 'systemic innocence' in relation to the 'conscience group' that guards belonging in systems, underpins this approach to working with people in life, in leadership, organizational development and coaching.

It's an aspect of this way of thinking and working that can be seen and experienced in almost every moment of daily life and all relationship dynamics. One of the roles of systemic coaching is to bring the role and importance of belonging to the surface and respectfully illuminate the loyalties and dynamics it creates.

The next chapter explores the need to belong and the dynamics that emerge.

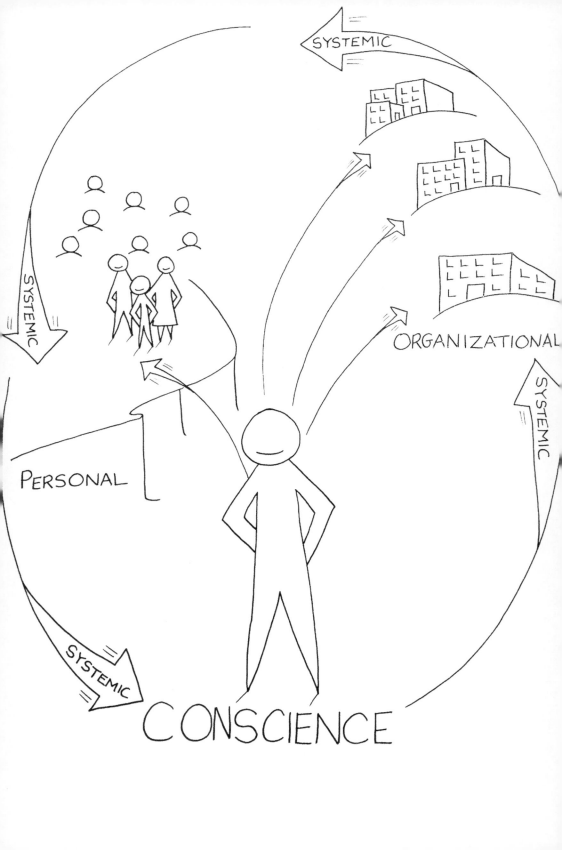

Belonging: Conscience, guilt and innocence

03

I wonder whether there is such a thing as individuality. Is it all a facade, covering a deep need to belong?

RABIH ALAMEDDINE

The need to belong and the dynamics that emerge

We all come from systems. Complex and overlapping relationship systems each with their own, mostly unspoken, rules of belonging. Our belonging in each system is unconscious but we carry with us an embodied sense of it, knowing when we are acting in alignment or out of alignment with it.

This awareness of systems starts at birth where we quickly learn the rules that protect our membership, that protect our belonging to the system into which we are born. This, our family-of-origin relationship system, is where we first learn about belonging – and leadership – and is the deepest pattern-maker for the rest of our lives and work. The family system is itself nested inside a wider social system, which also has a deep influence on our emerging consciousness.

We take this deep understanding of belonging into our life, our education systems and our work. We quickly tune into the rules that ensure our belonging in each system we join, testing to see how they align with us and with previous systems in which we have belonged.

Unspoken rules about behaviour are implicit and 'known' soon after we have joined each system. 'This is who and what we accept and this is who and what we exclude.' 'This is how we treat each other.' 'This is how we treat our partners, our suppliers, our customers. And those who leave.'

Belonging is everywhere; it permeates our language and our culture and is a key part of our sense of identity. When we journey through different schools as a child we quickly learn that the larger system is divided into sub-systems with names and colours that become a vital part of our sense of place and identity in the class, the group, the team, the school.

As adults we are surrounded by overt invitations to belong – the membership clubs in our supermarkets, gyms, restaurants and airlines. Each wants us to belong, to become and then stay loyal, each tries to build a strong sense of that belonging and keep us 'in'. These informal clubs bring out strong primary feelings in members and potential members and loyalty is rewarded.

The decline of family structures and the rise of social media have heightened the rewards and costs of belonging. The current trend in TV talent shows plays on our need to be 'in' rather than 'out'. The emotional impact of inclusion or exclusion is felt by the audience at home almost as strongly as amongst the contestants, tapping into our deep need to belong, to be included.

The role that belonging plays in our lives is also the subject of humour in popular entertainment, cartoons and feature films. The *Godfather* trilogy created such a powerful global following because it deals with the idea of belonging, of being 'in' or 'out' of the Corleone family, in very visceral and emotional ways. *Meet the Fockers*, with its idea of a family 'circle of trust', for example, speaks directly to the rewards and challenges of belonging in family systems and the extent to which families define their boundaries and defend their rules.

Another example is the 'People's Front' sketch in the Monty Python film *The Life of Brian*, in which the members of a group argue about its name and the rules of belonging. The sketch begins with the line 'Can I join your group?' and ends with a single word: 'Splitter!' This sketch cleverly expresses the need to be included in groups of belonging and the exclusion of others as an inevitable product of that. The importance to people of articulating precisely the name and boundary of their system is also highlighted along with the price people pay when they leave or are excluded.

At the end of the sketch they also show how groups (of belonging) often hold most animosity for another group that's very similar to them in almost every way except for a different name, badge or colour. The subtle but huge differences in belonging between two apparently close systems can be seen every day both on the battlefields of the world and also in all competitive team sports. The differences in what each side believes and does may be marginal but the loyalties, rivalry and emotions created are enormous. Choosing which system you belong to, to which you will be loyal, makes a significant impact on all your behaviours and actions that follow. And can be a matter of life or death.

~

So, attempts to meet our deep need to belong are everywhere – and perhaps especially strong in organizational and indeed coaching communities. People bring their skills, experience, motivation and talent into organizations but they will also bring their need to belong, especially if this was not fully met in another system, often the family-of-origin. This puts a strain on the organization that it's not designed to handle. Expectations and needs can't be met and this in turn leads to many difficulties and difficult leavings.

Challenging exits that don't respectfully honour the bonds that form through membership, and don't acknowledge what was gained and what was lost, create ties and entanglements that can reach forward for many years, through many systems, leaving an entanglement of unresolved dynamics.

Belonging in systems creates loyalties and understanding loyalties is central to this way of working with coaching clients. The hidden loyalties in systems are often a source of resistance and, once brought into the light, the key to lasting resolution and freedom.

As so many of us coaches are 'teaching what we need to learn', this aspect can be important in developing a truly objective, systemic stance and approach to client work and working relationships.

Belonging. It begins in the family

You can feel it if someone has a strong and deep sense of belonging in their family-of-origin. They are grounded; they embody a calm and calming energy. They have plenty of resources that they can offer to others, but they know and respect the boundaries of their offerings and are self-contained, resourced from within. They don't impose themselves or their ideas on others; they don't get over emotional when joining or leaving other systems.

Some of these individuals become coaches, using their secure base from which to work and be useful to others. But this is fairly unusual. For coaches, like many therapists and others who 'help', are often those who have struggled to belong. As a result, those who struggled to either find a safe place in their family-of-origin, or who judged their family as not good enough, may find themselves attracted to the belonging of a coaching association, federation or other professional community provides.

Alternatively they may feel safer holding onto the comfort of familiar separateness and become adamant about defending their independence from any group, in secret fear that they wouldn't be able to find their place safely or might be rejected.

If these patterns and dynamics are seen and resolved through compassionate systemic intervention, the entanglements can loosen and become a deep resource for the coach, enabling them to offer a systemic perspective to their clients, having been on the journey of insight and integration themself.

We inevitably bring our innate need to belong in to our work as coaches. When we do that consciously it can be healthy for the coach and client alike, creating deeper levels of awareness and growth in both. Done without conscious awareness it can be both limiting for the client and exhausting for the coach.

Coaching with belonging in mind can support us to be more fully present and aware with our clients, in our work.

- The deepest human need is to belong. Belonging can only occur with others, in a system, a relationship system. The process starts at birth as we bond and belong. This is the first system we encounter and belong within and we call it family.

- Families have rules that protect belonging. Some are spoken and known, some are unspoken but still deeply known. Without words being necessary we quickly understand what we need to say, how we need to behave in order to belong in our family system.

- Our family-of-origin system is the deepest pattern-maker for the rest of our lives and work. We stay loyal to our family-of-origin 'way', especially when we protest that we don't.

- Loyalty protects belonging. As an example, it's hard for people to allow themselves to become happier or more successful than their own parents were able to be. This is an example of a hidden loyalty and once illuminated, respectfully seen and integrated, can transform life and work.

- Modern life and the ease of international travel have created some challenging dynamics around belonging, some of which can be seen in people who describe themselves as 'third-culture kids', those brought up outside traditional family structures or who spent much of their childhood in residential or boarding schools.

- Through life we build an inner hierarchy of belonging and the loyalties that emerge from that. We refer to this hierarchy, mostly unconsciously, when there is conflict, confusion or disagreement about how to behave, how to belong.
- Belonging in each system has many rewards as well as being the source of hidden loyalties and entanglements.
- The 'rules' and judgements of our family-of-origin or 'primary conscience group' have no inherent moral value; they are simply the rules of belonging in our family.

Conscience groups

All systems are influenced by organizing forces which attempt to maintain the coherence of the whole. This is where the principles of TIME, PLACE and EXCHANGE come from – they are products of the systemic conscience. The systemic conscience attempts to maintain a coherence and dynamic balance in the system and creates a kind of framework for everything else to happen, rather like an operating system in a computer. Like an operating system it's invisible but if you ignore or violate its rules you'll feel its powerful impact.

Conscience

The invisible and often unspoken governing force which maintains the system at any cost.

Loyalty to one particular conscience group drives one set of behaviours, actions and responses. In another system you tune into a different conscience and quickly adapt to different rules that protect your membership. So, 'conscience' in this context means the need to protect our belonging to a group that drives us to hold certain beliefs and express certain behaviours in that group, and a different combination in another.

A conscience group that becomes a moral authority excludes those who don't agree with the judgements and so may cause damage and pain in relationship systems rather than safety and inclusion.

When we are children we can move from one conscience group to another easily and intuitively. As we get older and we develop a complex web of loyalties we may take a little longer to adapt.

- Each system is governed by a conscience that is created as a result of all the people and events that have belonged within it as well by systemic conscience which influences all systems.

- Our belonging in each system we join becomes conscious when we step over the boundaries of acceptable behaviours. We sense when we are acting in or out of alignment with it.

- When we act in alignment with the conscience group we feel 'innocent' and when we step outside it we feel 'guilty' in relationship to it.

- The conflicts we see in the world, in the world of work and as coaches are often due to a clash between different conscience groups. The need to defend belonging to one conscience group in the face of a perceived or actual dominance from another can be felt as, and sometimes is, a matter of life and death.

You can consider three different kinds of consciences when you work as a coach: personal, organizational and systemic conscience.

Let's take a closer look at each.

Personal conscience

The personal conscience emerges out of the lively cocktail of land-of-origin and family-of-origin bonding experience, innate personality type and events in our childhood. It's re-formed and reshaped as we learn how to belong in different schools and education systems and when we form each new group of friends. It's challenged, reshaped and moulded again as we enter the world of work and learn of the many other kinds of personal conscience, those we feel easily aligned with, those we feel strongly opposed to and everything in between.

We gather and internalize, deeply, sets of attitudes and beliefs about relationships, about work, about others. The attitudes and beliefs become our internal reference system.

Our personal conscience tells us whether we conform to or violate the rules of belonging and is formed only by the rules of the system in which we belong. Its function is to maintain the group as it is. When we act in alignment with it we feel we belong and therefore feel 'innocent'. Acting in alignment with our personal conscience protects our belonging and creates a feeling of 'innocence'. We then justify all kinds of actions and behaviours in its name.

Despite a sense of self-righteous belief to the contrary, our personal conscience is not a guide to right and wrong in a different family or a larger context. It's simply a set of reference points, an inner compass that tells us whether we are acting in or out of alignment with our systems of origin.

Personal conscience is like an inner voice that asks, 'Is what I'm doing and saying keeping me in the group or casting me out? Do I belong? Am I being loyal? If I'm disloyal can I tolerate the feeling of guilt or exclusion?'

Ask yourself: 'Where are my origins?'
It's likely that your personal conscience, in its most elemental form, will have begun to form there.

Guilt and innocence

The personal conscience often lies at the roots of interpersonal, organizational and indeed global conflict. Many people whose behaviour is considered 'bad' or 'dysfunctional' are motivated by deep loyalty that is protecting their belonging. Chronic stress, sudden exclusion from a group – or an opportunity to demonstrate their deep loyalty in relationship to the group – can be at the root of some very destructive behaviours.

I can still remember, when I was participating in a family constellations workshop 15 years ago, how the facilitator brought this idea to life by explaining that someone who perpetrates a violent act, like a suicide bomber for example, believes they are acting in deep accordance with their personal conscience – so they perpetrate these very damaging acts with a feeling of 'innocence'. Meaning that, for them, they feel aligned with and so innocent in relationship to their belonging within a particular conscience group, because their actions are an expression of their deep loyalty and so protect their membership.

> *The soldier fights not because he hates what is in front of him, but because he loves what is behind him.*
>
> G K Chesterton

This understanding of such difficult and damaging behaviour doesn't excuse it, or make it right in the moral sense; it simply illuminates one of the deeper motivations, the importance of belonging and the powerful loyalties that emerge from that. In this way one can see how moral judgements have limited value when trying to understand damaging actions; they merely condemn or support them. Moral judgements neither deepen the understanding or resolve anything in the system.

Painful and limiting patterns like this, when dynamics emerging from belonging underpin them, are likely to repeat until the source of the original loyalty is revealed and respected.

> *A moralist is someone who uses a small measuring instrument for the great world.*
>
>   Bert Hellinger

This single insight – that extraordinary and sometimes very damaging behaviour is done with feelings of 'innocence' out of strong, often partly unconscious loyalty to a conscience group – transformed my understanding of life and work and then my coaching practice.

After all, very challenging and painful behaviour is not that uncommon in organizational systems. Most people know what it's like to work with somebody whose impact may be described as 'toxic' or indeed to coach someone who we are told behaves in a 'very difficult' way with their peers or direct reports.

Guilt and innocence

Because we know instinctively what will jeopardize our membership in each system we attempt to stay 'innocent' in relationship to it, so that we protect our belonging. Not challenging, staying loyal to maintain the feeling of belonging and innocence.

When we act out of alignment and risk our belonging we feel 'guilty' because we have risked our membership of the group.

When you're coaching somebody who has difficult behaviours that hurt others it can feel hard to get past the story – or the 360 feedback – and coach without judgement on 'right' or 'wrong'. But if you can coach with respect for what is and with an understanding of loyalty to conscience groups in mind you will get a different level of contact with your coachee and increase the chances of them making a lasting change in behaviour. After all, all behaviour makes sense when you look at it in the context of the system to which it is an act of loyalty.

There is more on the subject elsewhere in this book, particularly where we explore the use of sentences to challenge and soften potential systemic dynamics. For example, the sentence 'To whom are you loyal when you do that?' can be useful when working with an issue that you sense may be connected to the dynamics around belonging. Or this: 'Who watches you and smiles in agreement when you behave like that?'

When you can coach beyond judgement on right and wrong then you can hold a safe space for individuals and teams to look at their challenges with great respect for everything as it is. All kinds of deeper truths and loyalties can emerge that release individuals, groups and teams to flow again.

Putting it another way, see if you can agree to everything just as it is. That doesn't require you to agree *with* everything. Simply agree *to* everything as it is and you will begin to adopt the radically inclusive, non-judgemental stance that makes systemic coaching a way of being, not a way of doing.

The Rumi quote that begins Chapter 5 sums up this inner attitude and intention very well: 'Out beyond ideas of right and wrong, there is a field. I'll meet you there.'

> People change their behaviour in order to belong in systems. Their attempts to stay innocent in relation to the system they work within may result in them becoming guilty in relation to another system.

The implications of belonging and the dynamics that emerge as a result of it for leadership and for organizational health are very significant and are touched on throughout this book. When leaders can lead with belonging and hidden loyalties in mind their leadership will have a very different quality to it. The implications for society and politics, both local and global are beyond the scope of this book.

> Feelings of guilt surface when we act out of alignment with any of our conscience groups because that endangers our belonging.

Many coaching and leadership books are underpinned with the idea that there is 'good' and 'bad', that there is a 'right' and a 'wrong'. These are moral judgements and take no account of systems and conscience groups, guilt and innocence.

In fact there is only 'what is', and looking at it all with compassion for belonging and an understanding of loyalty changes the perspective. This is a part of the non-judgemental stance of systemic coaching and one that underpins constellations themselves.

Looked at in this way it becomes clear why many of the traditional leadership development and other organizational interventions and coaching methodologies may sometimes struggle to have a lasting effect when such powerful and invisible dynamics as guilt, innocence and loyalty to conscience groups are at play. This is where systemic coaching can have an impact and add value.

Loyalty

There are many times within a coaching relationship and process where the understanding of conscience, loyalty, guilt and innocence are important.

> *I noticed my client's body language was incongruent with her words. A constellation revealed the hidden loyalty.*

For example when I think about my own coaching practice, I recall starting to work with a man, the leader of a technology company, who despite commissioning me as a coach found the idea of coaching itself very difficult to relax into. He was a deeply intelligent man and a pioneer in his field who had self-taught his way to building a company that produced world-class products. However, his resistance to getting any kind of 'help' or support made it almost impossible for him to engage in a meaningful way. Trusting that his request for coaching was genuine I found myself wondering to whom he was being loyal when he resisted being supported, so I asked him: 'Who would be pleased with you – who would smile on you – if they saw you resist in this way?'

'Oh!' he said. 'My father. He would say, "What on earth are you doing, son? You can do all this yourself!"'

He found this connection and deep loyalty to his first system, his family-of-origin system really fascinating as it was something he had not considered before. It enabled him to understand the concept of the deep loyalty that protects belonging. Belonging in his family-of-origin system meant 'do it alone'.

Most people understand that if they played a particular role in their family they're likely to mirror that in their working relationships. People who played the fool, the saint or the saviour are likely to play these roles at work. Those who struggled with an authoritarian parent are likely to have difficulties with authority figures at work. Some people have very complex relationships with their siblings and they are often the same people who later struggle in teams or with peers.

This playing out of redundant family roles is common and fairly commonly understood. But there is something else just as powerful but much less understood than this. Something that drives and something that limits personal, team, leadership and whole business success.

Loyalty. Hidden loyalty to the family system. Often unconscious and rarely discussed, these powerful loyalties play a very significant role in life and work.

I went on to offer him a simple table-top constellation in which he asked a representative for his father for permission to learn about leadership development. He found this difficult too – an embodied manifestation of his deep loyalty and attempts to stay 'innocent'. He was understanding that to grow and develop we must become 'guilty' in relationship to a previous system. This proved to be a breakthrough session that enabled real contact between us and between him and the leadership developmental journey he was embarking on.

As a coach, resist the temptation to become loyal to the client and their story instead of the system and its dynamics.

As an added benefit it also allowed him to translate an understanding of conscience groups, guilt innocence and loyalties into his marriage. When you form an intimate partnership with someone you will inevitably need to spend time negotiating around your personal conscience and need to negotiate an integration of each. In your attempts to remain innocent in the way we mean it here, you may take a stand on issues connected to money, eating times, raising children, entertainment choices and behaviour at social occasions. As you stretch out of your comfort zone and become guilty to your previous system you build a new set of rules, responses and behaviours in your new system, letting some aspects of your personal conscience go.

Belonging and loyalty

- Belonging expresses itself through loyalty. Loyalties run deep and their impact is far-reaching. Hidden loyalties can resource but also limit individuals, teams and organizations.

- Unconscious loyalties to previous systems – which often occur because of a judgement over them – bind us and limit forward movement.
- Inertia, feelings of confusion, resistance to change, difficult behaviour and 'dysfunctional' individuals or teams can often be expressions of hidden loyalties or unacknowledged bonds to systems. To a family or social system, to an original intention, to those who started the system, to those that have left or been ejected from the system.
- You can begin to explore questions of belonging and the hidden loyalties that develop as a result of it by asking yourself, then your clients:
    - 'To whom are you being loyal when you behave like that/stay stuck like that/react like that?'
    - 'Who would look at this "dysfunction" and be pleased?'
    - 'To which relationship system in which you have belonged is this a sign of loyalty?'
    - 'To whom would you be disloyal if you chose to behave differently?'
- When coaching with the importance of belonging and loyalty in mind you can work on, illuminate and support resolution of the dynamics emerging from it. In yourself and your clients.

Growth requires guilt

- The loyalties to your system, to protect your belonging and stay with your feelings of 'innocence' are sometimes stronger than the loyalty to your own growth and success.
- Staying aligned with your original systems may limit your capacity to support others on developmental journeys, the need to stay innocent will limit your field of view.
- If you stay loyal to your original systems then you may find that you attract clients who are loyal to the same or very similar attitudes, beliefs and values. In this way you may accidentally collude with the stories and judgements they tell you and then you will have lost contact with a systemic perspective.
- Alternatively, you may find you strongly disagree with your clients' values, morals or judgements, in which case you will also find it difficult to coach with the balance of the whole system in mind, agreeing *to* everything, especially including your clients' own systemic loyalties, just as it is and just as they are.

All growth will include guilty feelings.

Bert Hellinger

So, personal and professional growth and development require us to become 'guilty' in relation to the various systems in which we have belonged. If we stay 'innocent' in relation to our original systems (family system, spiritual or social systems) we may not gather the 'weight', the gravitas to coach (or lead) others, relying instead on a framework of rational ideas, tools and models.

In this way belonging within conscience groups and the loyalties this creates can be important in your development as a coach. Exploring to whom and to what you are privately loyal when you are working with an individual, a team or group can be a fundamental part of the journey towards systemic coaching.

> *It takes courage to make the transition from our original conscience group. When this movement into guilt is facilitated with respect and acknowledgment for what was given and what was received it can bring profound growth and strength.*
>
> Alastair Kidd

For if we bring unconscious loyalties, or if we bring judgements about good and bad into our ideas about life, leadership or coaching this can have an impact on the system with which we are working. This is an area that we explore in the trainings because it's an essential building block for developing a systemic stance – an aspect of this work that is also addressed later in the book.

Here is something Bert Hellinger said about resistance to change, which may help illustrate why we can struggle to develop and grow:

> *I'll tell you something about happiness. Often, happiness seems dangerous because it tends to make people lonely. The same is true of solutions to problems. Solutions are often experienced as dangerous because they make people lonely, whereas problems and unhappiness seem to attract company.*
>
> *Problems and unhappiness often attach themselves to feelings of innocence and loyalty, whereas solutions and happiness are often associated with feelings of betrayal or guilt. Not that such feelings of guilt are reasonable, but they are experienced as feelings of betrayal and guilt all the same. That's why the transition from the problem to the solution is so difficult.*
>
> *But if what I've said to you now is true, and if you accept it as such, you'll have to change your whole orientation!*
>
> Bert Hellinger, *Love's Own Truth*

Leaving and joining

Leaving systems and joining others is a fundamentally important part on the journey of life and work as it requires us to respectfully soften one set of loyalties and establish belonging in another system. That's a delicate balance because of loyalty to conscience groups and the associated feelings of 'guilt' and 'innocence'. For this reason leaving a system is often more complex than we like to imagine and as a result the tails of a challenging or difficult leaving can be long.

To separate from a system and be free to move and grow you first have to acknowledge your belonging and what you gained from that. In the case of a family system that is life itself; in the case of an organizational system it may be industry experience, skills, friendships, insights about yourself and more.

If you don't feel ready or able to acknowledge what was received from each system in which you have belonged, the balance of EXCHANGE, you may find yourself increasingly looking back with resentment or unsure of yourself, unable to fully join a new system.

To facilitate this approach with your coaching clients you will need to look back into your own systems, your own belonging, respectfully disentangling and then resourcing yourself from within the system even in separating from it. Take some time to map all the systems in which you have belonged, either drawing on a piece of paper, or by creating a physical map using representative objects. Notice to which systems you are most loyal, to which you felt a deep belonging and to which you didn't. Notice to which you act feeling 'innocent' and with which you have to tolerate feelings of 'guilt' in order to create change and growth.

What you judge you become.

The way you leave a system is crucial to your ability to develop and grow into others. If you consciously decide that you don't want to belong to a particular system, you don't want to be like 'them', and you leave without acknowledgment for what you gained, you are likely to end up becoming just like them.

Take for example your family of origin. If you judge them as 'bad' or 'not good enough' and design your life to be different, special or 'better' you may be frustrated by how many times you discover you are simply repeating the pattern or behaviour you are trying to avoid.

Or you may have been part of a business organization in which you felt bruised or disapproved of the leadership style and if you leave to set up a system of your own, or join one that is 'better' you may find the same patterns repeating.

If, on the other hand, you leave with respect and acknowledgment for what you've gained, balancing the EXCHANGE, then you can be free and grow. Happily this process can be completed long after you have left a system with which you still feel entangled.

If, as many coaches who have moved out of life in an organization do, you have a difficult leaving in your past and you don't process this difficulty, you will become entangled in it. You may then attract clients with the same or a very similar dynamic. If your own issue, your own entanglement remains unconscious and unresolved you risk re-entangling yourself and your clients in what can be an endless cycle in an attempt to resolve something in the system. This underlying dynamic can be *respectfully* revealed and resolved in constellations and is a familiar subject for those who travel on a systemic coaching training or developmental journey.

When illuminated and resolved as a conscious process it can transform your entanglements into your hidden resource, even your specialism. As with all aspects of this work this requires you to really look and keep looking at your own belonging in systems.

This level of understanding of the power and importance of belonging combined with a non-judgemental and inclusive stance which gives everything and everyone a place just as it is or they are, is hard to achieve but can make a significant difference to your work as a coach and the developmental journeys of your clients.

Personal conscience

- The deepest need is to belong. We belong in systems, relationship systems. The primary pattern maker for our lives and work is our family system.
- We know we belong when we act in a way that keeps us in the group, within the conscience group of that particular system.
- The purpose of conscience is to define and protect the system boundary and bond us to the group. It has no intrinsic moral value but establishes its own ideas about 'right and wrong'.
- Each system expresses its own rules of belonging through a certain mindset and attitude, its own particular language and actions unique to that group. We know we must adopt these in order to belong.
- We have an inner compass that tells us when we are within the boundary of the system conscience and belong or when we are outside it and risk our belonging. What is acceptable and feels right in one system may not be acceptable in another.
- Belonging within the conscience group creates feelings of connection and of 'innocence'; we know we have a right to belong and this results in deep loyalties.
- Actions and behaviours that don't align with the conscience of that group, that system, risk our belonging, separate us from the group and we feel 'guilty'.

- Every coach and every coaching client is nested within multiple overlapping systems and conscience groups. We all come from multiple belongings in many systems.

- We all come from family and this forms the foundations of our personal conscience and is our first experience of belonging. For growth we may need to *respectfully* expand beyond this primary system and become 'guilty', reshaping our personal conscience to include other truths and possibilities.

- People who stay 'innocent' in relationship to their primary conscience group often have strong views on 'right and wrong' and may make moral judgments based on these. They may adhere to strict doctrines, share absolute beliefs and prefer only literal explanations.

- People who become 'guilty' in relationship to their primary system without respecting and integrating what it has given them may suffer from feelings of isolation and exhaustion.

- People who become 'guilty' to their primary system in a respectful way – integrating what was useful and looking at what was not with systemic insight and compassion – will be able to tolerate and learn from a wider range of attitudes and behaviours without judgement over them. When we can take what has been given to us exactly the way that it is and with respect, we feel resourced and can expand what has been given and pass it on. In this way we don't feel isolated but extended, taking something valuable and growing it.

- People who have made this journey can work with and agree to what is, just as it is, working with insight and beyond judgement.

- Growing, tolerating feelings of guilt, is not an easy path but can result in a quiet authority and the capacity to coach, or lead, a wide range of people from many systems without partiality, intention or depletion.

Organizational conscience

A unique set of mostly unspoken rules of belonging or 'organizational conscience' emerges in each system as a result of the founding intention and relationship dynamics and then all the events, successes and failures and all the people that have been a part of the system. Each organizational entity has its own memory of all that has taken place within it. Some may call this the organizational unconscious or simply the culture but I sense it's more than that; it's a unique combination of dynamics within the organizational system that creates a set of rules that govern inclusion or exclusion, the flow of leadership and organizational health.

This is why I will often put in a representative for 'the culture as it's described' and another for 'the culture as it's actually experienced' in workshop and table-top constellations to open up the space that often exists between the two. It's in that space that you may often find the roots of the organizational conscience.

Naturally the personal conscience of each individual within the system both creates and also rubs up against the organizational conscience and when you join there is either a natural fit and alignment, or there is not. This is the source of much stress and conflict in organizational systems when an individual's personal conscience (they may describe it as 'my personal values') comes into conflict with the organization's desire for different attitudes and behaviours.

Take a moment to reflect on all the organizational systems in which you have belonged.

Starting with the first professional system you joined and the businesses or organizations that followed it. See where the tension rises as you recognize conflicts between your personal conscience and the organizational consciences you found yourself working in. Notice where there was strong fit, an alignment between the two and how that felt. Notice when there was not a comfortable fit and reflect on where that tension came from.

Then ask yourself: What was the benefit and cost of being a member of each?

To which of these systems are you still most loyal?

If you are familiar with the methodology and application of sentences that name what is then you may notice some emerging for you as you reflect. To take this a step further try the exercise at the end of this chapter.

~

Since writing the first edition of this book I have spent some time working with senior leaders and heads of division within a large European Union institution with global reach. I was invited into the system because a manager with responsibility for coaching and team development had seen me facilitate an introduction to systemic coaching and constellations at a conference. So the invitation into the system was explicitly a 'systemic' one, though the systemic issues were invisible for quite a while and remained unspoken until a systemic intervention (described in the exercise 'TIME: An exercise for use in team coaching' on page 20) revealed them.

What became clear was that when an organization has been started in a particular country with a certain mix of national identities or conscience groups, this creates a set of dynamics and behaviours that have a key role in defining the original culture and unspoken rules of belonging.

When the original cultural reference points of an organization are acknowledged and included and the rules of belonging that were originally so important are acknowledged and spoken about, then people can separate more fully from them and move into the future with a much greater degree of willingness to accept and adopt new rules and an evolving culture. The loyalties to the 'old way' soften and dissolve once seen and respectfully acknowledged.

That working relationship proved to be a useful reminder of the importance of looking back and acknowledging foundations and cultural reference points of a system if one is to truly understand its rules, hidden resources and unspoken dynamics.

~

If we choose to act out of alignment with an organizational conscience, we damage our belonging and often pay a price for that. To illustrate that, we can look at the impact of becoming disloyal to an organization by becoming a 'whistleblower'. Despite expressed support for honesty and the reporting of behaviour deemed inappropriate, individuals may find that their own behaviour – in 'good conscience' – threatens their place in that system. For many this means years of 'fighting the system' at great personal cost.

> *There can be loss of income, house, friends, marriage. There are health issues and sometimes even death because of the stress.*
> John R Phillips, lawyer for whistleblowers, Washington

The threat of being ostracized by the group is often enough to force compliance. Disloyalty is almost always punished by exclusion and the price of that exclusion illuminates how central belonging is to the human condition, at home and at work.

Fred Alford, professor of government at the University of Maryland, is the author of *Whistleblowers: Broken lives and organizational power*, a study of the impact of whistleblowing. Of his substantial sample group, most lost their jobs and never worked in the same field again; many also lost their families, as court cases and tribunals dragged on for 10 years or more.

The sanctity of whistleblowing may be written into law, both in the UK and US, but for most it is a traumatic experience. This can be the price of disloyalty to the group, the organizational conscience group.

Organizational conscience at work

- The personal conscience of the founders creates the foundations and this combines with all the people that work within the organization, all the events that take place, the purpose and intention, to form the organizational conscience.
- Each organizational system develops its own spoken and unspoken rules of belonging and this forms a field that influences those who come into its sphere. We may often refer to this as 'the way we do things here' or 'the culture'.

- In the world of work we quickly tune into the rules of belonging in each system in which we become a member. When we join a new system, a business, organization or professional group we are asking ourselves 'What do I have to do, how do I behave, in order to belong here?'
  - A useful question to ask your clients if you want to open a systemic perspective for them and your coaching: 'What do you have to do here, in this system, in order to protect your belonging in it?'
- As we learn the unspoken rules in each professional or organizational system we naturally attempt to stay 'innocent' in relationship to them, so to protect our belonging. These attempts however may clash with our personal conscience and we feel we are not quite fitting in as we try and find our place in between two differing conscience groups.
- Our sense of belonging and wellbeing in an organizational system comes in large part from our sense of what we have to agree with or compromise to belong.
- If we choose to be disloyal to the unspoken rules of belonging, the organizational conscience, we may pay the price of exclusion.

Systemic conscience

Systemic conscience works in the collective unconscious of all relationship systems. It's a force that works with the primary intention of sustaining the coherence of the whole system and creating a dynamic balance within it no matter what the cost.

Attempts to ignore or to violate the system's natural drive for coherence, entangles people and other elements in the system in efforts to restore the structure and systemic hierarchy.

The systemic conscience and the forces that arise from it, recruits people within the system in order to achieve the balance it seeks. From the perspective of the system everything and everyone has to be included, which is the principle of PLACE. So, an individual will be recruited by the systemic conscience to represent someone who has been excluded. Put it another way, the system will attempt to 're-member' them.

For example, when a founder is 'forgotten' or unfairly dismissed by those that join later, the system will entangle someone in that dynamic until the founder and their contribution are remembered with respect. This 're-membering' by systems is very common but not commonly or well understood. (See case study on page 180).

> Systemic forces are like gravity.
>
> When we agree with them life and work flow.

The systemic conscience has no interest in the individual or their personal conscience; it simply serves to protect the integrity of the *whole*. As long as it stays unconscious and unspoken it tends to create difficulties and complexities that are hard to illuminate or resolve.

This is where systemic coaching and constellations can have a deep impact as they're designed to give the system a voice and illuminate and resolve system entanglements.

Coaching questions that may be useful when illuminating the systemic conscience:

'Who started this system'? (TIME and PLACE)

'Who/what else belonged here, before now?' (TIME and PLACE)

'What is not being said here?' (What unspoken sentences exist and are being embodied here? The missing conversations. What has not been *acknowledged*.)

'What do you have to do to belong here?' (What is the price and benefit of belonging? What do you have to do or say to stay *innocent* in relationship to the organizational conscience?)

'What does this organization owe to others eg its suppliers or customers?' (EXCHANGE)

'Has anything happened here that is difficult to talk about?' (PLACE)

'Who has left but not had their contribution acknowledged – or acknowledged how they benefitted?' (EXCHANGE)

Much of the rest of this book, together with the case studies in it, further explains and brings the impact of systemic conscience to life in multiple ways.

Belonging and systemic conscience

- Beyond the personal and organizational conscience is the systemic conscience, which attempts to create coherence in all systems.
- Its effects are hard to see but clearly felt when the organizing forces (TIME, PLACE, EXCHANGE) are ignored or violated. These violations are at the root of multiple organizational difficulties, inertia and conflict.
- Organizational systems are more complex than family systems because they have the family systems and the personal conscience of everybody in them.
  - The mix of conscience groups and conflicting loyalties creates much of the tension, confusion and resistance to change in contemporary organizational life.
  - Systemic coaching and constellations have much to offer in this area as they are designed to respectfully acknowledge and separate out the differing loyalties, giving each a place and bringing the whole into balance.

- You can access and work at the level of the system and the systemic conscience, whether working with an individual, group or team by using the stance, principles and practices of systemic coaching and constellations.

How this might be useful for you as a coach

- Because all coaching will include systemic issues connected to belonging it can be important to tune into them and know how to access them.
  - Systemic issues are not resolved through linear interventions. Systemic issues require systemic awareness, insight and interventions.
- Because all coaches have resources and entanglements within several systems in which they have belonged it may be important to explore and soften these.
  - The completed leavings in your past will strengthen and resource you as a coach, allowing you to be useful, to coach the system, rather than helping at an individual or team level.
  - A bond to a system in which you belonged may need to be acknowledged and softened before your neutral stance can be fully accessed.
  - If your own need to belong is not satisfied outside coaching it will influence how you 'show up' as a coach, and how you coach. Fill your own cup first.
- Because working with all the resources, entanglements and loyalties in the systems that your client has belonged within requires you to explore the same in the systems in which you have belonged.
  - If you exclude any systems – and many coaches keep clear of the family of origin – you are excluding the roots and sources of the client.
- Because it's easy as a coach to become partisan, partial to the stories and judgements that your clients tell you.
  - With an understanding of belonging in conscience groups it is easier to maintain a truly neutral, impartial stance and work beyond the story within a more accurate context for the material your client brings.
  - The embodiment of this stance underpins systemic coaching and allows the coach to find and hold a systemic attitude in which there are no longer ideas about 'right and wrong' or 'good and bad'.

– Agree *to* everything just as it is. This deeply respectful approach to what is, just as it is, opens up a space for clients, whether individual, team or group, that allows truths to emerge and fresh energy to flow.

- Questions connected to belonging to ask yourself as a coach:
  - Who looks kindly on me when I work as a coach? (Within family-of-origin, land-of-origin, ancestors, teachers and previous organizational system leaders etc.)
  - In relationship to which system do I remain 'innocent' when I'm coaching? With which may I need to tolerate feelings of 'guilt'? (Family-of-origin, land-of-origin, ancestors, education and organizational systems etc.)
  - Am I prepared to tolerate the 'guilt' (act in a way that could risk my belonging in a system I belong/belonged in) required for growth and change within me as a person and as a coach?
  - Am I able to work beyond ideas about 'right' and 'wrong' and agree to everything, just as it is? Can I allow each person and each system to be as it is without 'fixing' it?

How this might be useful for your clients

- All coaching clients will have loyalties and entanglements within several systems (family, social and organizational) in which they have belonged, so all coaching will include systemic issues.
  - The illumination and resolution of these loyalties and entanglements in personal and organizational systems is one of the benefits of systemic coaching with constellations.
- All coaching clients come from family systems. Their roots and many of their resources, as well as some loyalties and limitations, are held within that system. They will also have had their first experience of leadership within that primary system.
  - When their leadership includes these truths – in themselves and in others that they lead – their authority can be followed and trusted.

- Systemic issues require systemic interventions if they are to be illuminated and resolved.
  - Linear solutions to systemic issues may appear to work at first but the inertia or difficulty will return, often deepen and expand, until a systemic perspective and methodology are used to dissolve and resolve it.
- When leaders understand their own belonging needs they expand their understanding of their own behaviours and patterns and those of others.
  - Recognizing that an organization cannot meet the need to belong that was not met in another system can liberate clients and reduce the cost and impact of working in an organization.
- The simple awareness of the importance of belonging can clarify and soften views of explicit sub-systems that are seen as 'difficult', for example groups of belonging like workers' unions, professional groupings and pressure groups.
  - A leader who understands the impact of personal conscience and hidden loyalties will be able to lead a safe and inclusive organizational system, allowing each to belong.
- Leaders and others who use coaching to develop themselves find it clarifying and liberating when their hidden loyalties to people and systems of belonging in the past are respectfully illuminated and softened.
  - For example a coaching client who gets to a certain level in an organization but can't seem to occupy the authority required at the next level may be loyal to a family pattern where leadership was avoided and success was elusive or cost too much.
  - These kind of unconscious attempts to stay 'innocent' in relationship to a primary conscience group can have a significant impact on people's lives and work.
  - Facilitating a respectful release from previous systems is something that this methodology can offer coaching clients. They are then free to move forward to fresh goals and levels of success.
- Leaders who understand the organizing principles of systems will be able to acknowledge what is, use the past as a resource to move into the future, honour who and what has contributed so others feel able to make their contribution, ensure each has a place and let people leave with acknowledgement and respect.

An exercise for you

To facilitate this approach with your coaching clients you may need to look back into your own systems, your own belongings. When you can see it all, like a peacock's tail of belongings behind you, then you can start to respectfully disentangle yourself from certain people, events and systems.

Constellations offer a particularly respectful and balancing way of doing this. Then you can resource yourself from within each system in which you have belonged.

If you are reading this book as part of a coaching circle book club or other peer-learning group you can open up your understanding of this important aspect by inviting those with you to stand up and represent people and events in a system in which you have belonged. If you are reading alone then you can do this with table-top representatives or floor markers.

Think of a system in which you have belonged and choose three or four representatives to represent the key people or events, and mark the system boundary, the 'conscience' of that system, with string or similar. Stand in front of them and see what emerges.

For example you could set up representatives (people, floor markers or objects on the table top) for a business or other organizational system in which you have belonged and with which you sense you may still be attached or entangled, due to loyalties and dynamics concerned with your belonging.

Perhaps as you drop down into your somatic experience in this exercise you will be standing in front of those who represent an organization in which you felt a deep sense of belonging, or one in which you could not. Perhaps it's a system in which you belonged but were then excluded, or you excluded yourself. In either case and for every other example in between these, find the true statements to speak the unspoken truths.

In searching for what's true you could experiment by trying sentences like these:

'I loved belonging in this system.'
'I felt excluded here.'
'I wish I could have stayed longer.'
'I had to leave.'
'Secretly I'm still loyal to you.'
'This was very painful for me and cost me a lot.'
'Here I felt diminished.'
'Here I grew.'

Use these as a starting point only, trust the words that emerge in you and express your own truth as you look at each relationship system in which you belonged. After expressing what's true in the context of belonging, start to open up possibilities for a respectful acknowledgment and softening of these bonds.

Sentences that may start to soften the dynamics may include:

'I stayed too long.'

'Thank you for what I learnt. I'll use it well.'

'You were just my employer. I was looking for something else.'

'I gave too much.'

'I'll leave what was difficult in this system that was yours with you, and will keep and look at the part that belonged to me.'

'I never thanked you for what I learnt here. Thank you, I'll use it all.'

Use these as a starting point only, then experiment with sentences that ring true for you but that are also respectful to *both* the system and yourself, acknowledging what was gained and what was lost, what was given and what was learnt.

This exercise can also be facilitated or self-facilitated in the way described on page 28, 'EXCHANGE: An exercise for yourself'.

You may also find the case study by coach Hazel Chapman on page 114 a useful example.

~

Belonging is a primary human need and drive, so every coach and every client has dynamics emerging from belonging. Your personal and professional journey will be enriched if you keep the importance and role of belonging in heart and in mind.

As you develop your understanding of belonging in practical application I encourage you to refer back to this chapter as it may offer you a deeper understanding of this aspect and the importance of it in coaching.

There is no house like the house of belonging.

David Whyte

The time is now

The intuitive mind is a sacred gift and the rational mind is a faithful servant. We have created a society that honours the servant and has forgotten the gift. ALBERT EINSTEIN

When to apply this approach and the benefits of doing so

In order to know when a systemic intervention may be appropriate, it is important to develop the capacity to tune into information coming from the system. They are subtle signals that gradually become clear the more attuned you become at listening for them. Even if you don't move into a systemic intervention – a constellation – you will develop your ear for the kind of information that emerges, and what it may mean in the context of your client's developmental journey.

In a constellation workshop setting, the facilitator has an opportunity to 'interview' the client or 'issue holder' before doing any work. The client has travelled especially to a workshop to look at issues through this particular lens. They will have read about constellations and prepared themselves for a day focused around this way of working.

In executive or team coaching on the other hand, you're working with clients who, even though they may have worked with you before and know a little about your systemic orientation, will not be expecting to do a constellation every time they work with you. Nor should they: constellations are not an intervention to use with such high frequency or for every challenging coaching situation. They will, however, talk, and after a while you will hear the system flags, the messages coming up from the system, and know when it's time to act.

There are many potential applications of constellations that come from the system-aware coaching stance and understanding of the ordering forces. The following summary is designed to provide an introductory overview of the contexts in which the principles and practices can be usefully applied:

- When there is a need to illuminate or clarify the coaching agenda.
- When as a coach you sense that one of the natural ordering forces of systems has been neglected or ignored.
- When there is something stuck or the same problem or issue keeps recurring.
- When you sense that there is too much talking, too many words, that rational analysis is not getting to the issue and/or that the client or team are stuck 'in their heads'.
- When there is something hidden, secret or taboo and you are given permission to look.
- When there is recurring conflict in the relationships with or around the client.
- When a skilled/experienced person cannot fully occupy their role authority.
- When as a coach you have a sense that there is something unspoken in your client's system that is affecting their ability to be present or to perform; something that is distracting them and drawing their energy away.

All systems seek coherence. Inertia, challenging group dynamics, unwelcome behaviours, 'politics' and difficult emotions in systems can be seen as messages that something is out of alignment and the system is attempting to re-establish coherence.

- When the symptom is very clear but the cause is not.
- When there is a lack of energy or focus and your coachee wants to know why.
- When individuals describe or interpret the same event differently.
- When there is conflict and the source is uncertain or doesn't appear to make sense.
- When your preferred model or intervention doesn't seem to apply or the benefits don't endure.
- When you need to support your client to get in touch with and align their resources.
- When you hear of frequent miscommunication.

- When your client needs to say something to another in their system but needs support to find their voice and speak their truth.
- When the client is holding or expressing something difficult on behalf of the system and needs acknowledgement or release.
- When the client is attached to their own story and version of events and a fresh perspective may be a useful step towards resolution.
- When your client is using words that include strong judgements on another element or person within the system.
- When there is a requirement to guide choices between options but there is uncertainty, ambivalence or ambiguity.
- When you hear of apathy, ambivalence or resistance in a system.
- When you hear of conversations going round and round, and which keep going back to the start even though a resolution has been offered and named.
- When people are defending each other as if against an invisible enemy.
- When there are rebels and 'black sheep'.
- When there are high emotions in response to rational statements or requests.
- When people say one thing and do another.
- When there are conspiracy theories.
- When there is a lack of respect in the team or organizational culture.

Messages from the system

The indicators of an issue for which a systemic perspective may be useful are the same whether you are only going into the initial mapping stage or a full constellation. So, when you hear an issue that sounds muddled, mysterious or stuck, for example, it may be appropriate to open it up and offer your client the opportunity to explore it in a fresh way. Examples of the kind of language that might make you wonder if a map of the system may be a useful framework to introduce could include some of the following.

Muddled or unclear issues

Issues that are influenced by some hidden system dynamics are often those that are hard to articulate. You may hear, for example, things like this:

'I'm not sure how to put this into words really, it's confusing...'
'I can't get this issue out of my mind and it leaves me feeling very muddled... I feel in a bit of a mist...'

Your client may simply be unable to find the words, may use their hands a lot to create their own spatial maps, or, after saying that they are struggling with something, then remain silent.

Lots of detail and/or a long story

When you hear a long or highly detailed account, sometimes along with judgements, beliefs or expectations, or when it seems to you that the coachee is becoming more attached to their version of their story and is likely to be getting lost in the detail, then this is often a suitable time to offer a different way of working. Clients are always relieved when the coach has the courage to step into the middle of their story and respectfully ask if a different perspective may be of interest.

These are good examples of messages from the system, system flags, and there are several ways of identifying them and bringing them into your own and then the client's awareness.

Other 'system flags'

As you become more and more familiar with the underpinning principles and ordering forces that operate in systems, you may begin to 'translate' what your client is saying into possible other system meanings. On other occasions you will hear clients start to use language that is a direct expression of the system. Examples of both follow:

'We've looked at this several times before and just can't seem to fix it.'
(Is there a hidden dynamic in the system that lies beyond the influence of the individual and/or the team?)

'I can't seem to get this sorted in my head. I just can't see my way out of this.'
(Are they looking for their place in or with a system issue?)

'There is something holding me back on this issue.'
(Is this about a hidden loyalty, an entanglement or another dynamic in the system that is beyond visibility?)

'My team have been working at the company for years and I'm struggling to persuade them to change their production methods.'
(Is the order of time – as expressed in length of service – being acknowledged in this system, by this client?)

'Sometimes I think about leaving... but I don't really want to. Do I stay or leave?'
(What might be pulling them out of the system, what or who might they be being loyal to, or what force might be trying to eject them?)

Often you may hear direct references to systemic issues as asides at the end of another comment or at the point when the client is tailing off. For example, you may hear something like: 'Yes, it's all a bit stuck here...' or 'Yes... but the last chief executive left nearly two years ago, so it can't be anything to do with him'. That's a common example of a clear and by now familiar system issue.

You will also start to hear the more obvious mentions of relationship systems as opportunities to offer an orientated coaching conversation or intervention. For example: 'We aren't close to the strategy in this team...' or even as clear as: 'I can't seem to find my place with this...'

Constellations are interventions that emerge from a growing system awareness in the coach and so are used when there is a need to include a wider field of information, to open up to the collective intelligence in a system and go beyond the individual in search of fresh information, insights and resolution.

Another way of thinking about the right time to apply them is to consider the benefits they offer in a number of settings.

Agenda setting

Supporting your client to set an agenda of depth and breadth that reaches beyond the individual and leads to a transformational coaching journey:

- Mapping can help surface and set a powerful coaching agenda. This energizes clients as it clarifies and simplifies complexity and connects them to their most pressing concerns and developmental needs.

- When setting or refreshing the coaching agenda, the first part of the constellation process, mapping, often allows coach and coachee to see the individual challenges in the context of the wider system and so enriches the agenda and process. It's also a very effective way of getting familiar with the building blocks of constellation.

Diagnosing

Supporting your client to diagnose an issue and the source of resistance to change or growth:

- When your client is struggling to find the words to describe a situation or challenging relationship dynamic, a constellation may help to reveal the hidden information and dynamics.

- Constellations can quickly identify deep or hidden issues and so provide a powerful diagnostic in individuals, teams and whole businesses at a refreshing pace. This energizes coaches and clients alike, as it bypasses the story, focuses on facts and gets to the heart of the issue quickly, creating insight, energy and motivation for action without blame or judgement.

Placemaking

Supporting your client to find their place in the system:

- Giving everything in the system a place will be useful when you sense that someone or something may have been excluded and needs to be remembered. The system settles and the coachee works with a systems perspective.

- A constellation is an effective way of supporting people to find their 'right place' in a system – an abstract quality that is often only 'felt'. Because constellations involve an embodied experience of right place, they offer a uniquely powerful way of internalizing this 'felt sense' of place.

Acknowledging

Supporting your client to face into what is, in their system and in them:

- In organizational life there is often a lack of respect for what is. A constellation will help individuals and teams to see what is in the whole system and face into that. Standing in the whole, in the truth of what's revealed, and then finding a better relationship to the elements allows an inner shift to naturally emerge, which leads to a clear and enduring resolution.

- Constellations and the language of systemic coaching are designed to support leaders to face into their own truths too – their strengths and limitations, their responsibilities, their hidden loyalties and entanglements. This degree of authenticity and coherence releases fresh energy for change and progress.

Relating

Supporting your client to ease challenging relationships:

- If your client is experiencing challenging relationship issues that seem beyond their understanding or resolution, a constellation provides a way of surfacing the hidden dynamics and entanglements that may be at the source of the issue.

- The language and methods of this approach have the potential to respectfully facilitate change in relationships that seem beyond redemption.

Communicating

Supporting your client to have 'difficult conversations':

- When your client needs to say something that may be difficult to hear and needs support to find their respectful stance and voice, a constellation can help them ground their dialogue in a way that will be heard.
- Because constellations create living maps of systems and reveal the true relational model, they offer coaches and clients a cut-through and a new way of looking at old or apparently intractable communication patterns.

Leaving and joining

Supporting your client to leave and join systems:

- When your client is leaving one system and joining another, a constellation can help them to internalize what has been received from the first and what can be offered to the second.
- The way that people join and leave systems is key to enduring organizational health. The systemic perspective, systemic coaching and constellations can support clarity and balance.

Resourcing

Supporting your client to find personal and professional resources within the system:

- When your client needs additional resources but the source or nature of the resources isn't clear, a constellation can show the location of existing resources available within the system.
- Sometimes the wider system needs resourcing and this approach offers ways of supporting that process, bringing renewed clarity and vitality to the flow of leadership and organizational health.

Developing

Supporting your client in their personal, professional or leadership development:

- Systemic coaching, mapping and constellations are not only useful when illuminating challenges to do with relationships, team dynamics and the wider organizational system. They have a powerful application in professional development, as they offer a fresh way of looking at the deeper motivations and blocks to development.

- The difference between talking about leadership, feedback, developmental goals and behaviour changes and mapping them, illuminating the hidden blocks and resources within the unconscious relationship system in which they exist, is often significant. Systemic coaching and constellations provide a way of supporting deep developmental movement and change in the context of the wider system in which the client belongs.

Resolving

Supporting your client to get free of limiting dynamics:

- When your client is stuck or there is inertia in their system, a constellation can show unexpected routes to release and movement.
- When an individual or team expresses ambivalence or resistance to change in an individual or at team level, a constellation can provide clarity and energy for resolution.

Constellations also allow the coach and coachee to carefully 'experiment' with alternative solutions to issues and see the effect of alternative approaches. The approach is also useful where personal or family system issues overlap with organizational systems, as it can help to reveal and resolve entanglements and separate systems that have become confused.

Contraindications

It is also worth noting when systemic coaching and constellations may not be the appropriate route to follow. These situations include:

- Where a fixed and agreed outcome is required and there are no options needed or blocks to completion.
- Detailed action planning aligned to a schedule.
- When exploring relationship dynamics in a system that the client is not involved in and so does not have permission to explore.
- When your client doesn't think that a systems perspective or intervention is going to be useful because they believe their influence as an individual is greater than that of the system.

Constellation time

Since the mid-1990s, coaches and organizational consultants have been using systemic coaching and constellations in large and small businesses to help establish flow and vitality in leadership and organizational life. There is now a growing body of work to look back on – experiences gained from multiple constellations in groups and one-to-one settings. The benefits are self-evident across the many contexts and systems in which they are applied and offer something more in addition to the clarity, insight and resolution.

> Because the approach is inherently inclusive and can be applied alongside and integrated with other ways of working, it creates a spaciousness and ease of use. This settles something in client *and* coach, as everything is included, seen and acknowledged as it is. Everything has a place.

The focus on 'seeing the whole' and 'acknowledging what is' generates high levels of trust and safety. Coaches and clients often report how easy it feels to start working in this way, because systemic mapping – the first stage of every constellation – can be done with relatively little knowledge or experience and yet reveals previously unseen connections and new insights. This creates a sense of confidence in the coach and allows their learning in this approach to develop. Because mapping and full constellations can be used in any part of a coaching programme to identify hidden blocks, find hidden resources and move towards resolutions, this makes them feel accessible and applicable in executive and team coaching situations.

You will also find that, once you begin to work with this methodology, something odd seems to happen to time. It seems to both stand still and move rapidly forward at the same time. That is to say that the work may appear, to an observer, to be moving very slowly, with long silences and nothing much appearing to happen. On the other hand, for the client, they are often in a deep level of contact with something that talking can rarely reach. They are in touch with something timeless – the underlying forces in systems that hide below the surface of the symptoms, challenge or resistance.

It's this distortion of time, in a particular way, that allows you to work so fast and so deep at the same time, illuminating, clarifying and resolving issues and questions that had previously seemed perhaps beyond reach, beyond resolution. This sense of timeless contact with something essential is another benefit often cited by coaches who use this approach.

> Leadership, team and organizational development is a huge field and is subject to a continuous stream of new ideas and developments. One of the reasons that systemic work is taking hold is that it offers access to a kind of timeless wisdom about human relationship systems that many interventions are not designed to reach. The time for systemic coaching and systemic interventions is now.

Inside out

05

> *Out beyond ideas of right and wrong*
> *There is a field.*
> *I'll meet you there.*
>
> **RUMI**

Coaching with the system in mind

The underlying stance of systemic coaching and constellations is central to successful systemic interventions and the understanding of the methodology. It's about finding your place, in a particular way, with the client or team and the systems they belong to. To support this whole-system approach, it's important to maintain a stance that allows the coach to find, and stay, in their own 'right place' in relation to the client and the system with which they are working. This stance requires practice and is one of the most important aspects of this work.

The inner orientation of the coach

To be able to rely on yourself as a coach, you will already know that developing a trust in your experience of each moment is an essential source of information and resource. The capacity to do that, to be grounded and fully present while not getting in the way, is the foundation of all effective coaching. Coach presence comes from maturity as a person, as an adult with wide personal and professional experience who has done a certain amount of work on themselves and explored their own issues. It also comes from the development of some specific qualities particular to this work, especially a heightened awareness of your own systemic entanglements and loyalties.

> The less the coach does, in a certain way, the more is allowed to happen.
> It's about being, not doing.

The following offers a summary of the key qualities that underpin the systemic coaching stance and are drawn from my own experience, as well as contributions and insights from teachers, peers and students. At this stage it may seem like a rather long list of qualities and inner attitudes to integrate, but the rewarding thing about this work is that it creates a kind of 'virtuous circle' where facilitating tends to surface certain qualities and encourages the stance to surface naturally in the coach and in turn the client. The stance emerges out of the practice; the practice emerges out of the stance.

Lean back, prioritize the system

When you look at your clients, try to see the people behind them: their peers, direct reports, boss and former bosses, their educational and family systems, the possible loyalties and entanglements. Look with great respect for all that they are and come from, all that you know and all that you will never know. Remember that you are only a momentary guest to their immeasurable system of interconnectedness.

- As a coach you already know the benefits of opening yourself up beyond your own frame of reference and can come alongside your client, looking at the world through their eyes. But when working as a systemic coach, you also need to open yourself to something beyond you and beyond your client's perspective and take a position that has an eye on the whole system. That way you will be able to see and work with all that is within and between those systems.

- If you lean in towards your clients, metaphorically or actually, you will get more easily entangled in their stories and the system dynamics. Lean back, metaphorically and actually, in order to maintain appropriate distance, objectivity and separateness. You will be able to see the system better from there, without judgement or partiality.

- When you begin to tune in to information that's coming from the system, rather than only from the individual, fresh information and insights emerge. It's like 'active listening', but to the whole system not just the individual. This adds another dimension, opening doors to insights and truths that lead your clients into new levels of understanding and insight.

- Your priority is not the client; it's the system in which they belong. This approach liberates your clients from the need to do everything alone and helps them find their place and their resources in the wider system. Coach with the whole system in mind. Then you are free.

What really struck me is how detached I remained during the whole session, in a way which I had not experienced on prior occasions with this client, and how much that helped. Because I was led to focus on the system, not my client. I had to experience this first-hand to be able to actually start to understand what was meant by 'Lean back and see the whole system. Your priority is not the client; it's the system in which they belong'.

Philippe Truffert, executive coach and student of this approach, applies the stance for the first time.

Give everything a place

Be willing to support clients to find a place for everything, especially the issues or people they are trying to exclude. This is a core process and stance of systemic coaching and constellations.

- 'Negative' is just as welcome as 'positive', especially if people in the system are trying to exclude that possibility. Both polarities, and everything in between, have a place. Include everything.

- Agree *to* everything just as it is. That's different to agreeing *with* everything.

As a facilitator you need to be able to stand still in fast-moving and difficult system dynamics. You must also be able to leave people and systems to their fate without stepping in to rescue them.

Stand in and name the truth

Supporting your client to acknowledge the truth of their current experience is a building block of coaching and leads to deep levels of contact between the client and their work.

- Standing in 'what is', the truth of the system, settles the client and opens doors to fresh resolutions. When you stand in 'what is', you also have to let go of your own interpretations, beliefs and judgements about the situation. Being neutral supports the impartial non-intentionality of this stance.

- When you support your client to acknowledge what really is, you will find yourself standing alongside them in the true underlying hidden dynamics of their situation. Instead of expressing empathy ('I can see that must be difficult for you'), invite your clients to stand in their own truth from their place in the system ('In this place it's very difficult for me to lead...').

- This requires a calm, strong but impartial clarity in the coach in order to create a safe holding space in which the client can really see and look at their issues. Staying neutral, even in the face of painful systemic truths, is a gift that your clients will gain great benefit from.

Let your body speak its mind

In constellations, staying in contact with your physical self is an important ingredient in your stance.

- If you develop this connection, you'll be able to tap into the information held within the system from different parts of the constellation, even in one-to-one coaching.
- This is somatic coaching in action and it's just as important to notice what your client is embodying.
- Like other aspects this takes practice, as the instinct at first is to keep your eyes on the constellation and emerging patterns. That is important, but vital information will be lost unless you also include the client's embodied experience in your field of view.

Deep insights are given to us, they show themselves. Phenomenological means to learn through experience but it requires a certain kind of giving up. Instead of grasping you take a step back. You expose yourself and experience a client or a situation exactly as it is. Have no intention and no fear and wait. Suddenly an insight is given to you.

Bert Hellinger

Work beyond the story

As coaches we can easily get caught up in the story and risk becoming partial and so a part of the problem. If the story had been helpful or useful for the client it would have led them to a solution. Then they wouldn't need a systemic perspective or constellation.

- This approach requires a certain fearlessness, a willingness to respectfully challenge, the story of how things are or were, then to name the truths within the system in service of the client's question or developmental journey.
- Staying free of the story and working only with the facts, without judgement, often requires the facilitator to respectfully stop the client telling their story of how things are. Allegiance to the story of how

things are is a way of staying loyal, and innocent, to the system from which the story comes and in which the problem exists.

> *Long descriptions of problems can be understood as an invitation to the facilitator to share the client's attitudes and convictions, which serve to maintain the problem rather than solve it. These stories often lower the energy and resourcefulness of the client and burden all involved.*
> Gunthard Weber

Not knowing

Many coaches are familiar with the phrase: 'If you know where the conversation is going, it's probably not a coaching conversation.' This way of working is informed by a willingness not only not to know where the conversation is going, but also not even to fully understand the question, or sometimes the solution.

- Questions and issues that belong in the system are rarely clear because they are entangled with confusion, hidden loyalties and hidden dynamics. That's one of the clues to a system issue.
- The methodology of constellations allows the coach and coachee to illuminate and disentangle system issues without the coach needing to know everything.
- A stance of respectful humility is therefore particularly important in order to maintain the safety and confidentiality of the client's process. A much higher degree of silence and quiet reflection is often characteristic of systemic coaching and constellations. Work blind and in silence and you will see and hear much more.

Reach for solutions rather than goals

For those who have been trained to believe that coaching is goal-setting, there may be some resistance and confusion with this approach. It is more concerned with revealing 'what is' and disentangling complexities in the system in a way that leads to solutions, rather than reaching for goals.

- Systemic solutions may be different to the expected or desired solution, turning a previously identified goal on its head.
- A shift in the inner stance allows you to integrate both approaches. For an example of this, see the goal-setting constellations on page 170.

> *Constellation work, for a minor part, consists of technique, and for a larger part of perception and inner attitude.*
> Jan Jacob Stam

Be useful, to be helpful

If our underlying intention is to help, rescue or heal, then there is a risk that your own needs will come before the client's.

- If your expectation of yourself as a coach is that you 'ought' to be goal-setting and you ought to be 'helping', you may find the journey of systemic coaching and constellations challenging. You may also find it simultaneously liberating and energizing.

- A willingness to stay in the observer or 'witness' place and be useful and resourcing rather than helpful can bring a great deal of clarity and insight to the client. A need to help or find solutions isn't as useful as we may like to think. Be useful because that's helpful.

Work on yourself as a person and explore your own system

Most coaches are working on themselves to ensure that they develop high levels of self-awareness and commit to continuous personal and professional development. And many coaches are also, often unconsciously, 'teaching what they need to learn'. To sharpen your systemic practice, ensure you maintain an active interest in your own systems – and the conscience that guards them – from your family-of-origin to your place in your past and present professional relationship systems.

- A central part of this work is to support clients to think about what, in the relationship system they are working or living within, they are unconsciously loyal to. To do that you need to develop your own sense of your hidden loyalties. Think about what and whom you are loyal to.

- This will usually include your family-of-origin, your preferred coaching interventions, your professional background, and social and cultural beliefs, behaviours and norms. Self-awareness about what and who you are privately loyal to will allow you to assist your clients to work out the same for themselves and respectfully separate you both from entanglements in systems.

We were talking about the space in between us all...
              'Within You Without You' by George Harrison, The Beatles

Remember the family system

Many executive, leadership development and organizational coaches are concerned with keeping away from and excluding the family-of-origin of their clients. Fearing that these are private matters or that they have insufficient training to deal with personal issues, they exclude the source of the client.

- If you exclude the fact that we all come from family systems, you are already back in an individual, non-systemic view of the world and your client's world, life and work.

- This approach, and this book, offer a way of including, when required and appropriate, the family system within a coaching process and relationship. This allows the families of origin to resource the coach and the client, leaving both connected back into their system of origin.

~

This aspect of the systemic approach to coaching, the inner stance, underpins everything else and, I hope, this book. Systemic coaching and the facilitation of constellations are all about a subtle integration of stance and methodology. Of course, this stance can also underpin your existing coaching interventions, adding a fresh perspective to all the frameworks you already know add value for your clients.

Facilitating this approach is a strange combination of knowing and not knowing, of learning and un-learning, of steps and no steps, of being and doing. It requires something even beyond stance that arrives in the coach/facilitator as a trust in their felt sense of systems and system information. This felt sense is something intangible but also something beyond emotion, beyond an embodied physical experience and beyond intuition. It's something that emerges in you as you inhabit the stance, practise the processes and access the knowing field of information. When combined and integrated in this way you will find yourself working with ease on issues such as those described in this book and will recognize yourself in the description of systemic coaching offered in Chapter 11.

My observation is that as soon as the issue holder has named the issue, it is that issue that then becomes the 'client', and both the facilitator and issue holder work in service of resolution, surrendering to the authority of the system.

Patrizia Amanati

PART TWO
Practices

An invitation
An experiential exercise

To climb steep hills requires slow pace at first.

WILLIAM SHAKESPEARE, *HENRY VIII*, ACT 1, SCENE 1

Mapping your own system

Because this work has to be experienced to be learnt, this section offers an opportunity to do just that. A more detailed explanation of the practices that underpin it follows.

~

Being a coach can be an enjoyable and enriching personal and professional journey. It's not only clients who benefit from coaching, after all. But for many, the pressure to get new clients, to develop, to network and to attend to continuous professional development can be challenging. Sometimes this feels like it takes up as much time and energy as the coaching itself, leaving you feeling under-resourced. With the pressures of coaching and being a coach in mind, it can be useful to resource yourself, find your place in amongst your work, in your own professional relationship system.

So, as you think about a journey into the application of constellations in coaching, I invite you to tune into something else. Tune into what's going on for you at an embodied level: in your body. Move out of your head, even as you read, and notice what's going on at a more visceral level. Get grounded, literally; feel the weight of your feet on the floor, the weight of your body in the chair. Just notice yourself, without any judgement on how you are; just be.

Coaching is, as you know, as much about using yourself as an instrument as it is about knowledge, process or technique. To be able to really rely on yourself as a coach you need to be able to develop a trust of yourself and your experience in each moment. The capacity to feel into your own presence, to stand in your own truth, is an important part of that. This systemically-orientated work in particular becomes both easier and more effective if you are able to tune into your 'empty centre', your being-ness rather than your doing-ness. Your felt sense.

So, as you begin to get more centred, present and aware, reflect on your current relationship to your own coaching practice. It may be that you are new to coaching and this is one of the first books you've read. It may be that you are an in-house coach in a large organization. It may be that you lead a coaching organization with a global reach. Whoever you are and wherever you are on your journey, this is an opportunity to illuminate something about your relationship to your coaching or coaching business. So, first of all decide which is the most important question or challenge you currently face as a coach. What issue bubbles up to the surface as you reflect on the breadth and depth of your work as a coach or your coaching business offer or operations?

Mapping your relationship with your work as a coach

Maybe you have a concern over your resources as a coach, your skills or experience; maybe you have a challenge in relationship to another coach you are working with; perhaps you have difficulties attracting new coaching clients; or maybe you are struggling to decide whether to focus on one particular kind of client or another. Whatever your question is, simply focus down into it until you have the essence of it articulated in your mind as a question.

Now identify the key elements that make up the relationship system around that question or challenge. For example, there will be you; that's the first element in this system. Decide if you are going to work with a representative for the whole of you, or you in your role as a coach. You can separate those out if you like.

Then there could be 'my work as a coach' or 'my coaching business', 'my business partner', 'my existing clients' or 'potential new clients'. Feel into your question and see which other elements are needed. For example, there may be 'the future' or 'my income' or 'all my other options'. Identify the three most central 'elements' in this relationship system.

Creating a relationship system map

Now, working with a clear space on a table in front of you, choose an object to represent yourself: 'me' or, as described above, 'me as a coach'. Ensure you've chosen an object with a sense of direction. In other words, if you use a coffee cup the handle can represent the sense of direction, of attention. Each representative object needs to have this quality – whether you use a Post-it note with an arrow drawn on it, a coffee cup or a stapler where the open end represents the 'face' doesn't matter, as long as you know which direction each is 'facing' in as you place them in this, your inner map of what is.

Give the representative for you a place, in the physical space you've identified, that simply feels true. Not right or wrong, just true to where you are with your current sense of yourself in the context of your question.

Then choose another object to represent the next most important element. Pay attention to the distance and orientation. Where feels most true to 'what is'? Just notice how far apart the two objects are and where they are facing – towards each other or looking elsewhere? Set it up, slowly, as it is, not as you wish it was or would like it to be. Stand in the difficulty.

After a while, working slowly, add a third representative object, paying attention to the same things – distance and orientation. Now just look at the relationship system between all three objects and look without judgement. You've made a map of the relationship system around your question and you may even now be starting to see a new perspective emerging.

This kind of mapping is the foundation stone for every constellation you will facilitate with your clients in the future. In various forms it's the start of every constellation and the beginning of a shift from verbal to non-verbal exchanges; between you and your material, and between your client and their material.

Even at this first stage a system map offers an embodied experience of a largely unconscious relationship structure that you didn't know you knew until you knew it physically; until you stood in your own truth. If you'd like to get a more embodied sense then set this map up again, but this time using pieces of paper with directional arrows on them as floor markers. Stand in each place and feel into what it's like to really stand in each place.

What you've done so far is mapping what is. The next step is to bring this map to life – to make interventions that turn it into a constellation; a living map of the system. That will bring in additional elements, get the system on the move and effect an inner change in the way you hold this relationship pattern. That inner change leads in turn to changes in attitudes, behaviours and actions, which open up new possibilities and fresh energy for enduring change.

~

That's what this book is about and you will have another opportunity to work on this, your own question about your work as a coach, as you explore this approach. The whole book is designed to support you on a journey through this work so you can use it with your clients, but you must keep experiencing it for yourself, in experiential learning environments, throughout this book and through this invitation to explore.

This exercise is developed and extended at the end of the book, where you have the opportunity to take it to the next level. This will leave you resourced with fresh insight and clarity about your next steps with your own question and perhaps with this approach to coaching.

Map making

06

Maps are one of the oldest forms of human communication. Map-making pre-dates written language. OKADA

Getting started

Most coaches, even those who spend most of their time working with groups and teams, seem to find that learning and practising through one-to-one application is a useful context in which to understand and develop skills in using this approach. A few find it easier to start working in a workshop environment, though that's less common because the facilitator's role is so different from most other kinds of group facilitation. This book addresses both applications but takes as its starting point the application in one-to-one coaching.

Mapping, the first phase of a constellation, can be done without a comprehensive knowledge or long experience of constellations. When it is done within appropriate boundaries and the limits of the facilitator's experience, mapping can be a profoundly helpful stand-alone intervention in and of itself. You can work in a way that feels safe for you and the client by 'mapping what is' and agreeing to have a look at it and then stop, either by naming that this is all you are offering – to take an initial look – or by agreeing a time limit. This kind of clear boundary-making is often a releasing experience for the client, allowing them to feel safe enough to take a fresh look at a challenging issue in the knowledge of the limits you've agreed.

Getting permission to work

When you feel that you may be dealing with an issue that could benefit from a systems perspective and intervention, you can ask permission to look at it in a fresh way. This is more about inviting your client to look at their issue or question 'in a different way' than naming 'systemic constellations' or anything to do with you or this work. In fact, by not naming 'a constellation' you create a space of expectation and the client is taken to a heightened level of enquiry with their issue. In just a few words you have invited them to move into a new way of looking at old or apparently intractable issues.

For example, when your client is facing into a challenging or very stuck issue, you could simply say something like: 'I can hear that you are really struggling to find resolution with this – would you like to look at it in a different way?' or 'How would it be for you if we looked at this in rather a different way, a way that relies less on words and more on relationship patterns?' or 'What would it be like to explore your inner picture of this and take a look at it in a fresh way?'

Very often the client will agree to look in a new way and then hand the next step back to you. Occasionally they will tell you how many different ways they've already looked at it and explain why it's not possible to resolve. Again, you can offer to look at it in a different way, adding that you are inviting them to come out of their heads and into another way of knowing about things that they may not have explored before.

There is one other aspect of getting permission to work that's important in this approach to system health. That is, does the person you are working with have permission to access the system? The permission we are talking about here is the role and responsibility to action anything after the constellation. If the client doesn't have that role and responsibility then there is a chance that they are just looking out of curiosity, or out of frustration with the one who does. In those circumstances it will be more valuable to offer a constellation that illuminates and clarifies their relationship with the boss, rather than trying to do the boss's work.

One way of checking for permission, apart from your own sensing into the question, is to ask your client to take a moment to 'go inside' and reflect on whether they have the permission to explore this issue. Not only does that refine their sensitivity to the system dynamics, but it also usually creates a deeper contact with the real issue and clarity about permission levels. This generates respect and a deeper level of work usually follows.

Moving into the first stage

This first stage, mapping, provides a relatively easy way into constellations for the client, but also for a coach who is at the early stages of learning about systems and needs to work within their own learning boundaries. Limiting the scope of your work with your client helps to make the opening up of the client's reference system safe enough for you both to step into the system and step out again before too long.

The mapping process is broken down into the 'interview', the 'mapping' itself and the 'closure' stage, though in practice the flow from one to another is seamless. The first stage, the 'interview', may simply be experienced by your client as no different to any other questions you may ask, but you are feeling your way – and inviting your client to join you – into a broader, system-wide perspective of their issue; into a different way of 'knowing'.

The 'interview'

In this part of the process, when you are at the early stages of your learning journey, simply ask three questions:

1. What is the issue, in just a few words?

This helps people to get free of the stories, the judgements and the attachments. By asking for the issue in 'just a few words', you emphasize that you are keen to get to the heart of it. You also create a level of permission to ask your client to reduce the amount of words they are using if you feel that they are reattaching to a familiar story.

The next question moves you and the client into a more solution-orientated space where the answer lies waiting – and will be briefly embodied in your client (ie breathing out, sitting up and so on) as they describe the picture of resolution.

2. What would be different, for you, if this issue was resolved?

The answer to this question will often contain the word 'feel', as in: 'I'd feel much more able to do my work', 'I'd feel free and energized' or 'I'd feel clear and strong and safe in my role'. So you can modify the question to include that, for example: 'How would you feel if this issue was resolved?'

The purpose of this question is to agree a destination, not the journey. It provides an anchor to return to and to test the usefulness of the constellation at the end. By this stage the client has already created an inviting glimpse, a taste of the resolution, and is invested in finding a path towards it. But unlike in many coaching approaches, you are not about to set a goal or visualize a path to that resolution. You are going to do something else, something that simply starts with an acknowledgement of what is.

3. If we were to create a map of this issue what elements would we need?

This is an invitation to list out the key elements (very often people) that are connected into the client's issue. You can invite them to start with themselves, ie 'So there's you... and who or what else?'. Or you can invite them to list the three or four most important elements or people around the issue. They may say something like, 'Well, there's my boss, the team objective and our main customer.' A mix of specific people and abstracts like 'purpose' is common and allows them to set up a useful relational map between the elements. In any case, you can now invite them to include themselves and notice the impact of that as it can often be part of the information in itself. Once you have agreed the most important elements – ideally no more than three or four, as you can add more later if needed – you are ready to begin mapping.

The 'mapping'

In order to set up a map that's going to be useful and allow an exploration of the system, you will first need to set the boundary. Setting the boundary and selecting an object to represent the client or their issue can be achieved together. Start by simply saying something like this: 'How would it be if this tabletop represents the whole company and this sheet of paper is the leadership team... ?'

Next, check for the client's own sense of meaning, relative size, position and so on. Continue your facilitation with something like this: 'Now pick up the representative for yourself and find the place in this map that feels true to your inner sense of what this is like for you... a place that embodies your inner picture of your place in this map. Just as it is, without wishing it to be different or better.' Note that if your client struggles to find their place within the system boundary – also information in itself – you can invite them to set up the first two representatives, in relation to each other, at the same time. For example, 'self' and 'team purpose'.

This simple invitation often creates a powerfully effective system map very quickly, and already the client is feeling their way into the core of their issue, their experience, their truth. The two things to highlight for a client who may be new to this way of working are *direction* and *distance*.

For direction you will need to help them indicate which way the attention is drawn in each object. With all of the available constellation stones, blocks and 'chips' (see photos and Appendix), a direction of attention is indicated by a notch or point. If you are using Post-its or objects like bottles of water, cups and other 'found objects', ensure that you are both clear about the directional aspect. Handles on cups or arrows on Post-its, for example, provide a very effective way of indicating the direction of attention.

As for distance, you can guide your client in this aspect like this: 'Just notice as you place each object how close or far away they are from each other. Just notice that, without wishing it to be any different.'

As long as direction of attention and distance are attended to, the client will be dropping down into a deeper level of contact with their issue once they set up their first image. It's often useful to check with the client for the details by asking: 'So, in this spatial relationship map it appears that you're looking directly at the finance director; is that right?' or when they appear to be looking beyond the adjacent representative object: 'Does this indicate that your attention is drawn out to something else?'

Think of yourself as a facilitator/coach, not just 'a coach'. This methodology requires you to do something else as well as coach; in fact, it requires you to hold back on occasions from coaching.

As a general rule of thumb it's almost always best to start small. For example, start with simply the client and their place in the system in relationship to just one other element. If someone is talking about a team, try to encourage them, at this stage at least, to select one object to represent the whole team. This keeps things focused and helps both the coach and client to stay at the central point of contact with the issue or question. You can get more granular later.

At any stage you can check that the coachee has created something that feels true for them by asking: 'Do you recognize this?' That question usually elicits a positive response but also some more information. You can also check for more like this: 'OK, and is there anything else that's important here? Anyone or anything else that needs to be included at this stage?'

Articulating one of the core principles of this work – that everything has a place – in this way is often the point at which somebody or something that has been excluded by the client or the wider reference system emerges: 'Oh yes, I've just remembered, there was a...'.

This way of working goes well when you take it slowly. The whole of the sequence above, for example, may take anywhere between 5 and 30 minutes, with all the reflection, new information, adjustments and insights that occur naturally when the map appears.

Very often mapping doesn't need to go too much further than this. This stage is often enough to reveal fresh perspectives and insights, along with a range of new information for processing and exploration in the coaching relationship and process. As this is just an initial mapping exercise, it's important that you feel able to bring it to a close, to ensure that the observations and insights are captured and that it doesn't go into areas that you and/or the client are not yet ready to work with. However, more often than not you will find yourself coaching from this new perspective and moving back into your usual or preferred way of working, with this new information informing a fresh path forward. It's not so much an end as a start.

The 'closure'

A good way to bring this first part, this initial mapping, to an end (or at least a pause) is simply to ask: 'So, what fresh information or insights have you gained from looking at the issue like this?' Another thing you can do here is to suggest that your client stands up and walks slowly around the table that you have been working on to get different perspectives on their own map. Then you could simply ask: 'What do you notice as you look at this?'

You can also give the boundaries their place and name them. For example: 'We agreed that we'd just look at this rather than go any deeper [or 'We agreed we'd spend just 10 minutes of our time on this aspect'] so is it OK if we draw this to a close for now and spend a little time reflecting on what you've already got from this...?'

In these ways you can move back into a 'head space'. The client can start to make rational sense of the map they have just created and you can help them process this. This 'sense-making' is an important aspect to include, especially when working with clients who may not be so familiar with illuminating their inner picture of a relationship system or trusting their 'felt sense' of their issue.

This kind of approach to mapping 'what is' often creates a very much more focused and lively coaching agenda than if the client had simply told you the 'story'. This makes it a useful thing to do early on in the coaching process and relationship.

On occasion the client may experience real difficulty coming out of the mapping, because they are already in touch with the deeper forces in the system and are attracted to the idea of continuing. This may also be true for the coach. In these circumstances you may need to go via an alternative, slightly longer route to reach an acceptable closure. The closure needs to be done with sensitivity, as coming out too soon or too late can have a weakening effect on the client.

In situations where there is a difficulty in finishing, invite the client to simply move one of the representative objects to a 'better place'. For example, you might say something like this: 'We've agreed to limit this first look, but I can see you'd like to move on a little further with this. So, choose one of the objects in this map you've created and see if you can move it to a place that feels like it is at least a first step towards a better place, a first step to resolution...' This kind of invitation will often result in clarity and insight in which the client identifies what needs to happen next in order to start moving towards a more settled system. Whatever they identify or do will change something and allow you to bring it to a close and move back into coaching and/or processing.

It can also be useful, particularly when seeing a complex or stuck initial image, to invite your client to pause to revisit and examine their central question. Another way of doing this is to ask: 'If this is the answer, what's the question?'

> At a point that feels appropriate in the mapping process you can revert to your preferred coaching dialogue style and work with the information and insights that have emerged. You can then invite your client to return to the mapping if you sense that may be useful.

Mapping may soon evolve into fuller constellations, but you will feel more able to develop your scope and skills as a constellator if you feel secure in the knowledge that you can respectfully close the process down and return to a more familiar style of coaching.

From mapping to constellating

To facilitate constellations you need to develop an understanding of four things. First, you need to know when it may be an appropriate intervention. We explored that earlier and your ear for messages from the system will be developing already. Second, you will need to build an understanding of the 'ordering forces' that guide systems. Third, you need to develop the stance of a constellations facilitator; one that allows you to tune in to those forces and work with them. Finally, you will need to learn about the processes required to illuminate, clarify and disentangle the dynamics that emerge in constellations. Each of these requires learning, understanding and practice in order to be effectively combined.

Once you've experimented within the boundaries of your evolving skills – with mapping the first phase of a constellation – you may soon feel ready to move into more substantial pieces of work. Your interventions will not only show and clarify the unconscious relationship patterns, but will also start to surface the collective intelligence held within the wider system. In these situations you will want to know about the core processes that facilitate this way of working, so that you can support your client to see and understand the dynamics in the system and then start to move towards resolution. If you simply leave the physical elements of the initial mapping exercise in their place while you are talking about what has emerged, it provides a natural opportunity to return and continue into a fuller constellation later in the same session.

> The distinction between mapping and constellating is actually rather an artificial one, articulated here in order to help you feel your way in a manner that feels appropriate for you. In fact, all constellations are mapping exercises, but the map keeps changing and the processes and experience required to read and influence them expand.

The key difference between mapping and constellating is that, in the latter, the hidden dynamics that emerge are, if appropriate, named, illuminated and disentangled. In addition, if appropriate and required, a picture of resolution is found. However, in a coaching and organizational context it is very often not appropriate or necessary to move to a 'picture of resolution' in the same way that is common when working with personal or family constellations. This is an important point and one that creates a certain freedom in this work, in the coaching context. Freeing yourself from the need to find resolution to challenging issues frequently achieves a great deal, and very often an unexpected path to resolution emerges as a result of not searching for one.

At this stage, simply remember that there is no one 'right' way to constellate and no need to get a complete resolution. The combination of principles, stance and knowledge of the core processes will be enough to begin with. You have learnt how to respectfully bring a constellation to an end if you feel you have reached the limits of your knowledge or comfort. You can now move back into your preferred coaching approach or methodology.

Core processes

To work with the emerging dynamics, two core processes are required:

1 movement;

2 sentences.

Let's look at the role and application of both, as they are key to illuminating and working with the hidden dynamics and intelligence in the system.

Movement

The embodiment of place and the orientation or direction of attention of each of the representative objects have special significance in a constellation, as they reveal the hidden information and enable the finding of 'right place'. Therefore it's important, as we've already started to see, to identify in which direction a representative is 'looking' in a constellation.

An effective way to do this is in the moment, as the client places each object. For example: 'As you place that into this map, just notice in which way it is facing' or 'If that was you standing there, where would your attention be drawn...?' or 'Imagine you are standing in that place. Which way would you be looking?' These kinds of questions can achieve clarity about direction of attention and create the start of an embodied experience of being 'in' the constellation whilst also observing it.

If you are using objects designed for tabletop constellations, the direction of 'face' is already indicated. However, most coaches start with (and many stay with) 'found objects' like coffee cups, water bottles and pieces of paper. This approach keeps the potential for resistance by a client to a minimum and reduces the feeling of distraction that some get when the coach unpacks a set of special stones or objects.

Once direction of attention is clear, you and your client can move the representatives in alignment with the insights that emerge as you move through the constellation. There are a few things to remember about making movements with representative objects in a constellation:

- Always make movements slowly to ensure that they are coming from the embodied sense of the issue and the place, not from the 'head space'.

- When the client wants to make a movement in one of the representatives, encourage them to say why first and then facilitate the movement, so it is done with clarity of intention.

- Decide if a sentence (see the next section) would be better or can precede a movement. This often surfaces the underlying motivation for a movement. For example, it can support a deeper inner movement in the client to say: 'You are the boss here; I withdraw' than to simply move the representative piece away from the representative for the boss.

- Remember that movements are not made at random or on a whim, but are made out of a search for balance and realignment with the natural orders. Other examples are to bring in someone who has been excluded; to bring a representative piece near to another so that acknowledgement can take place; to realign people in a team in a better order; or to test different options or possibilities.

- There is one important question to ask when exploring different relative positions in a constellation: 'Is that better, the same or worse?' You are always looking for what strengthens not what weakens, so this simple question will support finding the best place.

- The last move of every mapping exercise and constellation is when the process is complete and the pieces have to be put away. It can often be important to do this in a way that respects what the pieces and the pictures that have emerged mean to the client. Offering the client the opportunity to slowly replace the constellation pieces into a bag or to collect the Post-it notes into a pile, in the order they feel appropriate, can make a significant difference to the way in which they internalize and integrate their work.

Always watch where you are going.
Otherwise, you may step on a piece of the Forest that was left out by mistake.
Pooh's Little Instruction Book, inspired by AA Milne

Sentences – the language of the system

In Chapter 1 we looked at the universal language of systems, a language we all know when we hear it, but have mostly forgotten how to speak. This approach and this particular aspect – systemic sentences – give us and the system a voice. The use of short sentences forms an important part of the constellations methodology and can be used with powerful and lasting effect in systemic coaching. In fact, as we'll see later, there is a great deal of work that can be done without 'doing a constellation', but simply listening with a systemically attuned ear and offering these short-form 'sentences of truth' to acknowledge, illuminate and resolve the hidden dynamics. This is perhaps the hardest aspect to master, but also one of the most useful parts of this approach.

The purpose of these short phrases or 'sentences' is to:

- Provide a fresh way of communicating that goes deeper and integrates the body, the emotions and the mind.
- Illuminate and disentangle the hidden dynamics so that larger and less entangled pictures are revealed.
- Connect with and articulate 'what is' and the underlying truths in the system.
- Give everything a respected place, by naming things, so that the system can relax.
- Serve a larger purpose of systemic coaching – to return the responsibility and guilt to its source.
- Move to a picture of real and enduring resolution by testing different resolutions for impact.
- Align the system with the organizing principles.
- Reframe blame, pain and forgiveness and connect with something deeper.
- To join what has been wrongly separated and to separate what has been wrongly joined so each can stand in their responsibility and their strength.

Between what is said and not meant, and what is meant but not said, most love is lost.

Khalil Gilbran

How to offer sentences

If you sense that something is emerging for the client – an insight, a hidden loyalty or a powerful feeling, for example – then that may be an appropriate time to offer or invite a sentence. At first – and until the client is used to this way of working – sentences should be offered with great care. There are a number of ways of doing this, for example:

- 'I'm going to offer some words for you, to try to capture the essence of what I sense is going on here. Is that OK?'
- 'I'm going to invite you to say a few words – out loud, or just quietly to yourself – just to see what impact it has, OK? Try saying...'

- 'It sounds as if you may be saying...'
- 'This sentence is just like a thought bubble – see it as a test, an experiment. If it's not right you can adjust it until it is...'

Systems have a kind of universal language embedded in them dating from the earliest beginnings of mankind as tribes.

Matthias Varga von Kibéd

Another way is to invite the client to speak their own sentence. You can ask them if there is anything they want to say. However, you run the risk of them going back into their heads and the story. If you ask like this: 'Is there an inner sentence – just a very few words – that acknowledge this?' then you may get a more accurate and so more useful response.

Whatever the context these short phrases need to embody certain qualities. They need to be short, simple and spoken without intonation or emphasis. They need to be respectful of the impact that naming 'what is' may have and so offered with quiet respectfulness and without attachment to them being right. The sentences also need to support the client to stand in their responsibility for their own feelings, their requests and actions so there is real clarity and separation without blame.

Simple truth is like oxygen: with it we thrive, without it we suffocate in our stories.

John L Payne

When developing your practice, just experiment slowly and respectfully and don't worry if you or the client go into much longer sentences. This particular kind of language develops over time and is often the aspect that coaches new to this approach struggle with. That struggle is often connected to a concern that the words sound directive. That assumes that the words are the opinion of the coach. They are not, they are attempts to realign with the organizing forces of systems. Offered in that way the coach is experienced as offering respectful tests and 'litmus papers' to check for resonance. The sentences are the voice of the system, not the coach. The coach surrenders to the authority of the system when offering them, without personal opinion or attachment.

Responses to sentences

There are generally four possible responses from a client when as a systemic coach we offer a sentence:

- 100 per cent correct and spoken willingly by the client because it feels so true;
- 100 per cent correct but too difficult or painful to voice by the client, because it's 'too true';
- close, but the client needs to adjust to improve the accuracy;
- totally wrong, and the client suggests an alternative, usually the opposite.

These are all 'good' responses and can be useful in illuminating, clarifying and resolving. The last one, when the sentence offered is totally 'wrong', often provides the richest source of information and accuracy, as the 'right' sentence or phrase is then willingly offered. So, offer the sentences without attachment and with a willingness for them to be rejected and/or improved.

When to offer sentences

Discerning when a sentence may be useful comes with practice and the integration of all your learning, and in the moment. They begin to flow as you make the inner shift to a system-orientated stance and can be used to acknowledge, to name a truth, to illuminate and resolve entanglements, and to embed solutions.

Writing about sentences is fraught with challenges, as these sentences emerge, with experience, as you tap into the system dynamics and entanglements that surface as you work. For this reason any examples, out of context, are just that: examples.

Those that follow include the kind of sentences that you may consider offering simply to acknowledge what is, and others that turn the pressure up on the issue in order to bring it into sharper focus. In still other examples you'll find sentences that open up possibilities and dissolve judgements and resistances, for in this way of working you will already be beginning to sense that yielding strengthens.

> Many individuals, leaders and teams spend a great deal of energy holding firm, resisting or refusing to really acknowledge what is in place. However, when they are offered a way of doing so, of yielding instead of resisting, they and the system around them are often profoundly relieved and fundamentally changed.

Here are some 'sentences' to give a sense of what you may find yourself offering as your understanding and scope develop. These are roughly divided into various categories; however, it's hard to be completely clear about this aspect, as they will often overlap or be combined.

To acknowledge what is; to vocalize the facts; to name the difficulty in a few words:

- I'm beginning to see how it is here.'
- 'This is difficult.'
- 'I can see that this is difficult for both of us.'
- 'In this place I have no authority to lead.'

- 'In this place I have limited influence with the team.'
- I am stuck.'

To 'turn up the heat' on the issue:

- An issue of PLACE emerges in the constellation: 'I refuse to acknowledge your right to a place.'
- An issue of TIME emerges in the constellation: 'Because you were here before me you have greater weight and I refuse to acknowledge that.'
- An issue of EXCHANGE emerges in the constellation: 'By giving too much I'm looking for something you can never give me.'
- The constellation shows a resistance to really look at something/ somebody: 'I refuse to look.'
- The constellation shows a possible or actual judgement on somebody or something: 'Secretly, I judge you.'

To illuminate an entanglement more clearly:

- An excluded element is identified: 'We acted as if we could forget you.'
- And in acknowledgement of the behaviour or difficulty that arose as a result: 'We have found ways of remembering you.'

Important note:

These special sentence forms are designed to give the unspoken truths a voice and are only for use in constellations when neutral representatives, not connected to the issue, are involved. They can therefore form an integral part of one-to-one coaching constellations using objects or floor markers. They are also used in workshops where other participants, not connected to the issue-holder, act as representatives.

To begin a movement towards resolution of a system dynamic or entanglement:

- An issue of PLACE is resolved:
    - 'Your contribution to this system was important. Thank you.'
    - 'Because of what you have given, you have a place here too...'
- An issue of TIME is resolved:
    - 'Because of what you contributed, I was able to join later.'
- An issue of EXCHANGE is resolved:
    - 'For what you were able to give me, thank you. I will do the rest myself.'
    - 'You were just my employer. What I gave you, you may keep and what I learnt, I will keep. Thank you.'

- A resistance to looking is softened:
  - 'I'm beginning to look.'
- An excluded element is re-included:
  - 'We missed you.'
  - 'We remember what you contributed.'
- A judgement over somebody is softened:
  - 'I'm no better than you.'
  - 'In your place I may have done exactly the same.'

To make requests and test for movements:

- The constellation shows that more time is needed before a movement may be possible: 'Please give me time.'
- The facilitator wonders if a particular solution embodied in a movement may be emerging, so tests that possibility by inviting the client or representative to say: 'I will move closer/further away now...' or 'When I take this place I can occupy my authority in this role.'

To vocalize and embed a resolution:

A better place is found in the constellation:

- 'This is my place.'
- 'I will be leaving soon.'
- 'I agree to it all.'
- 'I am leaving this with you and I'm withdrawing.'
- 'Thank you.'

> *All great things are simple and many can be expressed in single words.*
> Winston Churchill

Whose line is it anyway?

Sometimes, particularly if sentences come easily to you or you are by now experienced in their use, one will come into your mind that doesn't immediately seem to belong to anyone. In these circumstances, in a workshop environment for example, you can simply ask: 'To who in this room does the sentence "I must leave" belong?'

The same applies in one-to-one coaching. You may be looking at a map that your client has created in front of them and a sentence comes to mind, the source of which is unclear to you. Ask your client something like this: 'I've got a phrase in my head and I'm not sure where it's coming from. May I share it with you?' You will be surprised by how many times your client smiles in recognition and then shares something they or another member of the system has been reflecting on and has not shared.

As with other aspects it's best to experience how these sentences emerge in a workshop setting where you can experience them coming up in you as a representative and also as a facilitator. It's often an area that people find hard at first as it requires a certain kind of letting go that allows just the right words to appear, and some find it easier than others. One student of this approach who found it relatively easy is Maren, a coach who lives and works in Switzerland and who attended a training I facilitated in Italy some years ago. It was clear from the start that she found these sentences easy to access as a representative and so I asked her, as she developed her facilitation skills and then joined the Coaching Constellations teaching team, to write something of her personal experience of finding and expressing them.

Giving voice to the system: A personal account

Coach: Maren Donata Urschel, Executive Coach, London, UK

For me systemic sentences ('sentences') are the voice of the system. Seeing the map of an issue or movement by itself can be immensely powerful and can be enough. But what sentences do is move things from the implicit and unspoken to the explicit. They enable clients to shift their embodied experience of a constellation towards a place where they can see, speak and process the information they receive from the system more clearly.

Sentences are one of the hardest things to explain as they appear from the system while the constellation is taking place.

They seem to me to defy categorization because they are mostly dependent on the context. Yet if categorization were possible, you could say that sentences serve to: acknowledge what is, articulate what has remained unspoken, disentangle, acknowledge what's been given and what's been received, express the underlying truth and initiate a movement towards 'better' or articulate a possible resolution.

I'll share my personal experience of how sentences emerge for me and then how I might craft them in a particular situation.

So, firstly, where do these 'sentences' come from? Well, the only thing I can tell you for sure is that they don't come from the head. When I 'receive' sentences they seem to go through my body first before they get to my brain. Yet they remain unprocessed in my brain. I don't think about them, I don't wait for them, I don't worry about whether they are right and I trust that they emerge. Sentences announce themselves a bit like an intuition, only they don't seem to come from me but through me, from the system.

When I facilitate or when I'm a representative, I act like a channel for what the system needs to say. Physically, I notice that my voice changes. It seems to come from a deeper place within me than when I speak normally. I don't try to be anything or to do anything in order to come up with a sentence. I just let go and relax into the system. If I had to illustrate this with a physical movement it would be something like breathing out, letting go of all the tension in my body (particularly in my heart and in my abdominal area) and having my feet firmly connected to the ground. My head feels completely clear of thoughts and assumptions, just ready to tune into the system.

I don't notice a difference in terms of how sentences emerge for me – whether I work with live representatives, objects or virtually or whether I'm a representative or the facilitator. However, I notice a difference between being a representative and a facilitator in terms of how I process sentences.

As a representative, I stay fully focused on my embodied experience and I articulate the sentence as soon as it comes up.

As a facilitator, I often 'hold on' to a sentence for a while because my responsibility extends beyond focusing on what I'm picking up from the system. In some way, my focus is divided between my brain and my body when I facilitate. My brain enables me to manage the process of the constellation/mapping. This includes holding the space and the client's question, being mindful of all the people and systems involved, looking out for disturbances of the organizing forces that sustain systems and opening up possibilities when things feel stuck. My brain also periodically prompts me to check whether I have become part of the constellation myself. For example, if I stand still for too long as a facilitator, I could become a representative for someone or something that's not been included.

My body enables me to tune into what the system needs to say, to offer a sentence with gravitas but also without attachment and to intuitively decide when to offer it. I can be most useful as a facilitator when my brain and my body collaborate. It's like having a continuous flow of energy that allows information to move freely between the two.

I'll give you a practical example of what this might look like from the facilitator's perspective. Imagine that a representative is about to turn away from another who represents someone who joined the organizational system long before them. I could, in these circumstances, invite the representative to acknowledge the unspoken motivation for that movement by inviting them to say to the other representative: 'I refuse to acknowledge you' or, if more pertinent because they are also their boss, 'I refuse your authority.' The words are spoken first, followed by the movement. As a result, a fuller picture of what really is emerges.

When facilitating it's inherently important to be mindful of any disturbances of the organizing forces that sustain systems. It's equally important to stay with 'what is' and the client's process. Sentences can be very useful in articulating both simultaneously. For example, I might add something like: 'Although you were here before me... I refuse your authority.' That way I'm able to respectfully stay with the client's process and at the same time invite them to acknowledge the order of TIME in this particular system.

Once the sentence has been spoken and integrated into the body of the representative, I might still perceive some stuckness. In my role as facilitator I hold a space for opening up new possibilities even if there appear to be none. As a result, I might offer something along the lines of: 'I'm not ready to acknowledge you, yet.' If this leads the representative to catch a first glimpse of possibility, I might propose: 'Please give me time,' and notice the reaction.

Offering each sentence that got from my body to my brain with lightness, free of judgement and with the willingness to let go, if it doesn't feel true to the representative, is my body's contribution. Holding an awareness of possible disturbances in the organizing principles, acknowledging 'what is' and opening up new possibilities are my brain's contribution.

Only the result of the collaboration between my brain and my body enable the sentences I offer as a facilitator to hold the potential of removing stuckness, catalyzing reconciliation and restoring flow where it previously seemed improbable or undesirable.

Being in a state of seamless collaboration and flow between my brain and my body is challenging as a facilitator – and as a human being in general. I know that I'll always be on that journey, as I continue to learn more about systems.

Maren Donata Urschel

~

I remember my first attempt to apply this methodology in one-to-one coaching, not for my anxiety about getting it 'right', but for the lasting impact it had on my client. He was a young management consultant keen to make an impact with his client. I sensed in what he said about the relationship that there was something else apart from a straightforward difference of opinion, beliefs or personality type. There were a lot of judgements in his language, a lack of respect and a sense of stuckness. He'd talked at length about his client in the previous sessions and we'd made little progress. We'd looked at the issue using personality type, discussion and all the coaching questions and frameworks I could think of. On this occasion, as he began to tell me about the relationship difficulties again, I quietly interrupted him. I invited him to choose an object on the table in front of us to 'represent' his client, and find a place for it.

In that moment, as though it was the most natural thing in the world, this rational man stopped telling me what an incompetent leader his client was and simply chose one of the many coffee cups on the table, placing it in the centre of the space between us. He had stopped talking and seemed suddenly reflective, calm. I was fascinated that such a simple invitation had affected him so quickly, so deeply. He had come out of his head and dropped quickly into a stiller, quieter place, clearly in contact with another way of thinking, feeling about, his issue and his client. So had I.

He stared at this cup as if it was something completely new and of the utmost interest and importance. He knew, at some unconscious level, that this coffee cup – this representative of his client – was in a place that felt, well, *true*. It belonged in this particular spot on the table, and nowhere else. It was in its place. After staring at it, transfixed, for some time without speaking, he very slightly adjusted the direction in which the handle on the cup faced and then looked up.

> A constellation often induces a kind of light trance where movements, words and insights come from somewhere beyond conscious awareness.

Unsure of what was happening, I decided to trust the process. I invited him to choose another object to represent himself and place it in relationship to the coffee cup, his client. He looked around the coffee cups, pens, pads and other clutter on the table. Then he stood up and, reaching across the table, took hold of a large silver coffee flask, which he placed right next to the coffee cup, his client. He sat back and looked at the two representative objects. A flask and a cup. I watched him closely.

It didn't take any experience of this approach to see that he was having a powerfully embodied experience. A direct experience of the underlying relationship dynamic that he could now see as if never having seen it before. He had created a kind of picture that expressed his own unconscious mental map of this relationship. An external picture of an internal, previously unknown landscape.

I was feeling my way carefully into my first attempt at working this way, but I need not have worried. Like with so many times that followed this first experience, my client saw what this map was showing him. In this case he voiced it without prompting: 'I'm too close, aren't I?' He paused. 'And too big.' I nodded in respectful agreement at this clear statement of truth, his truth. Less from the coach was rapidly turning into more for the client. I'd never seen him more deeply engaged with his material than he was now.

I had recently completed a day of training in which we looked at the use of 'systemic sentences': short phrases to help capture and embody the truths and insights that flow when working in this way. I tried the one that came into my mind. 'Try saying: "You're the client, I'm the consultant."'

Slowly, and with a great sense of presence, he said: 'You are the client... I am just the consultant'. After a while, without my prompting, he slowly pulled the flask away from the coffee cup. He looked at this new picture and breathed out. A sigh of relief, as he found his place.

The sentence is just ahead of the movement.

Nicola Dunn

In less than five minutes, and with only a few words, he had moved from a place of vocal judgement to a quiet and respectful humility. The insight and fresh understanding were not in his head; they were in his body. Embodied. He was in a better place, literally; one from which he could add much more value.

However, it wasn't just about him. By finding his own place, he had given his client his place as the client too. Both of them had an equally valued place in this small part of a much larger system and could flourish. This was borne out in the real world in the following weeks and months.

I had facilitated, or rather witnessed, something I had previously doubted had a place in serious coaching. This short piece of work, which initially appeared to be little more than a three-dimensional representation of the relationship, had been invaluable. It released him from the attachments he had been forming to his 'story' about his client. The judgements, assumptions and projections melted away as his inner image of the relationship dynamics emerged. The physical embodiment in the 'stepping back' movement impacted him in a way I'd not seen before. The non-verbal language exchange that constellations offer had really shown its benefits.

From that moment, everything changed – in his working relationship with his client, in our working relationship, which grew deeper and much more productive, and in my work as a coach with all my other clients.

Back then I didn't know much about the organizing principles that influence systems. I didn't know that this approach works as well with abstract issues as it does with interpersonal relationships, and I didn't know about entanglements, hidden loyalties or the broader ideas and many expressions and applications of systemic coaching. I just knew about the importance of place in healthy systems. That to flourish and for relationships to be in flow, everyone in a system has an equal right to a respected but different place within it.

I was impressed by the way that this first attempt had surfaced the hidden dynamic, so quickly and without pretention or many words, and by the way it had shown my client straight away in what particular way he was in the 'wrong' place in relationship to his client. The whole exercise had somehow surfaced the innate emotional intelligence, the system intelligence and resourced him with minimum intervention and a light touch. It also allowed me to stay in my place as the coach, as the witness, and it allowed him to find his place with his issue, with his client.

As you read this book, start to learn and to practise, you'll discover that you can relax into the process while you build your knowledge and skills, and then you will soon find yourself illuminating the invisible, working with the unknown and facilitating resolutions that are beyond your imagination.

> *Nothing you say stands alone or is complete in the present: it has its roots in the past and pushes feelers into the future.*
>
> Tim Parks, *Teach Us to Sit Still*

One of the constellation forms we teach in the trainings is called an 'integration constellation' and is designed to support deeper integration of the experiences that the client has had in their life and work. The purpose is to resource the client by integrating all that they've received, while also disentangling them from limiting dynamics and incomplete endings. It's important to visit both joyful, resourcing relationships, as well as painful ones that cost energy and had difficult emotions connected with them.

In the experiential training environment we use other group members to represent each key relationship system in which the client has belonged, in a structured form where each representative stands, shoulder to shoulder in a row and in time order.

We then teach how to apply this form of constellation in one-to-one settings using Post-its in a line on a wall to represent each system. This is usefully combined with the application of sentences and offers an effective way of finding and expressing them, as Hazel demonstrates in this case study.

Hazel is an executive coach working with leaders and leadership teams. She trained with Coaching Constellations in 2015 and started to integrate the systemic approach and constellations methodology into her thriving coaching practice.

'The Walk of Life': An integration constellation

Coach/facilitator: Hazel Chapman, Executive Coach
Client: 'Tricia', Head of UK Sales for a European company

One of Tricia's objectives for the coaching programme was to better manage her emotions, especially her frustration and anger in a current relationship within her organization.

This was the second coaching session and as her preparation Tricia had drawn her timeline on paper. I asked her how she had felt completing it and she said she was amazed how emotional she had felt. Even as she spoke tears immediately arose, quickly followed by anger that the tears had come.

'It's the break-up causing this, but it's completely over, I don't understand,' she said. I reassured her that it was understandable around such a big event and that letting go of the past is never easy. I asked if she would like to explore this. She rejected the suggestion with 'No, I can't today, maybe next time.' So I asked what she would like to explore and she said her timeline and turned to her journal.

As she started to tell the story of her childhood, I noticed she was pulled into her rational thinking – justifying and analysing her experiences. While she had rejected exploring her emotions over the break-up, I sensed that understanding her emotional connection to past events may be key to her managing emotion in the present. Because of the 'timeline' nature of the exercise and the level of emotional content I thought an 'integration constellation' might be a useful way of facilitating this process.

So I suggested we do something different. She agreed and then I wrote 'Childhood' on a large Post-it and put it on the left hand side of a clear wall at around her head height. I invited her to stand, facing it and at a distance that simply felt true for her. She started talking and I asked her to first 'Find your place, feel it in your body. Where do you belong in relation to this part of your life?' She stood very close and tears started to come up.

'Why am I crying – this is a *good* memory!' I invited her to just stand and reconnect with that time. After a while I invited her to tell her Childhood what she appreciated about it. I looked closely at her and felt some words come to me that might express what she seemed to be in contact with. I offered her this sentence: 'Thank you for the safety and warmth that you gave me.' She readily accepted and repeated these words, while nodding.

I asked her if she was OK to continue with this process.

'Yes.'

I referred Tricia back to her timeline and, as she described each stage, she drew it onto a large Post-it and put it up on the wall in line with the others. I repeated the same approach each time inviting her to just stand at a distance that felt true and simply reconnect with each part of her life. What did she notice? What was she feeling?

For 'School 11–16' she stood some distance away. There were struggles as well as happiness and she acknowledged the part they had played. I offered a sentence to condense the essence of what I sensed she was saying:

'My family and friends were always there for me as I found my way.' She repeated this and smiled and stood thoughtfully for some time.

At the next stage, '16–18', a conflict with her parents emerged and the distance grew greater. However her gratitude for her parents was self-evident. I fed this back to her by offering her this sentence:

'Thank you for sticking by me despite all that I did. I really appreciate what you did for me.' She happily repeated this – 'Thank you for sticking by me despite all that I did' – and then stood in silence for a while reflecting.

We continued to her university and gap year and she acknowledged being far from home and friends but finding her way nevertheless. The distance between her and each Post-it had grown greater at every phase. She too had noticed the pattern.

Her next phase was her 20s. She immediately said that work and home were different and so I created two smaller Post-its for 'Career' and 'Home' and added them to the bottom left and right hand corner of the larger Post-it that read '20s'. She stood in relation to each separately and we did some work with those.

The painful break-up was in the next stage. Tricia described her pain, her not knowing why he left. After a while I offered this synthesis:

'Your lack of explanation caused me a lot of pain,' which she immediately accepted and repeated. A little later I offered her:

'I leave your reasons with you, and will move on.' She rejected this, saying that that felt like she was forgiving him, which she couldn't do.

So then I said:

'How about "You had your reasons and I leave them with you. They are yours, not mine"?'

She immediately smiled and repeated the sentence several times. We stood there for a while in silence as she integrated this truth and the words.

'You had your reasons and I leave them with you. They are yours, not mine.'

A little later I also offered her something to try and acknowledge the balance of EXCHANGE: 'I will take what was good and the rest I leave with you.' This also resonated deeply and she repeated it strongly and firmly.

When the moment was right, we moved on to a Post-it marked 'Now' and she started talking freely about her current situation with optimism, which was very different from our previous conversations. I then invited her to turn around, when she felt ready, and take everything the past had given her and look to the future. In fact she said she wanted to stay in the 'Now' as this felt good. So she spent some time in 'Now' simply integrating everything she had just experienced and we brought the process to an end.

Benefits

This session proved to be a turning point in the coaching because Tricia separated from being in the grip of her emotions and instead gave them a place and so was able to start the journey of integration without blame, judgement or feeling so overwhelmed.

There were also noticeable observational differences in the following sessions. Tricia started to take more care of her own health, fitness and appearance, she started to dress in brighter colours and patterns and her language shifted from negative to positive descriptors.

Some months later, when I asked her for permission to use this as a written case study, she wrote to me saying:

'I found this exercise very powerful, Hazel. I call it "the walk of life" as it was so helpful to reflect and understand how each part of my life had led me to my current place.'

'The suggested phrases you offered made it easier to understand and integrate each and made sense of moments of pain, lifting an emotional weight off my shoulders.'

My learning

I learnt that when you give the exercise a go, even for the first time, the sentences reveal themselves as the experience deepens and develops. There was amazingly little effort in this, I just stayed present and tuned into Tricia's embodied experience and the words emerged.

When I offered sentences, if they didn't resonate, they were easily rejected and more information was given, or they were improved, so they were all useful. I learnt that there are no right or wrong sentences to offer. This surprised me and helped me to relax and focus on being present and simply trust the process.

After the coaching, I realized there were some sentences of EXCHANGE that I felt I could have used to go deeper, eg 'I gave too much' or 'I'll take my responsibility for what happened between us, and leave you with yours.' However, it was still very powerful for my client, even without those.

Above all, I learnt that by focusing on being useful to the coachee in each moment, and by trusting the structure of the exercise and the sentences to emerge and do their work, without the need to 'get it right', I could be truly useful.

Bowing

There is a third process, beyond movement and sentences, that you can explore when working in this way: bowing. Developed, like the rest of the work, in a family system context, this 'ritual' can have a profoundly connecting impact. In executive coaching settings this might seem impossible and even undesirable, but you may be surprised, as we briefly touched on earlier, by how often it happens of its own accord.

> Yielding strengthens. When strength is restored, the work of change can begin.

In family workshops it's commonplace for a facilitator to ask a client or representative to bow – to their parents, to their fate, to someone they are withdrawing from. However, in coaching my preference is to simply ask the client or representative to follow any movement that feels respectful and appropriate.

When someone finds a place in relationship to someone else who has a system or organizational precedence over them, when someone withdraws with thanks for what they have received, or when someone bows to a great difficulty in the organizational system, then you can invite them to embody that in a respectful way. Most times they will make a small nod of their head; sometimes, depending on their personal style and cultural reference point, it will be a full bow.

~

I'm often struck by how easily people with no previous experience will willingly get up and stand as a representative in a constellation, reporting accurately on their embodied experience and then accessing hidden information in the system being explored. I also notice how often the people who appear to be the most sceptical, defended or resistant in an opening round or in private comments to me before a workshop or training begins, will often be the same people who feel most drawn to represent and will most willingly offer to articulate their experience, follow inner movements and, yes, even bow without hesitation.

It's as if something else, a larger force, is recruiting them into the service of the constellation. Their highly attuned sensitivity to falsehoods, to dubious theories or belief systems, enables them to be open to very subtle information in the field that is of vital importance for the client.

Living maps

07

To understand is to perceive patterns. ISAIAH BERLIN

Once you have started experimenting, respectfully and slowly, with the processes that turn a static map into a dynamic picture, you are moving from simply 'mapping what is' into a constellation. The map comes to life and you have opened up many fresh possibilities.

There are a number of ways of working when the map starts to come to life, which it will, in your hands.

Seeing patterns

The best way of recognizing the various patterns that emerge in constellations is to do so by experiencing them. See them once and you may miss them; see them again and you'll remember. You can already imagine some of the patterns you will start to see as you invite your clients to map what is in a number of contexts:

- Leaving (the representative for the client is looking outside of the system as if saying: 'I want to leave.')
- Loyalty to someone/something else (the representative for the client is looking outside of the system and may be entangled with something/someone there as if saying: 'I'll remember you.')
- Out of order (the representative for the client feels 'above' that of their boss for example they choose a much larger object to represent themselves as if saying: 'I'm better than you.')
- Resource required (the representative for the client stands alone and looks under-resourced or expresses difficulty finding their authority as if saying: 'I need some additional resource here.')
- Conflict pattern (the representative for the client is looking in exactly the opposite direction to another key representative or is right 'in their face', looking at them very closely: 'I refuse your authority.')

- Different purpose (the representative for the client is facing away from the purpose or task of the organization or team: 'I'm here for other reasons.')
- TIME (the representative for the client is placed in a position of authority over people or roles that came before them: 'I refuse to see what came before me and will change things here anyway.')
- PLACE (the representative for the client is hard to place and, in one-to-one coaching, is held in the air above the map of others or tried in different places with no rest: 'I can't find my place/I don't know what to do to belong here.')
- EXCHANGE (the representative for the client is placed in front of the representative for the company or organization: 'I gave you too much/you owe me.')

You will see and recall many more relationship patterns. Even though no two constellations are ever the same, these patterns soon become familiar and you can respectfully offer your insight or emerging hypothesis to your client.

If your orientation is not to the visual patterns, then you can still identify and name them by recalling and exploring in amongst the natural organizing forces of systems. This is a good way of starting to illuminate the hidden dynamics.

Illuminating dynamics

Firstly, you can pay attention to the organizing forces of TIME, PLACE and EXCHANGE about who or what came first, who has their place and who or what may have been excluded from the system. You can also explore the balance of giving and taking; the level of exchange. In all of these you can now offer movements and sentences to carefully illuminate and explore.

Alternatively you could take a different route and work entirely through the experience, trusting your own and your client's feelings and emotional-level responses. This will move things forward and may often illuminate hidden dynamics at work in this particular system.

Finally, you could simply take what your client is telling you about the facts of the issue and work only with those, offering acknowledging sentences that confirm the essence of what is. That's a useful approach and a great way to learn when mapping and working with this methodology at the start of your learning journey.

So, you can work with the forces, the feelings or the facts. You may have a natural preference for one or more of these and that will provide you with a good starting point. However, to truly illuminate the dynamics, to be able to see and offer your client fresh paths to resolution while respectfully supporting them to stand in the truth, you will need to develop, over time, a full integration of all three of these approaches at the same time. This should be underpinned by your stance and facilitated through the principle of acknowledgement and the practices of constellations.

Facilitating solutions

Once you've experienced the potential for a constellation to facilitate a deep movement in your clients, once you've seen them understand the importance of the interconnectedness, you'll know that *not* reaching for a solution, a goal, or a measurable outcome is a solution in itself. This is one of the fundamental differences from goal-orientated coaching that not only releases the coach from the need to resolve everything but also frees your client to find their own path, in their own time, through the complexity of their challenge, dilemma or stuckness.

In a workshop environment or when working one-to-one, there can be a tendency for coaches and facilitators to feel that their work is incomplete if they don't bring it all together into a picture of resolution. The picture may well be the one that is possible, or it may not, but going there too early can often be experienced as too much for the client, who may not yet be ready to see, let alone internalize, the new picture. Less is more.

On other occasions the energy for moving to and seeing the picture of resolution will be strong and coming from the client. Even then, my preference is to encourage them to hold back from stepping in to the resolution too quickly. This is because, firstly, it can be useful and resourcing to reflect and deepen the contact with that moment of transition, and secondly because it can reduce the available energy to take the solution out into the real world, the real situation. Leaving the coaching client in the creative tension of not being able to stand fully in the solution can create a strong movement out into the real world where the need for the resolution really exists.

If it seems that a final resolving image would be useful for the client then use all that you know about movement, sentences and rituals to achieve that.

To bring this second part of the book to a close with an example of practical application I want to share with you a brief example from coach and facilitator Patrizia Amanati.

In this case study she describes how she weaves in and back out of the systemic mapping methodology as a part of an Action Learning Set with a client who is struggling to occupy his role authority. This case study also demonstrates the use of sentences to surface and express unspoken dynamics and truths.

Finding my authority

Coach: Patrizia Amanati
Client: A senior project manager in a regional division of a national organization

My client had recently joined the organization and had been invited to do so because of his impressive track record in a very similar role. However, he was having great difficulty in communicating upward, from himself to his managers, as if there was something in the way. He reported to two senior leaders but the communication with them and one particular direct report had slowed down to the point that he was finding it hard to bring his expertise and experience to bear.

It became clear that the questions from within the learning group were not helping him get clarity, but reinforcing the story of how difficult things were. So I suggested that he might like to 'have a look at things in a different way'. He was open to that despite the fact that he is a senior project manager and used to considering every problem through the lens of Prince2 or a similar model and with a strong need to consider the minutiae of every challenge. I sensed it might be a challenge to invite him to work with less detail and at the heart of the systemic dynamics.

The context of this session was an Action Learning Set and this, together with the physical layout of the small room, meant it was not possible or appropriate to use the group members as representatives. So I invited him to use a piece of flip-chart paper on the table top to represent the system and to choose two or three elements he needed to represent this difficulty. He chose a representative for himself, the two managers he wanted a better working relationship with and his direct report.

He placed the representative for himself – a small packet of sugar – right on the edge of the system that he had defined using the sheet of flip-chart paper. He indicated that his representative was facing inwards, into the organizational system within which he was trying to find his place.

He then added two drinking glasses to represent the two managers, one at each top corner of the paper. He then placed the representative for his direct report in the centre of the sheet. The two managers were facing each other and the direct report – represented by a large coffee cup – was in the middle of the piece of paper, the system, the three forming an equilateral triangle.

As soon as he completed this physical map he said: 'Oh, I see what's going on.'

In discussion and through questions from myself and members of the Learning Set it became apparent that the direct report was acting as if they were occupying the role.

I went on to explore the history of the role and discovered that the role was created and defined by the direct report and the expectation was that they would have occupied it. However, the organization advertised the role and this man was chosen to fill it.

On hearing this new information, I asked him to connect with the representative for himself and invited him to say this to the direct report: 'I don't have a place in this organization.' He listened to this suggestion, then said: 'I don't yet have a real place in this organization, but I want to do my job.' This was a powerful statement for him as it had been expressed previously only in a negative way.

I then connected with the energy of the representative for the direct report and offered a statement from what I was picking up: 'You took my job!' In that moment he was able to get a sense of the anger and disappointment of the direct report and this gave him a fresh perspective and understanding.

The map clearly showed a source of the difficulty and together we agreed that we would continue, in this session at least, to explore the relationship with his direct report rather than his managers. In that context I offered a number of sentences for him to say while physically connected to his representative and facing towards the representative for the direct report.

These included 'Thank you for creating this role,' which changed something in him as he said it and then he said: 'I was appointed to this role and that must have been painful for you.'

He also went on, later, to add: 'I am well-qualified to occupy this role and to deliver what the organization needs. Please allow me to lead.'

As is often the case some of the sentences I offered didn't always resonate but hearing my words allowed him to reflect and find his own words to express what needed to be acknowledged or spoken.

At the end of the constellation he had more clarity around what was blocking relationship and communication and a fresh perspective on one source of this dynamic. He also felt able, resourced and ready to speak with his direct report with a new understanding and a willingness to listen, while also being clear about his own authority.

He was physically much more settled and reflective and we returned to the Action Learning methodology and moved to the next person.

~

This example shows how effective the creation of a three-dimensional physical map can be in quickly surfacing the hidden relationship architecture and dynamics in the system without the use of lots of words. It also demonstrates how the client can easily drop into a systemic perspective and start to voice sentences and see possibilities that they have not previously considered. Possibilities and words they would have discounted moments before.

Patrizia, who was the first student of Coaching Constellations trainings to become a facilitator on our programmes, describes her integration of the systemic approach as her toolbox. A holding framework into which she can place all her other coaching tools, skills and methodologies. As a result systemic principles underpin her individual coaching and team facilitation and she weaves in and out of a range of methodologies in the moment.

This case study also shows the importance of always checking the origins of the role your coaching client is occupying, especially when they are having difficulty finding their role authority. You can't lead or really be effective in role if you didn't have permission. Sometimes roles are created that are not really needed by the system and people who occupy them usually burn out trying to find their authority. Or, in this case, the permission is not granted by another person in the system who believes it is their role.

This kind of issue can only be respectfully resolved when each person's truth is recognized and honoured, given a place. Then one can step back and one can step up and lead.

FAQs (A): Answers to frequently asked questions

In this section (and the other FAQ section that follows later in the book) I have tried to share the most common questions that I hear in workshops and trainings and provide the answers, some of which I've clarified and expanded for this book.

What do you mean by a 'system'?

- A system is a series of interconnected, interdependent relationships: a relationship system. This is as a result of our innate ability to tune into the rules of belonging, the conscience, of each system.

- The first system we are aware of and belong to is our family system, and then often our education and cultural system. Without conscious thought we know how we belong in each and what we must do to protect that belonging.

- We may remain loyal to those systems in all kinds of unconscious ways through our life and work. Living and working (and coaching) in alignment with them helps us to stay feeling 'innocent'. Try to identify the reference systems that you come from and live and work within, and that you are loyal to. Then consider inviting your clients to do the same.

- We are often not really consciously aware of the systems we live and work within and may refer to them simply as our 'reference system'. But we know exactly how to stay loyal to them.

- Systems are sustained by a consistent set of naturally occurring organizing principles. These principles are seen time and again and are experienced as balancing forces that move all human systems towards wholeness.

- When the naturally occurring balancing forces are ignored, the system attempts to bring itself back into wholeness, into alignment. These attempts to rebalance and align, to keep the system whole, create the dynamics within and between systems that have such an impact on life and work.

So, what is a 'systemic constellation'?

- The literal translation of the two words 'system' and 'constellation' means 'a group of objects that stand together to form a pattern'.
- So, a systemic constellation is a visible relational map of the client's invisible inner image of the relationship system. This image is, through a facilitated process, illuminated, disentangled and brought into better balance through the application of the insights, principles and practices of this work.
- A constellation creates a living map of a system and so is useful when looking at improving the relationships and interconnectedness between the parts.
- A constellation allows you access to complex relationship systems in a manageable and respectful way. In this way systems can be realigned and changed to give better flow and function.
- A constellation can illuminate relationships between people, teams and abstract qualities and elements, including organizations, products and brands.
- A 'systemic constellation', often simply referred to just as 'a constellation', leaves the client with a new map, a new picture, which is then internalized and integrated into their life and work.

How can constellations be useful in coaching?

- Constellations can help surface and set a powerful coaching agenda. This energizes clients and coaches, as they get clarity and sharp focus with real depth.
- Constellations can identify the roots of very challenging issues and so provide a powerful diagnostic in individuals, teams and whole businesses at a refreshing pace.
- A constellation is an effective way of supporting people to find their 'right place' in a system – an abstract quality that is often only 'felt'. Because constellations involve an embodied experience of 'right place', they offer a uniquely powerful way of experiencing and then internalizing a new picture of resolution.
- Constellations can be used in any part of a coaching programme to identify hidden blocks, find hidden resources and move towards resolution.

- The focus on seeing the whole and acknowledging what is, just as it is, without judgements, generates high levels of trust and a feeling of safety. This level of inclusiveness, agreeing to everything as it is, settles the coach and the client as everything is included and given a respectful place.
- This approach can be integrated with other ways of working with a light touch. It can create a useful framework for coaching conversations and all other interventions.

So, what is 'systemic coaching'?

- Systemic coaching is coaching that enables coach and client to see patterns and illuminate hidden dynamics in systems. The application of constellations allows access to complex systems so that fresh and enduring solutions can be found.
- Systemic coaching attends to the whole and restores a place for everything in the system. When everything is respectfully included, the system relaxes and allows access.
- Systemic coaching is coaching that is working in the service of the whole system. The focus is wide, beyond the individual and on the systems in which the individual belongs. Priority is given to the system.
- Working with the whole system in mind provides additional insights and resources that can illuminate dynamics and behaviours that may not have their source, or resolution, within the individual or team.
- Attempts to coach only at the individual developmental level may get stuck, or the solutions and new behaviours not endure, if the wider system view is not included.
- Systemic coaching also offers to enrich individual and team understanding of the forces that sustain and balance systems so that the insights and system intelligence remain and grow in the system in which you are coaching. This creates organization-wide behavioural change and moves the system towards organizational health.
- Coaching with an intention of affecting organizational behavioural change necessarily requires a system intervention. Systemic coaching and constellations provides one such opportunity, amongst other system-oriented methods and interventions.
- When organizational systems are in dynamic balance and moving towards health, it feels easier to find a reliable place, fully occupy personal and role authority, and make a valuable contribution. Systemically-orientated coaching supports leaders and teams to align with the naturally occurring forces in systems so that change is lasting and behaviours contribute to the well-being of the whole.

When could I use systemic coaching and constellations with clients?

- When there is something stuck at an individual, team or whole system level.
- When there are a number of complex relationships and relationship systems around the client. (Because the great benefit of constellations is that they allow you to access large or complex systems in a manageable way.)
- When there is no apparent path to a solution or previous attempts to resolve the situation have not been successful.
- When there is something hidden or secret, or when something 'just doesn't feel right' but the source isn't clear.
- When there is a need to illuminate or clarify the coaching agenda.
- When a preferred theory or model for working doesn't seem to apply or work, but you'd like to realize its potential in the system.
- When your client wants to get in touch with and align their resources in order to relax into their authority in role.
- When you have come to the limits of words, discussion and development and a fresh perspective is required.
- When as a coach you have a sense that there is 'something else' in this client's system that is affecting their ability to be present or to perform; something that is distracting them and drawing their energy away but that remains unspoken.
- When as a coach you detect that a natural organizing principle has been neglected or ignored. For example, when someone 'crashes into' a system because they have refused to acknowledge those who are already present and the importance of their contribution.
- When your client needs to say something challenging to another person in their system and needs to speak their truth in a way that can be heard.
- When on requesting more detail about a brief you don't get a meaningful response. This is easy to mistake as resistance or reluctance but is always a clear sign that the challenge is in the system, 'beyond words', and cannot be expressed. The lack of words is always rooted in the system and so, inevitably, only an intervention that includes the whole system perspective will add value.
- When the client is attached to their own story and version of events and a fresh perspective would be useful.
- When you, or your client, are stuck in your head and need to access a different way of 'knowing'.

Is this approach 'solutions focused'?

- Yes, but you can't make solutions happen in systems if they are not the right solutions for the system! Despite this simple truth, some organizations pay coaches and consultants many times to 'put something right' or 'sort something/somebody out' that is not possible. The systemic perspective allows a different path to be found, a path that gives a place to what is and what is not possible and supports organizational flow.

In what ways does this approach facilitate transformative coaching?

- The reason that this methodology is sometimes referred to as 'profound' by those who have experienced it is that constellations illuminate what has previously been invisible and apparently unknowable. They create a new inner alignment, a new inner constellation, in the client.

- This is achieved through a combination of the coach's stance, an understanding of the underlying principles and the application of the processes.

- When we use constellations we can stop *talking* about a situation and instead make it visible, tangible and three-dimensional. This creates the opportunity for a new vision of 'what is' and what's possible, which in turn facilitates a deep inner movement. Coachees see the interconnectedness in the structures of their relationship systems and experience the non-verbal language exchange that a constellation creates.

- Constellations tap into the interconnectedness of elements within and between systems. Accessing the invisible field of information allows the coach and coachee to use the invisible, implicit information, rather than only the visible and explicit. The invisible information is often the most crucial, particularly when looking at disentangling complex dynamics, stuckness or inertia. Working with both supports flow and integrity.

- Constellations free coach and coachee from their familiar perspectives, encouraging both to stand in the truth of 'what is' and see the client's issue in the wider system. This leads to the development of coherence and integrity through the system and the possibility for transformation of understanding, insight, behaviour and action.

When should I use constellations for my own development as a coach?

- When you require supervision or self-supervision to support your own clarity and resourcefulness as a coach with a particular client situation, or in relationship to your coaching offer or business.
- When you need to explore potential resources for choices and decision points.
- When resourcing or preparing to introduce constellations.
- When you want to explore your own family-of-origin patterns.
- When you want to integrate your previous professional expressions and bring their resources into your current work.

When you talk about 'systemic issues', what do you mean?

- Systemic issues are those that arise because the natural 'ordering forces' that govern coherence and sustain relationship systems have been violated or ignored. Systems naturally attempt to maintain their integrity and remain in dynamic balance by making corrections to realign with the forces.
- Systemic issues arise because the underlying organizing principles have been disregarded, which results in system dynamics. Those dynamics appear as symptoms or behaviours in individuals, teams and whole organizations.
- The symptoms of systemic issues emerge in individuals and in organizations in a way that may appear to have no root cause or obvious source. This is why thinking and working with a systemic awareness and the application of constellations is a particularly effective way to reveal the patterns and connections, surfacing the roots of apparently intractable stuckness, resistance to change and other system issues.

What are some common signs of systemic issues in organizational systems?

Some of the more common signs include:

- Difficulty performing or finding authority in role when the experience and skills seem to be present.
- Inertia in a part or the whole of the system without visible cause.
- Difficulties with authority or leadership without obvious cause.
- Team conflict, stress or challenging behaviour without obvious cause.

- A culture of conflict, secrets or exclusion.
- Frequent internal competition, with political power struggles.
- Unexplained low levels of loyalty and/or motivation.
- Low levels of respect for the organizational hierarchy.
- Subjects or people that are taboo.
- Stuckness and/or repeating patterns that don't support flow and clarity in the individual, team or organizational system.
- Leadership decisions that manifest as actions that don't make a difference.

What are these natural organizing principles that sustain systems?

An example is the organizing principle of TIME:

- What comes first comes before what comes afterwards. When this organizing principle is disrupted or disregarded, systems fall out of alignment, out of balance. It's often easiest to recall these forces at work in family systems. So, for example, you can see this in intimate relationships when a first wife's 'position' (as the first) is not respected and she is 'replaced' by a second wife. Without respect in the system for the first wife in her 'first place', the second marriage will become imbalanced and hard work – until the first is given her place and acknowledged.

- It's the same in an organizational context when, for example, someone takes on the duties of a role that already exists in the organization and was occupied by someone who left, or was forced out, without respect for their contribution. If the new role holder doesn't hold an inner respect for the previous one, they will struggle to find their authority in that role or persuade people to follow their lead. Time and again we see that lack of respect for what came first in business systems and it causes significant disruptions.

- This is a good example of something that coaches, new to this way of working, can listen out for. Is the natural hierarchy, the organizing principle of TIME, being disregarded and causing difficult dynamics? The idea of priority in systems, for what came first, is very important for system health.

Another example is EXCHANGE, sometimes referred to as the balancing force of giving and receiving:

- In intimate relationships, for example, when one person gives too much (love, energy, attention, money) the other may feel a need to leave the relationship. This is because they feel burdened and indebted and they have not been willing or able to give back enough to balance what they have received. It's too much to bear and they feel a need to leave the system so they can feel their own 'weight' and strength as an individual again.

- In organizational systems very similar dynamics can quickly establish themselves in relation to the balance of pay for work done. Overpaying people, more than they are able to repay in their professional time and efficiency, weakens the system and causes lower levels of motivation and loyalty, not higher levels. People who are paid too much often lose their motivation and talk in negative terms about the company, becoming rebels or secretly wanting to leave in order to get back into balance.

Are all issues 'systemic' and can all issues benefit from this intervention?

- Not all symptoms and problems are rooted in hidden system dynamics – other issues may cause them. However, most can be mapped, illuminated and resourced through this methodology. The systemic principles still apply when mapping and clarifying non-system issues because everything takes place within a relationship system.

- Take, for example, 'incompetence' or a 'mistake'. If you set up a constellation, a relational map of the incompetence or the mistake and the system around the individual or team responsible, you may discover a hidden connection. This could be an unconscious loyalty, for example, connecting the behaviour to something much deeper or unseen and out of consciousness.

- In this way the systemic approach and perspective can become a useful framework for looking at any issue, and constellations a useful tool for illuminating, clarifying and resourcing any system issue.

From where/whom did this work originate?

- The interventions of a systemic constellation are based on the work of Bert Hellinger in the context of family systems. Bert and then others developed and tested the insights, observations and interventions in organizational settings where the same need for systems to find a kind of dynamic balance and completeness, the same hidden loyalties and dynamics, appeared.

- One of the people responsible for migrating the work from family systems to organizational systems is Gunthard Weber. Others also pioneered and passed the work on, and so it goes on.

Do you talk about or work with family issues when working as a coach because you are using this methodology?

- While an understanding of family systems and the dynamics within them is very useful when training to facilitate this approach, it is not necessary to name or work with family dynamics when using systemic constellations in coaching or organizational interventions.

- Whilst the approach was originally developed in the context of family systems and was found to support the flow of love and life in families, its value in business and organizational systems is very similar – to support the flow of leadership and organizational vitality.

- When working as a coach, hold in mind the fact that we all come from family systems. You can go further but do your own work on your connection back into your roots and sources first, before doing that with clients.

I've heard this described as a phenomenological methodology. What does that mean?

- At its simplest, a phenomenological approach simply means one that allows for the study and trust of experience in the moment. That is, if you experience something as true for you, then it is true for you. In this way it's profoundly respectful of the individual's sense of self and their experience of themselves.

- Applied to systems, it allows us to see that we are all influenced by the same 'organizing principles'. So, while we are having individual experiences, there are common themes and threads and all our experiences are linked to everybody else's in the same system.

What is representative perception?

- In constellation workshops or when working one-to-one, people standing in the place of a system element will have distinct experiences including changes in emotions, physical experiences ('strong' or 'weak') and body temperature changes. They often also have sudden insights, as well as images and words coming to mind. This is the result of a phenomenon called 'representative perception'. It forms a source of information in workshops and coaching. There are several ongoing studies to explore its source and workings in more depth.

- Representative perception is triggered in part by the manner in which the person is placed in the constellation as well as where they are placed in relation to others and the holding circle. If the client is in a collected inner state then the representative will have enough information available as a result.

- Representative perception is useful as it points to dynamics and resources that can lead to a profound realignment of the system. This is the source of the power of constellations to deliver fresh information, insights and resources. Representative perception is accessible in one-to-one work just as it is in workshops and includes perception of events in the long distant past, as well as identification of future possibilities.

- A constellation offers a route out of secondary emotions and allows the client – through a representative for themselves – to move towards their primary emotion. Representative perception offers a unique insight into the primary emotions of the person they are representing. It's as if all the 'story' and ideas about the situation have been washed off, leaving the simple elegance of the, often quietly spoken, primary emotion.

What's the difference between 'representative perception' and 'role-play'?

- Firstly, yes, there's an important difference and it's incumbent on the facilitator to be able to tell them apart. Role-play is coming from the individual and arrives with stories and ideas about how things should be, projections, beliefs and judgements, and the other is reporting information that's coming from the system.

- To discern the difference takes experience and practice but it can be seen, and felt, in the manner in which somebody is speaking and in their physical presence, as well as the content of their words.

- To see the difference, try being in or facilitating a blind or double-blind constellation where you don't know the story and neither do the representatives. This makes it easier to discern what is coming from where or whom.

- No one is ever asked to 'act as if' or 'role-play' in a constellation. There is no placing of representatives in poses or requests to stand or move in a particular way; no acting or acting out.

- However, it's important to remember that people naturally bring their own 'stuff' to their representative experiences. This can often be an important part of the process and is why that particular person was chosen to be a representative by the issue holder: even though they have never met, they can pick up the pattern and dynamics in the other with no conscious awareness. This is one of the reasons why workshops are usually equally interesting and engaging for the 'observers/representatives' as they are for the 'issue holders'.

- What's also influential is the way that the issue holder collects and centres themselves and then the way they touch and move the representative during the 'setting up' phase. Enough information is usually gathered in the setting up process for any representative to illuminate the underlying dynamics, no matter what their 'neutrality', ethnic background or gender. However, if the client is still coming from their heads, not using their 'felt sense', then they may set up a picture of how they *think* it ought to look, or what they *think* it's like. This may encourage the representative to 'act out' the sense of the story they are picking up. An experienced facilitator will be able to see this and may invite them to take a different approach.

- Representatives often go into something like a light trance – often only perceptible to the facilitator – which allows them to forget what they consciously know about the system, or the story of the system and access a state of attention that surfaces unpolluted system information. By accessing the same state themselves the facilitator can walk through a constellation and tune into information from the field of information that is particularly accessible during a constellation. Collecting that information is an important part of the facilitator's role.

OK, but how do constellations work?

- Although, like me, I imagine you will never get asked that question by a client (they are too occupied with a new level of clarity), I recognize that it's a question that inevitably emerges in a learning environment.

- Constellations work because we each carry around within us an inner image of every relationship pattern we have been in or are in. They give us the opportunity to express that inner image in an external, three-dimensional manner; this is why they are often called 'living maps'.

- Because we hold that inner image at a deeply unconscious level and because we set up the map of it intuitively, using our 'felt sense', we create an external physical image of our inner unconscious map. The precise relationship between the elements in the system map reflects the precise way that they are 'held' within. Things that were previously unspoken and 'unknown' appear as fresh information and insight and emerge naturally once we can see the inner map externalized. We are then looking at our unconscious map.

- The impact of standing in a particular place is felt deeply and when expressed – through movement or words – has powerful meaning for the representative, the issue holder and others in the constellation. This is somatic coaching.

- In the same way that we 'know' if there is an approaching danger, through the limbic system in the brain, we are also able to access the field of information that exists between parts of a system, from the spatial relationship pattern and the verbal and non-verbal communication within a constellation. Standing in the field gives us access to it.

- This phenomenon, of being able to access what is often described as 'the knowing field', is of course rather challenging for the rational mind. British biologist Rupert Sheldrake offers an explanation by describing what he calls a 'morphogenetic field': the invisible balancing forces that create patterns of behaviour in systems like schools of fish and flocks of birds.

- As far as I'm aware, Dr Albrecht Mahr first used the term 'the knowing field' to describe this field of information and he also coined the phrase 'representative perception' to describe the way that information is drawn out of that field. Albrecht is a highly experienced and soulful facilitator who also developed the phrase that sums up the idea of giving everything a place: he called it 'radical inclusiveness'.

- I'm an applied practitioner, a coach, so am happy to know that neuroscientists, academics and researchers are rigorously exploring and testing this approach. It's a relatively new field of practice so research is emerging all the time.

When you talk about working from your 'felt sense', what does that mean?

- Yes, some of these expressions can sound whimsical can't they? I was also sceptical when I first heard that expression, but over time it's come to mean something very important. I would describe it as our 'other way' of knowing, beyond emotion or physical sensation; it's a kind of 'sixth sense'. When setting up a representative – either in a workshop or one-to-one – it's working from this sixth sense, this 'felt sense', rather than the idea or story in your head, that surfaces so much information. Placing representatives using your felt sense illuminates a new picture.

- There is a US philosopher and psychotherapist called Eugene Gendlin who has done a lot of work on this idea and talks of the felt sense as a living interaction with the world. In his work he has developed ways of connecting with and expressing our 'felt sense' through a process he developed with Carl Rogers and calls Focusing. His understanding of the human body as an instrument of 'knowing' is very closely aligned with our understanding of why and how constellations work so reliably.

- One of the reasons that experienced facilitators find it hard to explain what they are doing – and will often not be able to recall the details of a constellation that they have only just facilitated – is that they have become used to dropping down into this other way of knowing, their felt sense, and can pick up information from the system without fully knowing how. This is why an important part of learning the nuances of facilitating systems is a lot of practice in letting go of the usual ways of knowing, so you can access this 'felt sense' in yourself.

When you talk about this approach 'giving everything a place', how does that impact on our personal judgements, for example when working with a dysfunctional team or client system?

- Whose judgement is it that it's 'dysfunctional'? Yours? The staff who work there? You both have a choice – you can leave the system. You can't work effectively with people or teams you secretly judge.

- When we hold a judgement over an individual, a leadership team or a business system, we have already lost part of our capacity to support organizational health or make interventions that serve the whole.

- There is a difference between 'agreeing *to* everything just as it is' (the systemic approach) and 'agreeing *with* everything' (the rational/moral approach). You don't need to agree with some of the judgements your client or other consultants share. When you can agree *to* everything just as it is then you can be useful.

- Agreeing to everything, as it is, allows coaches to have much more influence on the system, because nothing can be hidden and everything can be illuminated.

- Another way of looking at 'dysfunction' is to see the behaviour, conflict or inertia as a signal from the system. It is a flag that's waving and trying to show something in the system. Very often when someone says that a team is dysfunctional, a constellation reveals that it is in fact highly functional – the function of the behaviour is to show something, point to something or someone in the system, often in the history of the system, that has not been fully acknowledged, or has been somehow disrespected or other kinds of entanglements.

- When you are working with a systems-orientated supervisor, or giving yourself supervision through constellations, you can experiment with including a representative for your judgement over an individual or team – of being 'dysfunctional' – you may see what's trying to be shown in the system and open up a fresh path to working with it and them.

What's the most effective way to learn how to apply this approach safely?

This work is phenomenological – the investigation of experience. So the best way to learn about the work and how to facilitate it is to experience it:

- Have as many experiences of being a representative in constellation workshops as you can.
- Experience the benefit of constellations by bringing your own issues – personal or professional – to a systemic constellations workshop, learning environment or systemic supervision.
- When working with clients one-to-one, invite them to map the current reality, the current experience of what they are describing, and start from there, slowly expanding your horizons while keeping the client and relationship within safe boundaries.

Aside from the learning experiences provided in training exercises, what are your 'top tips' when starting?

Well apart from learning about and observing the naturally occurring organizing principles of systems and starting to notice where and when they are out of alignment, here are four things you might consider 'tips' as you start to use this methodology:

- **First and last:** Listen to the first and last sentence the client says in the 'interview' stage. If you really listen to the first 15 or so words, you will be able to work at the core of their issue and later take the client back to that point and check progress. If you also listen to the last 15 words, you'll hear something else that's important, different every time, and always relevant later in the constellation.
- **Stop early:** As you become more experienced in this way of working it may be important to remember not to overwhelm clients with too many insights. Do this by asking: 'Is that enough for now, or would you like to go a step further?' Simply 'mapping what is' will illuminate something so fresh for the client that even this first stage can often be enough.
- **Small is beautiful:** Adding many representatives is rarely useful, especially when learning to apply this approach. Apart from the complexity, you may also be being seduced into the client's story about the facts, rather than staying with the simple truths that will exist between the first two or three representatives.
- **Use your head:** This approach requires you to trust your body, your felt sense of the situation, to tap into unspoken dynamics in systems. You'll find that you and your client go into a very contemplative

place, almost a light trance, when the system dynamics emerge. This is useful deep space and requires that you come out of your head and into your body. However, one of the skills required in a coach who uses this methodology is the ability to support a client through a more rational, cognitive sense-making stage after a constellation. Many people in business settings are unused to working at the embodied level and so a return to some verbal processing, reflecting, and discussion for suitable follow-up actions can be very important and useful. So, you need to be able to move out of your head and right back in again.

Tell me more about 'permission', 'acknowledgement' and 'respect' – they all sound very old-fashioned...

- Yes, they do. And many of the ancient wisdoms that we have tried to ignore or forget had their feet firmly planted in this way of thinking about systems. They're not so old-fashioned; but they are ancient, essential, fundamental. This work allows a contemporary expression of the timeless qualities and attitudes that are given little attention these days, especially in many business settings.

- Let me give you an example. I was facilitating a workshop recently and an executive coach asked if she could explore an issue around a team she was working with. To make a 'long story short', she had unconsciously 'agreed', as is so easy to do, with the team to label their leader as a 'controlling and autocratic boss'. We were in a workshop and the team members were represented by people, but I didn't allow her to set up a person for the boss because of the vocal judgements over her and because the coach said that if the boss knew she was doing this sort of exploration she would be 'horrified'. As a result we didn't have permission to access that part of the system. But she kept asking to include the boss, so we set up a chair in the place for the boss, in relationship to the team, who were standing in a configuration near the centre of the workshop space.

- Some time later it became clear that the team were all transfixed by something we'd placed on the floor to represent 'what the team are really looking at'. This resulted in fresh information emerging about some team members who had been forced to leave in very difficult circumstances. We did some work to acknowledge them and this settled everybody in the constellation. The coach was invited to join the constellation and as it came towards what looked like an ending, she picked up the object off the floor and threw it onto the chair, the boss. As she did so she said: 'And this belongs to you!', and then turned quickly away again.

- I invited her to turn slowly, respectfully back and say instead: 'You took responsibility for this.' As she said these five words her whole demeanour changed and she added of her own accord, speaking softly and with great respect: '...and it cost you a great deal... personally and professionally'. With this new truth out, I then invited her to say: 'I see the responsibility for and horror of what you are carrying and leave it with you, with great respect for what it cost you.' She did so, willingly and with a powerful humility and presence that affected everybody in the workshop.

- In that moment everyone in the room knew that this 'controlling and autocratic' leader was in fact carrying a great weight. She had had to take responsibility for implementing cuts that hurt her and her team deeply, and had been left isolated and excluded by the events and the continuous judgements made about her.

- The coach completed the constellation in a very different way and with a palpable sense of respect for the difficulty of leading complex systems. She reported learning something very useful about permission, acknowledgement and respect and left the workshop saying that she was in contact with a new and fresh source of energy and a completely different inner attitude towards the boss and the system she led.

- This level of non-judgemental inclusiveness, where everybody has a respected place, is the foundation stone of this work and of systemic coaching.

A one-to-one tabletop constellation in which two members of a team are looking away from the team leader and beyond the system boundary to something excluded.

A tabletop constellation in which the client is connected to their place in the system while exchanging system-orientated sentences with a representative in the system.

A tabletop constellation in which the leader of one system finds a position in relationship with another system before a possible merger.

A self-supervision constellation resourcing a coach to face into significant organizational challenges with a client who is protecting an organizational secret.

A client maps their leadership team in a one-to-one coaching session and starts to illuminate the resistance he faces.

A tabletop mapping and constellation using a mix of Post-its and figures to support separation and clarity between personal and professional systems for a company director.

A coach participant demonstrates how to place the first representative of a constellation in an open workshop setting.

An open workshop constellation exploring top team dynamics moves towards completion.

Mapping in a one-to-one coaching session to identify personal qualities, a place and order for each.

A mapping exercise that led into a constellation for a US executive director of a global engineering firm who realized that several of his team were 'not on the same page' as him.

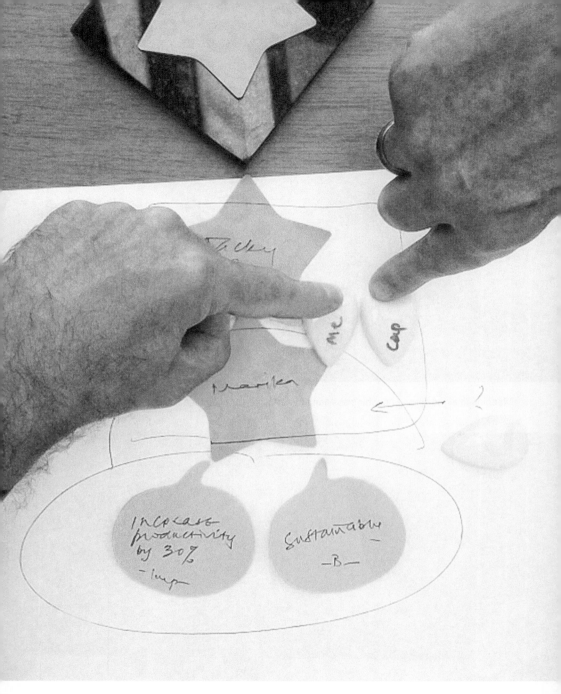

Two coaches who work closely with a senior team of a large government department explore 'best place' from which to work with a team in difficulty in a supervision session.

A table-top constellation using wooden representatives to reveal the hidden architecture of an organizational relationship issue.

Self-supervision exploring the best alignment of resources for a coach exploring options and the balance of life and work.

Mapping the 'organizational chart' of the team

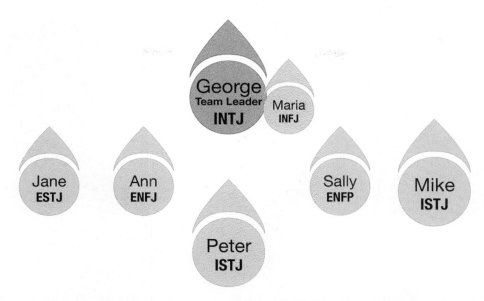

A team leader maps his team from the organizational hierarchy and personality-type perspective, but then asks for a fresh diagnosis as to why the team gets frequently stuck.

Mapping the team relationship system

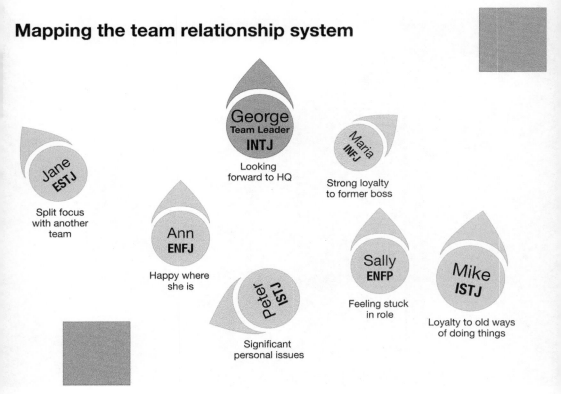

The leader is invited to map the team again, guided by the approach described in this book. This reveals the underlying relationship structures and sources of inertia, setting a fresh agenda.

Executive coach students of this approach practise the application of systemic coaching and constellations in telephone coaching where the coach cannot see the constellation.

A client harvests permission and resource from an unexpected source. Please see the penultimate case study in this book, 'The heart of the matter' in Chapter 12.

PART THREE
Application

From tabletop to workshop

08

Principles and practices in action

> *All fixed set patterns are incapable of adaptability or*
> *pliability.*
> *The truth is outside of all fixed patterns.* BRUCE LEE

There are examples of application throughout this book – examples of the systemic coaching stance, principles and practices in action. In this chapter we'll explore some more in-depth case studies, which will show the common themes that emerge in systemic coaching and the contexts for application.

We will look first at some examples in one-to-one coaching, including selection or 'chemistry check' meetings, and then go on to hear about application in one-off sessions, coaching pairs, three-way sessions, teams and workshops. In amongst the case studies are some more exercises to try for yourself and with your clients.

One-to-one application

Common contexts, themes and case studies

Creating chemistry

Selection meetings, or 'chemistry checks' as they are sometimes known, are now commonplace at the pre-contract stage in executive coaching, particularly when working as an associate for a large coaching business. Initiated by corporate HR, L&D and OD departments, there are strong and varied opinions on their effectiveness but they are seen by many as a crucial stage in the process of selecting a 'good' coach.

Coaching is clearly a relationship as well as a process, so there is logic in checking that the 'relationship chemistry' is likely to support the process. However, looked at from a systemic point of view, I would suggest that the job of the coach is not to focus on the relationship between themselves and the potential coachee, but to think about making a good connection between the coachee and their system and so give them some insights into their current challenges.

Many coaches have also achieved high levels of success at the selection meeting stage because they know that this first meeting is an opportunity to give the potential coachee an experience of working – in other words, to start coaching. Systemic coaches can do this by working with the client in a particular way, combining system-orientated questions with physical three-dimensional mapping. In the following case study we hear from executive coach Gerry Brannan as he applies his growing understanding of this approach to great effect in a selection meeting.

Creating chemistry

Coach: Gerry Brannan, executive coach, London
Client: 'James', a senior manager

At a chemistry check I met a senior manager – let's call him James – who had originally been hired for his highly respected technical skills and quickly became one of two key people relied on by the Managing Director for day-to-day advice. When James started to exhibit aggressive behaviour it was ignored as out of character, but when it persisted with colleagues and his own team he was challenged by the MD and a programme of coaching was suggested.

When I met James he didn't deny or hide from his reported behaviour but he couldn't explain where it came from. He showed remorse and wanted to manage his emotions better. We explored how he might feel and what his colleagues and staff would say about him if he were successful at changing this behaviour. This possibility seemed to relax him and I felt we could explore his situation more fully. After establishing that he had been in his role only 10 months, I asked what he had heard about his predecessor. His response was illuminating.

His role had been occupied by a long-serving member of staff who it was decided was not capable of growing further, and who had been quite clumsily squeezed out of the business, without respect for his long and valued service. James, who replaced him in the role, told me he felt constantly frustrated at what he considered to be a lack of cooperation and understanding from his colleagues and staff. I began to wonder if there were still hidden connections and loyalties in the business to James's predecessor.

I asked him, 'Where do you stand in this business? What's your sense of place?' This question caused some confusion so I suggested, 'Perhaps you could create a map to answer that question?' The table we were sitting at then quickly came to represent the business system and he made a map of his place using coffee cups and glasses as representatives for the various elements and people within his relationship system.

I asked him to place himself on the map first and gradually add more elements, including his team, then the MD, and lastly the other departments. When placing his team on the map, he used a coffee cup to represent them. I just asked, 'Which way are the team looking?'

He looked at the cup and said that the team were looking away from him, to beyond the edge of the table, beyond the business system. 'What are they looking at?' I asked. After a while and a little hesitation he replied, 'At their old boss.'

This was a revelation for him and provided the basis for a rich and fruitful discussion about his own frustrations and difficulty in finding his authority since taking this role. It became clear to him that his frustration was the main source of his aggressive behaviour.

By the end of this brief 'chemistry check' he was totally engaged with the insights that had emerged, the process I had offered him, and therefore me as coach. This led to a high trust and a rewarding coaching relationship and process, in which he made great progress. Even in that session I got a tangible sense of an inner shift, which grew into a deep behavioural change that developed as we worked together.

This example illustrates the simple elegance of this approach when applied in selection meetings and the benefits it offers coaches and clients alike. Gerry knows that the larger purpose of these sessions is to make a good connection, a good chemistry, between the executive and their system, not between the potential client and the coach. If you do one, the other follows naturally.

This example also serves as a useful reminder of the frequency of the system dynamics and behaviours that it revealed: exclusion, organizational disrespect for contribution, identification, and burdened roles. Other case studies in this book also bring this to light, and the frequency reflects the number of times you are likely to come across this in coaching situations in all kinds of contexts.

You'll also see from these case studies that many examples demonstrate an overlapping mix of the organizing forces. Once you become familiar with the three system forces we've identified in this book, you will find it easier and easier to work with them at the same time and see other forces, first cousins of these three, starting to show their faces.

Agenda setting

Let's look at an example of application in a situation where a client approaches a system-orientated coach for a one-off clarifying session. In this case an executive comes to a coaching session with a 'presenting issue' that soon turns into another issue altogether. This is a good example of the use of a brief constellation combined with a system-orientated question to illuminate the underlying truths and the real agenda.

Challenging for the truth

Coach: Jan Vos, executive coach, Madrid, Spain
Client: Cristina, executive in a large property company

Cristina, a senior manager for an international property group that offers real estate services and investment management, had been assigned to a leading commercial centre in Madrid to improve rentability/m². Her role sat between the landlord of the venue and the head office of her company.

During a coaching session, she described a difficult situation and explained that she would like to know what would be the best option for her. Cristina was working on a project that would be interesting for the commercial centre, but was not, she felt, in line with the goals of her company. She had doubts about sharing this information with her boss, especially because of the very different vision they have about how to handle the landlord–service provider relationship.

I suggested using a tabletop constellation with the Carl Auer grey block figures (see photos and Appendix for examples of these and other representative objects), to see what dynamics were playing in this situation. Over some time she set up figures for herself, her boss, the company goals, the project she was working on and the commercial centre. I asked Cristina to place her finger on the different figures and feel each different piece in relation to the other pieces. It quickly became clear that neither the representative element for the commercial centre, nor the one for the company goals, were very interested in her or in the constellation! There was no energy there.

This was an unusual situation but, trusting the process, we continued. As an experiment I asked Cristina to try changing the positions of some elements, but this didn't seem to change anything. There was still no energy in this part of the constellation. As part of a short series of interventions and experiments, I invited her to place a representative for 'something – we don't know what it is'.

Then, very shortly after, something significant changed when I noticed the distance between her and her boss, followed an intuition and asked her: 'Do you respect your boss?' Her answer was quick: 'Of course I respect my boss!' But when I asked her to put her finger on the object representing her and say out loud to the element that represented her boss: 'You are my boss and I respect you fully for that,' she wasn't able to say it. She just opened her mouth but nothing came out. I also noticed her skin colour change very slightly.

Instead of asking what this meant for her, I decided to leave her with just this. We talked a little about respect for 'what is' in systems and the session ended. I told her not to think too much about it for the next couple of weeks because there would probably be some inner work going on during this time. She should not try to force anything, just go with the flow and pay attention to her body and inner reflections.

Three weeks later I met Cristina again. It soon became clear that she had made a decision to leave the company and that this was partly as a result of the constellation and her difficulty in saying the words that respected 'what is'. She was very clear-headed and also excited because of a job offer she had just received. She explained that it was only now that she really understood and acknowledged the previous situation and her position in it. Reflecting on the constellation together, we remembered the lack of energy in some of the representative objects and the object that represented 'something – we don't know what it is', and discussed the clarity she now had about the meaning of all this.

In this example Jan stayed with the process, trusting that no information was information in itself. He combined that with an observation and insight that led to a question and so allowed the deeper truth to emerge. This was in service of the wider system rather than the individual's stated need or presenting issue. This approach serves systems and the people in them well and frees up both to act with integrity. Jan tells me that Cristina went on to a company where she felt very much more in her 'right place', and that the company she then respectfully left thanked her for her contribution and also told her that she would be welcome back at any time.

Joining and leaving

When individuals don't arrive well in an organizational system they may never find their place. Joining is almost always connected to leaving. The person who occupied the role before them, the one who came first, has an impact, in the way they leave, on the one who joins.

In most cases it's important to really acknowledge what the person who is leaving has contributed. Even in circumstances when their contribution was limited or compromised, it's important to publicly thank them for what they were able to contribute whilst also acknowledging that what they did was not enough in other areas. This respect for what was given leaves the path into the role clear and open for another person. In some circumstances, it's important to communicate that the person did not (or more likely was not able to) make a full contribution and so it was better for the system that they left. I've come across several examples of that in my work as a coach.

I was coaching a new CEO and he expressed his feelings of being 'in the mist' in his new role, despite the fact that he had been the deputy CEO for two years and felt more than able, as far as skills and experience were concerned, to occupy the role and deliver on its objectives. I asked about the way in which the previous CEO had left. It soon became clear that it was sudden and recent, with the board asking her to leave with immediate effect. This was followed by almost no communication about the change, simply a mention in the company newsletter that the CEO had left and had been replaced by the deputy.

This was a new coaching relationship and my client had little knowledge of the systemic perspective. I shared with him the idea of acknowledging what was contributed by his predecessor and he said: 'I'd really struggle to do that – she didn't really make a contribution in her short time in role'. This was said with humility and respect and was followed by an explanation that they were in fact good friends. Holding this confusion was weighing heavily on him. So I asked about the way in which the previous CEO had taken the role, joined the system, and it soon became clear that she had applied for leadership of another division of the same company, specializing in a different aspect of the business, and had only accepted the CEO role under political pressure. In other words, she was fulfilling someone else's agenda and tried to occupy the role with that deep compromise built in from the start. She never stood a chance of success with that kind of hidden agenda; the system health was bound to suffer and, finally, eject the role holder.

So, to free the role up and allow my client to fully 'take his place', he needed to break the company silence around the predecessor. He needed, outside of the coaching, with the real people, to share with her and with all others the truth of the appointment, the truth of the impossibility of occupying the role successfully, and the fact that she would refuse to collude with this kind of systemic secret-making. This worked well and the system, and everyone in it, breathed out, and in again.

Leaving well

Few employers and fewer employees consider the importance of leaving a system well, but for organizational system health it can be vital. As you know, it's connected to the organizing principle of TIME. What comes first takes precedence over what follows in a system. Always. This is simple to remember, but harder to implement in fast-moving, complex systems.

> It's of real value to coaching clients and the organizations that they are leaving if the coach is aware of the importance of and potential damage caused by poor endings.

This means noticing when an individual's contribution to the business isn't fully acknowledged when they leave. Noticing attempts to 'forget' all the useful and valuable things someone has given to an organization. This often happens when there have been behavioural or performance issues or a change in leadership that has led to interpersonal tensions. Somebody who was making a powerful contribution gradually (or sometimes very quickly) becomes 'persona non grata' and exits. In the hurry to get them 'out', and to 'move on', they are 'helped' out in all kinds of ways. Few of the common methods of doing so make any lasting or positive impact on the system and organizational health.

> Systems don't tolerate 'moving on', 'forgetting' or otherwise excluding, and will entangle another person in the resulting dynamics until the issue is properly attended to. Yet organizations around the world still give people more money to leave than they did to join, believing that this will help them to leave the organizational memory. It has exactly the opposite effect on the system, which will 're-member' them.

Organizations pay money to the very people they no longer want or need in the belief that it will somehow keep them silent, and keep them out of the system. In fact it risks simply deepening the connection. The case study transcript, in a bespoke workshop environment, on the Business Constellations website gives a vivid example of this in an international consulting firm. In that example you can also see how simple, and cost-effective, it can be to get somebody who has not delivered in crucial areas to really leave a system with respect.

Joining and leaving are times when you are perhaps most likely to see the most overt expressions of TIME, PLACE and EXCHANGE in evidence. If a leader leaves in circumstances that ignore or violate these underlying principles then they will not only leave behind them a role difficulty, but also risk creating another one in the organization they join. This dynamic can go on for years until it is identified and settled.

When coaching a senior leader who's managing an ending, it's useful for them to know about this dynamic. In general, everybody who has employed somebody else will, on prompting, be able to recall a significant number of things that the person contributed before the reasons for them needing to leave emerged. When the leader is back in touch with those contributions, a new level of respect and understanding emerges. These qualities lead in turn to a reconnection with the original levels of respect that the individual earned on joining. Then the leader can have a conversation with the person who needs to leave from a different standpoint, and this leads to partings that are easier and relax the system. Psychological safety returns and the new role holder is able to really occupy the authority required for success.

Additionally, the person who is leaving will naturally often have a wide range of mixed feelings about leaving themselves. They've invested themselves, often for years, in a job, a role, a career. They've 'made it their own'; they've given extra time, attention and care to ensure they did it as well as they were able. And yet they are being asked to leave. It's only human to feel a degree of frustration or anger at being asked to leave, or realizing that it would be best to leave. Organizational systems are powerful and complex and are full of tensions, dynamics, hidden fears and loyalties. Leaving brings up a lot of emotions for people, both those who are leaving and those who are being left.

There are many, many circumstances associated with difficult leavings, but no matter what leads to the leaving, it can still be achieved with a mutual respect for what has been exchanged. This includes a respect for the person at an individual level, a respect for the wider system needs, and a respect for the truth around the reasons for departure.

~

A couple of years ago I was working with a woman at a senior level within a significant organization with international reach. She was the head of the largest division in the organization and had recently applied for the CEO position of the whole group. After some time it became clear that she was not going to be appointed and we began to process this, alongside her desire to leave that system and take up an alternative position in another organization.

In one session we looked together at the reasons why she had not been successful. We got past the story of how things were ('political') to the deeper truth that, at this time, with the needs of the organization as they were, she was not in fact the best candidate. A distinguishing aspect of systemic coaching is supporting clients to stand in the truth, the whole system truth, of their situation. Acknowledging what is. Resisting the temptation to get 'seduced' into stories and allow natural empathy to turn into collusion. It's important to be able to tolerate the truth and then help your client to do so too. Done with respect for the difficulty of leadership and the human condition, this always leads to growth, humility and increased levels of emotional intelligence that serve the client well, usually for years after.

Once this particular client was able to stand in this simple truth, it created fresh energy to really look at what she'd achieved in her current role and attend to a 'good' leaving. It also allowed the truth behind the story to fully emerge – that she was a very popular and well-liked leader who many in the organization would miss.

On asking her if she'd be willing to write something about this process to share in this book, this is what she wrote. It's her personal experience of a systemic coaching approach and a brief constellation using the small, white 'Touchstones' seen in some of the photographs in this book.

My decision to leave a job I really enjoyed was made after careful thought and a realization that I was not actually ready to take on the top role. This simple truth settled me and, after a short while, I actually felt good about not getting the job. However, I was still anxious about leaving what felt like a safe, 'family-style' environment I had created and about the next role in another organization.

It was useful to be invited to go back, in that session, before moving forwards again; in fact this made a difference that has impacted all the moves I've made since. The exercise helped me understand the sense of loss I was feeling about leaving, explore what those feelings were really connected to and then explore the leaving in a much more thoughtful way. In fact the way that I subsequently handled it all also helped my colleagues, many of whom, it became clear, were sorry to see me go.

I set the white stones up showing me in the centre at the front, with my partner one side and 'being me' the other, as the job had very much enabled me to be fully myself in it. This was a useful reminder in itself. Close behind I placed a number of stones to embody a range of feelings such as validation, working relationships, a sense of family, security and belonging. These were the things I identified as those I would miss most, along with three particular members of my team who I was very close to.

Acknowledging to myself the importance of the qualities I'd been able to access and manifest in this job helped me understand better the emotion I was feeling in 'losing' them. And, actually, it wasn't so much the job I would miss as the team culture or 'spirit' I had created, which was so important to me. But I was also able to see just how much this job had given me. It had allowed me to return to myself, my full professional competence and expertise, almost without compromise. And I'd enjoyed the journey very much, and it was good to feel so proud of all that I'd achieved. My initial confusion at not getting the job was turning into something much more useful – a sense of pleasure about moving on to something new and a growing sense that I could leave all the value I had created in the business, but take with me all the qualities and relationship values I had fostered and been allowed to foster whilst in the role.

This process also changed my attitude to the organization and I found myself remembering all the good things, all the opportunities it had created for me, the many friends I'd made, and the much wider network of contacts in this particular sector. Yes, they'd given me a lot too. This really was feeling like a good balance of 'giving and receiving', as you would say.

This in turn led to a very respectful leaving where both 'sides' were able to really acknowledge what had been exchanged and all the good relationships could continue, even grow, with the less good ones left respectfully behind. It felt really 'complete' by the end of what was a great leaving process – and party!

Back to the session itself, I remember that I moved the small stones to the final configuration, which enabled me to move forward and out into the front. I was ready to face what was then a rather uncertain future, knowing that all that experience, support and resource was behind me and still there in place. This may have looked like a simple movement of those white stones but it actually had a profound impact on how I saw myself, my relationship with my team, how I planned my leaving speech and how I approached my next job. It changed what could have become a sense of sourness and loss into a celebration of what had actually been a hugely successful period for me. I was able to leave whilst wishing them all well and taking a new sense of myself, as well as a deeper understanding of systems, into my next role.

It's relatively unusual to get an opportunity to work with a senior executive in this crucial transition phase, at least for me, so it was a particular pleasure to support this client with system insights through this leaving process. There was a strong sense that the work she was doing was supporting health in a number of systems: the one she was leaving, the one she joined and others she may join in the future. This client, now thriving as the CEO of another organization, went on to share how she now pays particular attention to 'joinings and leavings' in her new role, having experienced first-hand the benefits of getting it 'right'.

Leaving a system in a way that supports organizational system health is a delicately balanced matter that often has a profound influence on everyone in the system, as well as the one or ones who leave. In a coaching session or a constellation workshop where a senior executive is sharing their difficulties with taking their authority, it's common to discover that the person who occupied the role before them left under difficult circumstances, or often hasn't really left the system at all. Their influence is still very much alive in the system, even though at a contractual or legal level they appear to have left.

Working as a coach to support people to leave well is always particularly satisfying, as you can feel the system settle around them. This leaves their role truly available for the next person, and leaves them free to move on to a new organization or role.

~

In coaching sessions where you come across this situation it can be useful to offer your client phrases to say out loud that address the underlying balancing forces. For example, when working with somebody who is planning to leave an organization and who feels embittered, exhausted or otherwise reluctant to look back with respect, you can invite them to say to the company (using a representative object like a pot plant, a Post-it note on the wall or floor markers if this helps them focus): 'Everything I've given you – my time, my experience, my hard work – you may keep.' And then also: 'And everything I've learnt and benefited from while working for you I'll keep and make good use of in the future. Thank you.' This ritualized dialogue around the principle of EXCHANGE supports a more settled system and allows for bigger conversations and fewer entanglements.

Application in leadership development coaching

Much executive coaching is concerned with developing self-awareness, emotional intelligence and leadership presence. While constellations were originally developed and have built their reputation around 'issue resolution', ie specific challenges faced by an individual or team, they also offer a rich source of fresh information and resource as part of leadership developmental interventions. The following examples are some of the more common applications in this context and show how this approach can often act as a catalyst for developmental coaching to have its full effect. You may also like to review the 'double-blind' constellation on page 160 in Chapter 7.

Delegation

I recently came across a situation where a leader who was otherwise delivering good results had great difficulty delegating and was at risk of burning out as a result. Inviting him to choose an object to represent himself, I followed that with an invitation to choose another object to represent his direct reports. He set them up and reported feeling 'proud of them, but stuck'. In that same moment he had an insight: without me making any further intervention, he said: 'Oh, I just remembered.' With that he took another, larger object and placed it right behind him. 'My old boss couldn't delegate either!' he said as he 'looked' up at the old boss from his representative position. This led to a conversation about the influence of his former boss, his loyalty to him and his difficulty of reporting into him when his delegation skills were so underdeveloped.

I invited him to place something behind his old boss that represented the resources and skills he would have liked him to have had in order to develop his delegation skills. This led to a very private process that had a deep resonance for the client. Suffice to say that the very brief mapping of the system issues around his dilemma about delegation shifted something in him, which we may not have got to through coaching dialogue alone.

By offering short sentences that included 'You couldn't, and so it was difficult for me' and later 'I will try a different way,' he was able to internalize an integration of acknowledgement, respect and new behaviour. This brief intervention, informed by the principles and practices of this approach, allowed us to move back into a coaching conversation where we could look at the subject of delegation in a new light and then also apply a more traditional framework and approach to the subject in detail.

360 feedback

It's possible to use the processes of this approach, combined with the stance and your emerging insights into systems, to support and bring to life other frameworks and methodologies. This especially applies to those that often involve a lot of talking and risk staying at the level of the head and the rational mind. This exercise, designed to bring 360 feedback to life, gives your client an embodied experience of the feedback, and so they are more likely to take it in a way that will stay with them and to make good use of it.

A 360 feedback exercise

Use this exercise when working with a client who is facing into some challenging 360 feedback. Find a large enough floor space and then invite them to stand up in the middle of the free space. You then place four large sheets of paper around them on the floor, on the four 'compass points'.

Name and write on the paper to the client's left (west on a compass, 9 o' clock on a clock face): 'Affirming feedback'. Name and write on the paper to the client's right (east on a compass, 3 o' clock on a clock face): Developmental feedback'.

As they are standing in the centre, invite your client to look to their left, to the sheet, and summarize their sense of the affirming feedback. Support them to recall all the positive feedback they received and help them internalize it. You can do this in part through using the kind of brief statements, the language of systems, that you are now familiar with to acknowledge the truths they recognize.

You can conclude this first part by inviting the client to look at the affirming feedback 'place' and say something along the lines of: 'Thank you'. Those two words can shift someone from disassociation or rejection of the positive feedback to a powerful internal experience and acceptance.

Repeat this process with the marker to their right, the developmental feedback. Following your sense of the best brief acknowledging sentences (to assist an integration of the feedback), you can conclude this part by inviting the client to look at the development 'place' and offer something along these lines: 'Thank you. I'll use what I've learnt here.'

Now write on the piece of paper in front of them (north on a compass, 12 o' clock on a clock face): 'The opportunity'. Invite them to step forward and write down two or three bullet points of ideas about the opportunity that this balance of feedback presents.

Finally, invite them to return to the centre and look again at all three places. Then ask them to look behind them and share with you what 'hidden resources' they have that they can access to help ensure they are able to maximize the opportunity. This usually leads to a period of quiet reflection while they dig down and find long forgotten and otherwise hidden resources. They may also, along the way, remember and articulate more obvious conscious resources. Include them all.

Invite them to write on that sheet what hidden resources they have realized are available to them. Now you can invite them to pick up the piece of paper with the hidden resources written on it and take it with them as they stand in the middle again.

Conclude the exercise in an appropriate way, for example by inviting them to look around, take it all in and then, if appropriate, step towards the opportunity.

It's possible to facilitate that exercise using objects on the tabletop, but it tends to be one of the exercises that offers more if you and your client stand up and work at a more embodied level. Like all the exercises offered here it is likely to develop a life of its own and you will find ways of enhancing it to suit your clients and your own style.

Goal-setting

Another question I often hear is how to integrate this approach alongside a preference for goal-setting. Systemic coaching and constellations are solutions-orientated but sit at the other end of the coaching spectrum from goal-setting. Or so it appears. However, many coach facilitators find that setting up a map of the goal can be an extremely useful way of revealing blocks and hidden loyalties on the path. Further, a constellation around a goal can be used to find fresh resources within the system, so that the chances of reaching the goal are greatly increased.

Here is a framework for a constellation form that you can use when goal-setting, when goal-setting needs to be set in a larger context, or when a previously set goal or objective is not being reached.

The goal-setting constellation visualized here includes a number of options that you can include when working with a client who is clarifying their path to a particular goal or objective. When you try it with a client, or try it for yourself, I'd recommend using floor markers and standing in each place, using the full length of the room you are working in (the larger the better).

Start by setting out the goal, the place for you or the client, and then an obstacle between them in whatever feels like the right place for the goal you are thinking about. These are indicated on the illustration by the rectilinear shapes. So, you now have a 'classic' map of a goal.

Now, let's take a brief tour of the various additional elements that can be offered in addition. These are indicated on the graphic by the four circular shapes. On some occasions it may be appropriate to include all of them in the goal-setting exercise, though that's unusual. You will know what's appropriate and in what order as you work with your client.

For the purposes of this explanation, free of the context of a particular client or issue, let's start with the floor marker for 'what's excluded', by which we mean 'what's excluded by this goal'. This follows the principle that if you give *everything* a place, so nothing is excluded, then the system comes into coherence and can settle into a dynamic balance and move forwards. It's always fascinating to see what emerges when you invite your client to consider what their goal excludes. It often reveals a block to reaching the goal that they and the goal-setting process are trying to ignore or exclude. This tends to make contact with the goal deeper. Try this yourself and see what emerges for you.

Then, following the same principle, move on to the 'hidden benefit' of the block to reaching the goal. The flip side of the apparent conscious block to

WHAT'S
POSSIBLE

WHAT'S
EXCLUDED

GOAL

BLOCK

HIDDEN
BENEFIT

HIDDEN
LOYALTY

reaching the goal may be very valuable. This idea may already be familiar to you, but working in this way allows the client to really stand in that aspect and dig into the hidden benefit of the block.

Next is the third option, the 'hidden loyalty'. You may like to introduce that to your client as 'the hidden or secret benefit of not reaching your goal'. This often brings a smile to the face of the client as they recognize and reveal the 'secret reason' they may already be struggling to set off on the journey towards the goal. This is a systemic dynamic or entanglement, as the hidden loyalty is one that will probably be an unconscious loyalty within their system of relationships, an idea you are now familiar with.

Finally, as is often the case in effective goal-setting, a larger goal comes into focus as a result of standing in the truth of your current, conscious goal. This can be given a place in this exercise with the floor marker for 'What's possible', meaning what else is possible as a result of reaching this goal – what larger purpose or further goal emerges.

This simple goal constellation has been an illuminating process for the coaches and clients who have used it. One of the reasons for this is that it embraces one of the fundamental principles of this approach: everything has a place. By including a representative for 'what's excluded by this goal', you are allowing everything to have a place. This allows a bigger and clearer picture to emerge without the accidental exclusion that can pull energy away from the goal. By including a representative for hidden benefits of the block, you are allowing yourself and your client to remember that the solution to most system problems or blocks lies within the same system, hidden under or as part of the apparent obstacle. And by placing a representative for the hidden benefit of not reaching the goal, the 'hidden loyalty', you surface the unconscious connection, the unseen payoff – often a deep loyalty in another system to something the client is partly entangled with but may not have previously fully acknowledged.

You will have already realized that this element, the one that illuminates the hidden loyalty, is one of the main blocks to behavioural change. For example, when the objective of the coaching is a significant behavioural change, some coaching approaches hope to drive this by modelling and encouraging the client towards it. The approach described here offers an alternative and complementary intervention if that doesn't work or endure. In this way the real source of the unspoken resistance to change is respectfully surfaced. Once revealed it can be illuminated and, if appropriate, resolved.

If you are feeling familiar with this methodology and comfortable enough to try using some of the sentences designed to illuminate and resolve system entanglements, then this may be a good opportunity to offer something. For example, the hidden loyalty option often reveals a deep connection to a person close to the client who wasn't able to enjoy the options that the client has access to. Because of their need to remain 'innocent' to that conscience group, to stay loyal, to protect their belonging, they feel unable to reach out and move towards their goal. To do so would mean they have to suffer the guilt. This is the power of hidden loyalties.

If that's the case then you might offer a sentence, as your client looks back towards the hidden loyalty floor marker, similar to this: 'Please smile on me as I take a different path/explore options that were not possible for you/reach for this, my goal.' If it's a family connection and therefore a deep loyalty that they need to honour in order to become free, then you can offer this sort of sentence structure also: 'What's possible here for me I will move towards gladly – and will do so in your honour.' This sets the behavioural change in a completely different context, beyond right and wrong.

Finally, as one further option in this exercise you can add, in a place that feels true for the client, a floor marker for 'what's really distracting me'. This tends to surface a more conscious but unspoken distraction or block that the client feels embarrassed or ashamed of, but that may be the route to resolution of this particular challenge.

You can safely experiment with these options as long as you can hold a respectful, non-directive space for the client to explore in, as any coach should be able to do with ease. And this exercise is one that you can gain great benefit from by doing it yourself using your own goals, objectives and behavioural change. Enjoy experimenting and be prepared for a few surprises!

Difficult conversations

On a number of occasions it's likely that you will come across a client session in which the client needs to prepare themself for a difficult conversation. They are perhaps nervous, and sometimes angry or resentful. There are many well-known and useful methods designed to support this situation, and the systemic approach can also play a role.

Role-play can be a useful tool to use in this situation, but the risks include getting unintentionally caught up in the argument or 'taking sides' in terms of either your attitude or tone of voice. Role-play can work but it is often coming from an individual, actual or imagined story perspective and may entangle coach and coachee.

An exercise you can try is to ask your client to sit or stand directly opposite a representative for the person with whom they need to have the challenging conversation. If sitting this can be another chair; if standing, a floor marker and the use of 'the cataleptic hand' technique described in Chapter 9 works well. Then facilitate the exchange but at the level of the system truths, not the story and opinions. In other words, don't get into long dialogue and exchanges of opinion but offer alternatives that bring the truths in the system to light. Use sentences that acknowledge what is, then turn the heat up on the system dynamic (often very different to the apparent one), and then offer sentences that allow for a respectful real-world conversation.

An understanding of the difference between primary and secondary feelings is useful here. Primary feelings are those feelings that arrive and are felt first. They are the instinctive responses that mean, for example, that if we are threatened we feel fear. However, the primary feeling only remains for a while, sometimes literally only a few moments. It will often quickly surface as another emotion – anger, for example. This is commonly understood but the understanding is not always applied in coaching. Working in this way allows you to support your clients' access and work safely with their primary feelings.

The challenge with secondary feelings is that they disguise the primary feeling, making it seem like one thing when it is really another. This makes the job of identifying the first feeling harder. The secondary feelings are often a result of much thinking and confusion. They may deepen and get more and more entangled as they develop over time. People can stay in secondary emotions for a very long time, sometimes their whole life. They provide a misty picture of the individual's mental processing of the first emotion and the underlying emotion may come back as a surprise to them.

It's commonly understood that to blindly accept the secondary emotion may be to miss what's really going on. The special language of systemic coaching, expressed through the short phrases or 'sentences' and the methodology of constellations, offers one of the most effective methods for reaching and expressing these primary feelings. It's this shift from secondary to primary feelings that's essential when offering sentences in circumstances where there are likely to be many emotions mixed up with the essential content. This understanding and the application of system-orientated sentences are a powerful combination when preparing a client for a difficult conversation.

Application in coaching sessions with two people

The constellations methodology can be used to support clarity between two people as well as teams and whole organizational systems. Before we look at team application, let's take a look at the application of this approach when illuminating role clarity between two senior leaders.

Finding my place

Coach/facilitator: Katia del Rivero Vargas, coach and consultant, Mexico City
Client: Two directors who are also close friends

Context

I was called to have a meeting with two area directors of an international organization based here in South America. Both had recently been appointed to their positions, and both had been working in the organization for around eight years. Before starting in their relatively new positions they had also both had management positions in the areas in which they were now directors. They had a good professional relationship marked by service, mutual support and high achievement, and had become good friends after several years of professional success. The reason I was called was that after taking the positions as directors, they began to have professional friction – so severe that it put the credibility of their new positions, their results and their personal relationship in danger.

The constellation

In the private session with them both, I asked them to make four cards – two each – with the name of their role on one and their own name on the other. Then I asked them to place these cards according to their relationship. Where were their roles? Where were they? How did this reflect their current issue and connection?

First they positioned the cards for their roles, which they placed quite a distance apart and opposite each other. Then they positioned themselves, in relationship to their roles, and to my surprise placed them exactly opposite the role that they actually occupied.

When I asked them how they could explain why they had placed themselves in opposite positions, they both replied that in practice they were performing each other's roles more than the tasks ascribed to their own roles. In fact, at this point they realized that this was the reason for the problems they had, though they weren't sure how they could have ended up in this strange position. So, my next question for each one individually was: how did you get into your current role?

Director A said that she had come to her role on the recommendation of the previous director in that role, who had hired her eight years earlier. This previous director had decided to retire and leave the company, and as a farewell had recommended her for the position. So I asked her to make a new card with the name of the previous director and place it on the table. As she did so, she also removed the card of Director B and placed the card next to her place.

When I asked Director B how she got to her role, she mentioned that there had been a previous director who was very difficult to work with and had apparently committed various injustices against the staff. Director B, who had been part of that team, decided to get involved with a group of personnel filing a formal complaint with the management. As a result of this and other complaints, the previous director had been removed from her position. The role that she had occupied, the director's position, was offered to Director B, who had accepted. So I asked Director B to make a card representing the previous director and place it on the table. She made a similar movement to Director A. She removed the card representing Director A, putting in its place the previous director, and put the card representing Director A next her to her own position.

I asked them what this meant to them. Director A responded that she felt a great weight in the position of the director; she felt that she didn't belong there because her previous director had been a great leader and she felt she could 'never take her place'. Director B responded differently, saying that she felt very guilty, that she had not supported the letter of complaint with the intention of having her manager leave, only to bring the problems to light so they could be resolved.

Movement to solution

After listening to them both, I asked Director A to look at the piece of paper that represented her former boss and to thank her for at least three things that she had taught her. After some reflection she said: 'Thank you for choosing me from amongst so many candidates; the opportunity has made me grow, learn and have a job that I like. Thank you for everything you taught me; you were my first boss and everything I know is thanks to your dedication and commitment to my learning. Thank you for everything you did in this area, because now it is much easier to continue to work.'

I asked her to take some moments in the position of the previous director and share what she thought she would say. Her response was that 'she is very proud of me, and this is no longer her place'. So I asked her to return to her own position, to look again at the place of the previous director, and to tell her: 'Please, look on me kindly if I take the job and, in honour of you and how much you gave me, I will do something good with it.' After this, without being asked, she moved places, leaving the previous director behind her and taking her own place in her own role with a new dignity and calm.

Then I asked Director B to tell her previous boss: 'I'm sorry. I didn't want them to fire you.' She then added of her own accord: '... and I feel very guilty about having your job.' After that, I asked her to take the place of the previous director and asked what Director B thought her former boss might answer. She said: 'It was nothing personal.' At this moment she left that place and started to cry, saying that it hadn't been personal and that in fact they had had quite a good relationship.

So, I asked her to look at the place of the previous director and thank her for three valuable things that she had taught her. She said: 'Thank you for being the boss that you were, because I learnt what I don't like to do. Thank you because I learnt a lot from you about this business and know what I know thanks to you. Thank you because when you left you said goodbye and told me that everything was fine with me.'

When she had finished, I suggested that if she liked she could say the following phrase: 'If it is possible for you, look kindly on me if I take the job and do something good with it in honour of your contribution.' On saying this, she moved again and responded that this was what the previous director had asked on leaving: that she do something good with the post. Then she took the place of the previous director and put it behind her, carefully and with respect, and then little by little moved into her own position.

I asked them both to take a few seconds to return again to those who had previously held their positions, to take a few seconds for what they needed: to look, to thank them again, whatever they felt they needed to complete this process. After several minutes of silence and shared glances, each returned to her place. When they returned they expressed in unison: 'Now I can see you!'

To close the process, I asked them to express gratitude for each other's support and willingness to try to take on the duties of the other, given that neither of them were able to take their own positions.

Burdened positions

This case study is a good example of what a 'burdened position' looks like in an organization. When people take up and occupy a role, they may not be aware of the history of that role. Feeling strangely unable to really fill the role or struggling to find their authority, they may believe that it's their own lack of experience or competence. That may be a factor but other dynamics are usually at play, as we can see in this example.

This kind of entanglement with the system dynamics, an unspoken or unexpressed admiration and thanks or, at the other end of this colourful spectrum, guilt and shame towards the previous occupant, is common. In the case above it's touching that from the desire to resolve this, both people changed places in an unspoken way, so that they could continue to operate and contribute. But that leads to friction, loss of place and, if left for too long, a risk of burn-out.

When people do this in organizations, it is as if they are saying: 'I'll do it for you' and it's just the kind of hidden dynamic that systemic coaching and the application of constellations methodology can illuminate and resolve. Only by seeing the whole picture, honouring the history of the role and those that occupied it, can leaders really bring themselves fully to the organizational system. As systemic coaches it's our role to help them identify these deep and hidden entanglements.

Application in three-way sessions

This way of listening, thinking and working, combined with the mapping techniques that begin each constellation, can provide a useful focus for three-way meetings when you have a coachee and their manager in the room. As they are still at an early stage of the coaching journey, this context presents a good opportunity to look at any differences in the internal maps each person holds of the coachee's place in the organization and the key developmental issues.

Using Post-its or other objects, you can invite one and then the other (depending on the context and circumstances) to create a map of their place in the system as they experience it. This is useful when the brief is about a sense of losing place or authority in role but it's also just a very useful and illuminating way of respectfully surfacing some of the deeper issues to do with their system. After some review and discussion of the map of Post-its or objects, invite the line manager to repeat the same exercise from their perspective, placing the coachee in the system in a way that embodies their inner picture.

You can significantly lighten the load for coaching clients who are feeling overwhelmed by developmental demands when you illuminate the system dynamics and separate them from the personal and interpersonal in this way. This provides clarity and differentiation between what belongs in the organizational system and what belongs at the personal or professional development level.

As with all mapping and constellations, I'd encourage you to invite your client to take pictures on their mobile phone of each stage. It's particularly useful doing this in this three-way context, as it leaves you all with the two inner images of 'how it is' and sets a rich coaching agenda. This image can then be reviewed in a closing session with the line manager and the exercise repeated if appropriate to map what's changed.

Resourcing clients in one-to-one coaching

Many coaching sessions reveal a need for fresh inner resourcing for the client. The use of the systems perspective and methodology can be useful here as it allows the coach and client to come out of their heads again and tap into another way of finding resources, in the space around them.

The following exercise creates a kind of multi-dimensional constellation all around the client, providing a physical embodiment of the resources available to them within the system. This is particularly useful when resourcing yourself or a client to support a developmental journey or objective.

A resourcing exercise for you and your clients

This is a resourcing exercise that allows you to use the physical space around you to place each resource, with yourself or your client as the central focus. So, when you find yourself or your client reflecting on a situation in which you feel under-resourced, try the following.

Stand up and face towards something (a Post-it note on the wall or a floor marker, for example) that represents, for you, the situation or person that evokes this feeling of being ill-equipped and under-resourced. Take a moment to allow the feelings of this relationship to develop in you.

After a while, reflect on what resource you need most; what quality or mental, emotional or physical resource would be of most value to you, even though you may imagine you have no access to it. Let's imagine it might be something abstract like 'wisdom'. In this example, simply write the word 'wisdom' down on a sticky Post-it note.

Now find a place for the sticky note in the space around you. There is a lot of space around you and each place will have meaning. There will be a 'right place' for your Post-it note that only you will know as you feel into it.

I remember the first time I tried this with a client, a senior executive leader in a large corporate: she placed the first sticky note on her forehead. I was tempted to laugh because it surprised me and, frankly, looked funny. But this exact place was very important to the client and brought tears to her eyes as she connected into what that meant for her. In an instant she had connected to a quality she had thought eluded her, but found that it had a place within her; a place, once remembered, that she could access with ease.

Repeat this process, slowly, with each resource you identify. You can also respectfully suggest some ideas in line with what you know of your client and their developmental journey. It's often the case that they end up with Post-its around the room, under their feet, behind them or in their pockets.

As with all these exercises, it's useful to have tried it yourself first, and as all of us coaches need resourcing in order to be fully present and available to our clients, this simple exercise can be very helpful. You can try it before meeting with a coachee who you find particularly challenging, for example. Identify a door or picture on the wall opposite you to represent them and then stand and face it. Gradually identify resources you need to strengthen you, resources that allow you to stand in your competence and experience as a coach, and find a place for each.

You may like to end this exercise by making a 'tour' of each of your resources. Simply look at each Post-it note, reflect on what it is offering you, adjust its position if needed, and try saying something to each that embodies the sense of resourcing. I've been privileged to witness clients say 'Thank you for being there, I'd forgotten you,' or simply 'Thank you'. The sentences or brief words come naturally if they are going to and can be a vitally important part of the integration process.

If you have the space and the Post-it notes are spread around the room, you can also go and stand in the place of each resource and look back at yourself, perhaps offering a sentence like: 'I'm always here for you' and see what impact that has. You can also experiment with sentences like: 'You will have to look at me, and remember me, if you are to have access to me as a resource'.

You can also make a quick drawing of the map you have created to support your recall of this spatial relationship model. Many clients take photos of these resourcing maps on their phones spontaneously, as well as keeping the Post-its.

As we complete this introductory tour of application in one-to-one coaching, let's take a look at one more case study. This one explores the application of tabletop constellations combined with sentences and movement to illuminate and disentangle a complex situation that goes well beyond the individual.

No heart

Coach/facilitator: Judy Wilkins-Smith, coach and trainer, Tyler, Texas, USA
Client: 'Harry', the CEO of a US manufacturing company

I was invited to meet with the CEO of a manufacturing company. On the outside it appeared to have the qualities of a flourishing company but it was ailing. In particular, the production department was losing personnel at what was described as 'an alarming rate'. At his request we met in the conference room at the heart of the company building.

As I arranged my papers and markers on the large conference table, Harry moved to three different chairs before settling on a fourth at the head of the table. I wondered out loud why they were so uncomfortable that he had to move and was struck by the grimace on his face and the way he moved his chair to one side of the top position. 'I'm still trying to get used to this,' he muttered.

This sounded like a message from his 'place' in the system, so I offered him this sentence: 'I can't get used to this position; I can't find my place.' He nodded as he said the words and told me he had been the VP of production, the department that was now struggling. He was conflicted about whether to go back and save his department or honour this CEO position.

Aware of not exploring systems without permission, I asked if the founder had given his consent for us to take a look at the situation. He nodded but there was a tightness to his response and I asked him to place a chair to his right to represent the founder. He placed the chair behind him, to one side, then moved it right back against the wall. After some hesitation he also turned it to face the wall before resuming his seat, running his hands through his hair with a look of defeat. 'He's lost the will to even be around and it's a shame. This was... is... a great company.'

Again I noticed the ambivalence and commented that he seemed unsure whether his former department or indeed the company would survive. 'Not at the rate everyone keeps leaving.' He shrugged his shoulders and blew out a heavy breath. 'I've been here 20 years and counting...'

'And counting...?'

'... down the days to retirement in case I can't save it.'

He kept looking around him and it became clear to me that something or someone was missing. He repeated his sense of struggle between his loyalty to the company and to his department, referring to both as though they were people.

At my suggestion, he set up markers for the VP of production, the team leader and the team itself. They were all facing in the same direction and not in contact with one another. I asked who they might be looking for.

Harry immediately leaned forward and placed a marker in front of them, identifying the marker as himself. His breathing slowed and deepened.

'I like it there,' he acknowledged. 'This feels right.'

We sat for a while so that he could really feel the weight of what he'd said, even though it did nothing to lessen the tension. Then I asked him to identify the members of the executive team and set up markers for each of them.

The markers I use have a way to indicate direction so that I have a clear view of the way each one is facing. I am often struck by the ease with which clients transfer characteristics onto these markers. It's a relief, as though the truth can emerge more easily when places or roles are represented, rather than personalities.

Harry chose markers for the roles of Founder, CEO, HR, VPs for sales, marketing and production, and finally, CFO. He used a second marker for himself, as the CEO, without removing the marker for his position as leader of the production team. I indicated a line between the two positions and suggested he point to where he was drawn. He stopped midway but looking at his team, and still couldn't remove either marker.

The positions of the executive team were almost identical to that of the production team. I asked him to sit back and take a look and he could see it immediately. As is often the case, what shows up in a junior department may actually be a representation of what's happening higher up.

'Just like the production team, the executive team is also looking for someone... and you don't seem to know where you belong,' I offered.

'Nobody knows where they belong any more,' Harry said slowly as he looked at all the markers. 'We're all out of place. It's chaos. I didn't want this position but it was my turn. We've all had a go at it.' He nodded at the executive team.

'Go at what?' I wasn't sure what he meant.

'Being the CEO. Trying to save the company. But none of us can put the heart back into it. We've all tried but after about nine months we can't go on. I am at the eighth month and the stress is unbearable.'

'Who's the "it"? And what happened?' Again I indicated the empty space in front of the executive team.

Harry stared at the empty space for quite a while. The heaviness in the room was palpable and I wondered if we might stall here. However, the silence gave the issue a chance to clarify and find its voice.

'Jim left,' Harry said, as he reached for a marker and placed it in the empty space in front of the executive team. Immediately there was a change. He sat back in his chair, breathing out deeply. His entire focus had suddenly shifted to the 3D map in front of him. The person who was missing had been identified.

He looked at Jim's marker and then began to sneak a look at the marker for the founder, then back at Jim. It took a while before he could really look at the founder, and a little longer for a measure of respect to creep in. It was as though he was finally looking at what had happened and feeling its effects instead of ignoring it and trying to simply fix what was broken. After a long while, he leaned forward and placed Jim closer to the executive team with the founder at his back.

'This is how it was,' he said. 'We were a thriving company with a great culture, until four years ago. A rival got wind of our new product and our founder heard that they were trying to design a competitive product.'

I waited.

'He accused Jim of leaking trade secrets to them. Jim put his heart into that product and this company and we thrived. He would never have sabotaged any of it!'

Now I knew who the 'heart' of the company was.

'We beat the competition to market. That product is our finest piece... but for some reason... it just doesn't do as well as it should.' He stopped and looked up at me as a thought struck him. 'Jim was the production VP before he was promoted to CEO. In fact... he conceptualized the original product.'

His attention was drawn back to the spatial map in front of him. 'We all tried to reason with the founder but he was convinced that Jim wanted to take the product and run. Nine months later he fired him. They marched him out the door like a criminal. He left town soon afterwards.'

Harry's face was heavy with the loss. I asked him to touch Jim's marker and try these words: 'When you lost your place, the company lost its "heart" – and we all stopped breathing.'

The relief at expressing what he'd been containing was evident.

'You keep telling me that you've all tried to save the company,' I ventured, 'and that after nine months you have to leave...'

'... but it's really Jim we keep trying to save, isn't it?' Harry leaned forward. 'We keep trying to fill his shoes but the truth is – it never feels right. It's not our place – just like this place...' he touched the CEO's position '... isn't mine either. When I took the position my department said they'd lost their direction and heart too.'

I suggested that he say to the marker representing Jim: 'We all lost our places and we don't have the heart to go on.'

Harry complied and his shoulders tightened. It was clear that there was a lot of emotion in the words and for the first time a conscious acknowledgement of what had happened. The truth had been spoken exactly as it was. Now it needed a place to go. I asked if Jim had ever received recognition for the product. Harry shook his head and his eyes widened. 'No he didn't and none of us can really look at that product. We always feel guilty about it. We have a market winner and all he received in return for it was an unfair dismissal.'

I briefly explained how, when success is achieved at the expense of another, the system will look for ways to restore the balance. Failure to do so may result in inexplicable failure of a role, department or product associated with the person who paid an unfair price.

Harry pointed to the founder. 'He hasn't been able to show his face here since. He's a good man but he made a mistake and then he didn't know what to do about it. Jim really was the heart of the company.'

The repetition of the word 'heart', the other words Harry had offered, and the picture in front of us all pointed to a loss of life force. It seemed that the company had no will to live. I could see that Harry was stuck but open. I had him connect with Jim's marker again and I offered the words: 'We see you in the product you gave us, every day. That is your place. Please bless us when we all take our own places and do something good with your gift. In your honour we will help it to thrive. When your heart beats in this product... we can all breathe.'

Harry couldn't get the words out of his mouth fast enough. For the first time his smile reached beyond his mouth and lit up his eyes. He took a brightly coloured marker, pronounced it 'Product', and set it down in front of the production team.

I asked if anything needed to change or move and he began rearranging the markers, sighing with relief when he removed his marker as CEO. He turned Jim to face the representative for the product and smiled broadly.

'With a piece of Jim here, I could really take my place and make this product shine,' he said enthusiastically, giving himself permission to really look at the product for the first time. 'Everyone will be pleased to get back into their own positions too. The new VP of production was furious when we promoted him... Jim got fired after he was promoted.'

I was curious as to what had allowed Harry to remove his marker as CEO.

'I can do something here,' he said enthusiastically, pointing to the production department. 'Over there I just feel ready to leave.'

Harry had identified both his true position and perhaps a hidden loyalty to Jim or Jim's position in the wanting to leave... after nine months, like Jim had been forced to do.

I asked him to identify the original trauma in the system and without hesitation he placed the founder and Jim opposite each other. He sucked in a deep breath and I asked him to move his own marker closer and then further away. After a while, he moved his marker all the way back to his team and then looked up at me.

'This is not my problem, is it?' he said suddenly. 'I can't resolve this. None of us can.'

'What can you take care of?' I asked. Harry turned his marker to face the product and his shoulders relaxed. At my suggestion he rested his hands on the executive team and said to Jim and the founder: 'We can't take care of this. This is between the two of you and we will withdraw.'

After a while I gave him the words: 'Now we will all take our own places.'

He let out another sigh of relief. 'Nobody talks about this. The injustice of it all just about killed us. The founder withdrew soon after. We lost them both and you're right... we stopped breathing.'

He looked at the markers. 'I'd be happy to buy you a new set,' he offered. 'But I think these ones need to stay in place. I have an executive team that needs to see this and understand it.' He looked at me and said: 'We've all been trying to follow Jim out the door, haven't we?'

Harry had what he needed. In my mind's eye I could picture a heart beating steadily again within the company. A month later he was pleased to report a happier production department and increased sales. At their request the product would bear Jim's name. The CEO position was being advertised.

The founder had met with the executive team and heard what they had to say. At his request they had agreed to leave the dispute with him.

Jim's unfair dismissal had created a burdened position. Members of his original department had left, fearing the same fate if they tried to excel. In this way they unconsciously recreated the trauma and showed a blind loyalty to the one who had been unfairly dismissed. This is a common theme in systems and is sometimes described as the 'I will follow you' dynamic.

Blind loyalty almost crippled this company. Acknowledgement of Jim, his contribution and his rightful place created the catalyst for it to flourish again.

This case provides an example of where the natural order in a system has been disturbed. Everyone stepped out of order and tried to 'get bigger' by moving up into positions that didn't belong to them in order to fix the problem, makes things worse, as no one can then find their place. In this case the client was able to really see that he could only create effective change from his own position. He therefore returned to it and in doing so freed the whole system.

Integrating alongside your existing approach and methods

I want to address a question that arises as you journey into this approach. That is, how systemic coaching and constellations can be used alongside and as a catalyst for other interventions and methodologies and how they can be integrated into your existing approach. For example, if your preference is to use psychometrics frameworks, emotional intelligence models, goal-setting or any other kind of developmental model, how does this systemic approach support or enhance these methods?

When I trained as a coach, I also trained in the understanding and application of personality type, through the MBTI® model. I found it illuminating and became proficient in bringing its benefits to life for my growing client portfolio. I was loyal to that particular way of looking at and understanding the human condition and the way that personality influenced life, work and leadership.

As a relatively new coach I held onto this framework for thinking about my clients and enjoyed facilitating insights in one-to-one coaching and team workshops. I still use MBTI, except that the systemic perspective, amongst others, has added something without taking anything away from what I had before. It's like fresh oil in an engine – it was already going well, but the new oil has given a fresh fluidity and ease to the whole car, ensuring it is capable of more things and greater distances. It may well be the same for you, as you can be confident that the systemic coaching stance and the constellations methodology will often liberate the fuller potential of other approaches.

As I integrated MBTI with the systemic perspective, I imagined I'd leave one behind. That was neither necessary nor what happens naturally. I quickly found that they could sit alongside each other to the benefit of me as a coach and my clients. After a while I found myself mixing the two perspectives, until I could see that MBTI is itself a system of interdependencies and hidden relational dynamics.

Over the past several years I've had a number of opportunities to experiment with a mix of MBTI and constellations. The first was at a UK conference hosted by The British Association of Psychological Type. My co-facilitator Simon and I were able to explore working with type and type dynamics amongst a group of about 50 coaches who had little or no experience of constellations. To support our explorations we developed a form of constellations we called a 'type compass'. We invited the person bringing a question about their personality type dynamics to ask four neutral representatives to stand, in representation of the four mental functions (S, N, T and F). That forms a useful framework from which to move from a structural approach to something more fluid and phenomenological. That basic framework is something I've used several times since and it's created a robust way of working with and exploring type and type dynamics through constellations.

Working with a mix of MBTI and constellations has proved to be a rich journey of discovery for my clients. But working this way has raised an interesting question for me. Is our 'innate' personality type really innate or are we called into the service of our family-of-origin or another system, to complete it? That's a large subject but it illustrates the point that the systems perspective often raises some fundamental questions about existing assumptions!

Back to the practical application of constellations alongside another framework like MBTI, a simple exercise you can use with clients, combining mapping with your existing framework, is expressed in the graphic on page 151. This is simply a double mapping exercise where you invite your client to visualize the organizational hierarchy and perhaps add, in this example, the personality type of each individual. You then invite them to map it again, though this time from 'felt sense' perspective, where the system dynamics then emerge to make a fuller picture.

The contrast between the organizational hierarchy and the natural system hierarchy is usually, as it was in the example illustrated in the photo, quite revealing. This leads to a much richer agenda and the opportunity to coach at the level of the system, not the organizational story of how things are.

Many readers of this book will not have used MBTI but will have other loyalties, other favoured frameworks and interventions. So let's look at the broader question of integration.

The great advantage of the constellations approach, and the system insights it reveals, is that any element that is in relationship with another can be set up as a constellation. For example, you can take the key elements of the EQ framework, set them up and explore the interdependencies and relationships. That is not to treat constellations as a 'fit for all' methodology, for it's the underlying question or issue that a constellation serves, rather than the intervention itself.

The point is not that you 'can constellate anything' but that you can set up a map of any combination of elements that are in relationship to each other because they form a relationship system. So you can, for example, invite your client to set up representative objects for themselves as team leader, their current level of self-awareness and their key developmental objective. Simply setting up two or three elements like this will reveal a previously unseen, unknown relationship pattern. You could introduce into this map, if appropriate, elements of the emotional intelligence framework or another resource or model and find a place for each, exploring and illuminating the dynamics between each element. As long as you work slowly and in the service of a larger question, and work within the limits of your experience as a facilitator, all will be well and you will be using this approach in the service of your clients' journeys. You'll find that the systemic perspective and the constellations methodology weave effortlessly in and out of other ways of working, sitting discreetly alongside and without need for special attention, often clarifying tensions, blocks and paths forward.

Phone and VOIP coaching

It often surprises students of this approach how applicable it can be to remote coaching, over the telephone or Skype, for example. In fact, in many coaches' experience the lack of direct contact adds something that allows for a different kind of connection – between the client and their constellation. Having to describe the map they are creating, for example, can often surface information that may be assumed or implied when in face-to-face contact.

This is a growing area and one that requires more study, but with the popularity of the various VOIP systems it's an area that's on the increase. The photo on page 152 shows executive coach students of this approach practising application of the principles and practices without line of sight, in preparation for application in phone coaching.

Team application

Common contexts, exercises and case studies

In an open workshop setting, constellations rely on the use of other workshop participants as neutral representatives. These people are unknown to the client and know little or nothing about them or their organization. When working with a team, people who are already in relationship to each other, it's very important to adjust the way of working. For example, you do not ask one person to represent another who is in the room or in the team; this could risk revealing or exacerbating interpersonal tensions and closing permission to access the system.

There are several very effective ways of working with teams with the insights and understanding of this approach and with an adapted form of constellations. As with any team intervention, it's important to only work in response to a specific request, with permission from the whole group and with everyone present. Careful contracting combined with an understanding and experience of group dynamics is always important.

A particularly effective way of starting to work with constellations in teams is to gradually introduce aspects of the work into your team work-shops first through exercises relevant to teams in general. Then, later, the approach can be made subject and context specific through more substantial exercises that directly address the core issues the team is seeking to explore or resolve. In this section we will look at exercises to support an introduction to this perspective and methodology for teams, so that you can gradually introduce this approach in an appropriate context and with a light touch.

While you read this and as you explore with your clients, always remember that teams will often embody and enact dynamics that belong at the level of the organizational system.

> If a team is experiencing difficulties, lacks energy or focus, is locked in repeating patterns or conflict, or if developmental coaching and team facilitation haven't made a lasting impact, then you can be almost certain that they are expressing something on behalf of the system.

So, just like in one-to-one coaching, much odd or 'difficult' behaviour or conflict may make more sense when seen in the context of the system to which it belongs. Look out for this aspect as you work with teams in this way and use your new systemic insights and experience to give this possibility a place.

Start thinking about working with system issues and teams by simply working at the non-personal level, the level of the function or role and the level of the system. This allows a great deal of useful system awareness and energy to flow without risk of surfacing interpersonal tensions.

Get out of your head

Here are some experiential exercises, which you can build on and integrate into your own style, that will invite team members to 'get out of their heads' and into their bodies. These are not full constellations, in that you are not facilitating issues to a resolution, but apply the principles and practices to enable you to work with a team in a safe and respectful way while tapping into the invisible information held in their system.

The first couple of exercises are good 'warm-ups' and enable people who are unfamiliar with working this way to be more comfortable with getting out of their heads, using their bodies as 'markers' in a field of information.

Team exercise: Standing in a field of information

Create three 'word fields' on three separate flip charts set around the room to form an equilateral triangle. These could be the team values, team purpose and team behaviours, for example. Alternatively they could be three aspects of the team strategy or other issues you are exploring, like different communication styles, customer segments, and so on. For the first time you do this with a team, as a warm-up, they could be three aspects of the agenda that this team workshop day is designed to include.

Invite the team to walk slowly around in the space in between, noticing what they sense about their relationship to each from different places. Then ask them to find a place that embodies their current sense of their relationship to all three flip charts. They can ignore the other team members and just take care of themselves and their relationship at an individual level to each set of words. When everyone is standing still again, just invite them to notice where they are standing, what they are facing, and what they can see and not see.

Ask those who would like to, to speak from that place, sharing their observations, insights and intuitions. A useful amount of personal perspectives and insights will follow.

After a few minutes and some sharing and reflection, invite them all to follow any inner movement they feel drawn to make that embodies a 'better place' for them as a result of hearing the words from their colleagues. However, this time they should do so with an awareness of other people in the room and a sense of the whole team, the whole system, in mind.

Invite members to speak from that new place and then sit in a circle within the triangle and discuss. By allowing the team members to find their place, using their felt sense, they will have a lot of fresh information and an unspoken sense of embodied place in a relationship system. Some team members may even talk about this aspect – how they've noticed how much information is available within their bodies simply by placing it in relationship to other elements within a field of information.

In order to introduce this way of working to a team – and connect them respectfully to a truth for this team – you can invite them to experience one of the core underlying principles of systems. This exercise, exploring the organizing principle of TIME, was described in a particular application in the first chapter and is expressed here for team application. This exercise works very well following on from the introductory exercise above.

Team exercise: Who came first?

Invite all team members to stand up and then ask them to move, in silence, to stand in a circle (you define where 12 o' clock, the start of the circle, is). The person who joined this team first should be in the first place with the others, in order of joining, following on. No words need be spoken – this is an invitation to work somatically, trusting the body, the physical experience and the 'knowing field' to deliver the right information.

In large teams (15 plus people), it will often be the case that the explicit knowledge of date of arrival is forgotten or very unclear. This exercise surfaces the real 'order' for this system, not the imposed one. You will usually find that the boss is not the 'first place' in this order.

After everyone feels 'in the right place', invite them to check with their neighbour and make any adjustments according to the actual dates joined. Whilst many will be surprised that they 'knew' exactly where they belonged in the order of time without 'knowing' in their heads, others will not have found the correct place. When they have adjusted according to the facts, ask them to notice the difference between standing in the 'wrong' place and the 'right' place, as defined by date of joining (and therefore length of service in) this system. You can then say a little about the importance of working and leading from the right place in a system.

Then you may want to get the people who joined later to look around to the start of the circle and say: 'You were here first' and even perhaps, depending on context and team dynamics: 'If you were not here before me, I would not be here now,' or 'All the work and time you've contributed to this system, before I joined, created the opportunity and space for me to join later. Thank you.' You can then invite the ones who were there first to offer something to those who joined most recently. Start by offering something like this: 'What we have learnt from being here first, we will pass on to you gladly...'

You may be surprised by how readily people say these sentences, or adjust them slightly so they are more accurate and true for them, despite the fact that they can look odd 'on the page'. Some very moving and connecting words usually emerge in these exercises as people connect with a much larger context for their work and life in the team.

The principles and practices of this work can be applied with great effect and a light touch when there is a need to align with a team purpose. A clearly expressed and commonly understood purpose needs a clear place in an organizational system. Each role needs to be aligned with the purpose in order that it can serve the purpose with clarity and vision. Each person in the business needs to have an inner sense of their relationship to the purpose of the business and how their role can serve that purpose.

If leaders don't create, articulate and refresh the purpose, then people in the system will fall back on their experience and skills and the business only becomes a sum of the competencies, failing to live up to expectations. Creating a high-performance team is not an end in itself, only the beginning of focusing on the team purpose and aligning in service of that.

Using one of the ways you are already familiar with to generate the purpose, perhaps supplemented by the 'word field' exercise offered above, invite the team to write their agreed purpose on a flip chart sheet, card or other large piece of paper.

Team exercise: Aligning with the team purpose

Once the purpose is agreed and written down on a large piece of paper, place it in the middle of the floor, in alignment with a sense of orientation around 'past' and 'present' or in another way that has meaning for this team. Then invite each person (in order, from the longest time in the team or company to the shortest time) to stand in a place in relationship to the purpose that represents where they feel they are in relationship to it today, in this moment.

After checking in and some discussion – there is often a lot to say – invite those who feel they can or would like to, to move to a place that represents where they sense they could best serve the agreed purpose in the future, as a team. Gradually they will build up a relational map of all team members and find themselves standing in a new picture of interconnectedness around the shared purpose.

Once again, sharing and dialogue are always illuminating here.

If you work with this team again, six months later, you can invite them to stand in that relationship pattern again. They will be able to remember it exactly. It's embodied.

Team exercise:
Finding place in relationship to something new

If you are working with a team who are to create something new, like a product or service, you can invite them to choose some objects to represent the entity. This could be a number of chairs, for example, arranged in a way that has meaning for them.

Then, as you agree them with the group, invite people to represent the different functions or roles that they believe may be required to support success for this new product or service. See where each role needs to be in relationship to the new offer, product or brand and also see what experience each representative has in each role or place.

Find out which roles are needed and in what order of priority. Ask: 'What's missing here for success?' One or more of the team will know if there is something missing and can be invited to represent it, using themselves or a floor marker or chair.

If you are working with a team who are about to have a new member, or a new leader, you can support their preparation for this in such a way that they create a meaningful space for the person and role to flourish.

Team exercise:
Creating space and place for a new team member

Invite the existing team to stand in relationship to their team purpose (see the earlier exercise) and then put a floor marker or chair in to represent the role that is not currently occupied. Working with the whole team and using yourself as a walking litmus test for the 'best place for this role', find where that is and then place the floor marker or a chair in that place. If the team can't agree on the 'best place' for this role then a useful discussion can be had that illuminates what else is to be resolved before the role can find a place.

This exercise can surface issues around the previous role holder and the function and place of the role in the system, and reveal what's needed to support success for this role. Your facilitation skills and understanding of this approach will serve you well in these circumstances.

You can also try this exercise when a new team leader is to join, finding a configuration for the team that allows each person to have a clear line of sight to the leader and their own peers and responsibilities.

Neither version of this exercise should be done with the new team member; these are explorations to make *before* their arrival. They create an inner shift in the team and space for what's new that the person will feel embodied as they are welcomed by the team.

If you are working with a team in which there is a history of leaving and exclusion, where people who have made a contribution have left without appropriate acknowledgement, then you can give them a place and settle the team system.

Team exercise: Place and belonging

Invite the whole group to stand up and then ask about half of them to represent the existing team, as it is today. They can stand in the middle of the space and find a relationship to each other that has meaning for them.

Then define another area of the floor where those who have left are represented. Invite the other team members to represent individuals or groups of people who have left – for example 'the people who were made redundant two years ago' – or as appropriate to the context and facts.

You can then invite each person and group of people to speak from their place. They may well be surprised by the fresh information they are able to access from each place. This can be followed by a simple ritual and/or a sentence to show respect for those who have left so that the remaining system can return to balance. The particular form of 'sentences' as described in this book is useful here, for example: 'We were trying to forget you' names an underlying truth. 'Thank you for all you tried to do' and/or 'Thank you for your contribution; you made a difference here' acknowledge contribution. A different kind of truth is voiced by the sentence: 'For the survival of the whole system we had to ask you to leave'. Articulate, through co-creation, whatever is true and then what acknowledges and releases those who were excluded.

This is a good opportunity to practise non-attachment to the sentences you offer and to use the representatives for those who have left the system to refine them. They will know the exact words that acknowledge and release. For example, in a recent workshop the people representing those who had been excluded said the following: 'What we did first, before you, allowed you to make your contribution later. We all made a contribution.' This is an expression of the deep system truths of TIME and PLACE.

At whatever point you sense is an appropriate ending, invite everyone to sit down again and facilitate a discussion to help ensure sharing and meaning-making for all.

Teams and conflict

I want to describe a constellation exercise that's useful when a team is in chronic conflict; the kind that appears to have no source or keeps eluding those who try to resolve it. When in this kind of conflict, it's possible to work with this methodology if safely held within a systems perspective and by an experienced group and constellations facilitator who senses that the reasons are systemic, not purely personal. The purpose of including this exercise is so you can see what else is possible after training and experience.

> *When a team experiences difficult conflict it is possible that it's enacting a conflict on behalf of the whole system. Only when we enlarge the problem context to include the whole can we hope to find a resolution for the team.*
> Marcus Birkenkrahe, Berlin School of Economics

Teams often have difficulties and conflict that do not belong to them but are expressions of system-wide issues that remain unacknowledged and unresolved. Simply letting teams know this is a useful introduction to systems thinking and will often surface something that has previously been left unsaid.

To explore this idea and to illuminate and ease team conflict – after some experience of constellation facilitation – you can try the following exercise. Again, please note that this particular exercise is likely to raise significant system dynamics, and you will need experience of facilitating group constellations before attempting this with a team in conflict.

Team exercise: Illuminating team conflict

Working with the whole team intact, invite them to name, at the abstract not the personal level, the qualities or elements of the difficulty or conflict they are experiencing. You can give them a sense of what you mean by suggesting words or phrases like: 'De-motivation'; 'anger'; 'disrespect'; 'conflict'; 'shame'; 'fear'; and 'lack of energy'.

Invite each of them to write the words or phrases on separate sheets of paper until you have them all expressed and written down. It's likely that you will need to encourage people to stay away from the story of how things are and from any individuals being named. They should just stay with the words and short phrases that name the experience of the conflict, not their ideas about its source.

When the group have expressed them all, invite those who would like to, to stand up and 'represent' each of the elements, with each finding a place in relationship to the other elements. To support clarity and focus it will be important to have the company or team purpose clearly stated and expressed in the map too, so there is something agreed and shared to orientate around. Of course, that in itself sometimes becomes part of the reason for conflict without obvious source. Keep building the picture until you have a map of the elements in relationship to each other.

Ask each representative in turn what information they have from their particular 'place' in the system. Ask them all to name what they are representing, what word, quality or concept, before they speak. This means that, as far as possible, it's very clear that they are reporting from the place in the system and not their personal agenda. To support this, ensure that you encourage each to speak very briefly.

It may be important to add other elements from the wider system around the team – such as departments, functions, and the history – as these elements naturally emerge. Later in the process, and as you grow comfortable with illuminating and then working with the information that emerges from systems using this approach, you may like to offer other elements like:

- 'the real reason for this conflict';

- 'what this conflict serves';

- 'the hidden benefit of this conflict';

- 'who would benefit if this conflict was resolved';

- 'who would be disappointed if this conflict was resolved';

- 'the path to a solution to all this'.

After you have facilitated what emerges, using the principles and practices you have learnt, invite everybody to slowly follow any inner movement they feel able to make that supports a resolution for the whole team. Ask them to move in silence. It may be at this stage that some people require, and name, additional resources, qualities or elements that will support resolution. These can be represented by chairs or floor markers.

To end, invite each person to speak in just a few words, from their place, in the manner of a 'wisdom circle'. Each speaks, briefly, about what the system needs or has to 'say' from that place, to bring clarity and resolution to the conflict. You can also follow that with an invitation for all to follow, slowly, an inner movement that feels authentic and that supports coherence and flow in this system. Then invite everybody to sit down in a circle, and facilitate the rich discussion that will follow.

~

Beyond the examples and exercises above are other developments of constellations, including 'structural' constellations. These offer further frameworks and constructs with which to work and are the subject area and focus of other facilitators and books. Some of these are included in the training and recommended reading section at the end of this book.

Workshop application

Examples of workshop application: common themes and case studies

Some coaches begin their journey with this work through working one-to-one; others begin by facilitating in team workshop environments. There is no 'right way' to journey into and with this approach, any more than there is one 'right way' to constellate. Trying to do it 'by the book' and sticking rigidly to everything you have learnt about constellating will leave you stuck and inflexible when something you are not expecting happens. Likewise, being too 'loose' about how you integrate this approach into your existing one may lead to a dilution of its impact and may risk creating difficulties in individuals and teams.

Whichever way you find yourself developing with systemic coaching and constellations, ensure you allow yourself plenty of experience in workshops where you can observe and participate. In this section we will look at the application in workshop environments. This is, after all, the environment in which this work was originally developed.

However you develop and express this approach and methodology in a workshop setting, it's always going to be important to do so within your existing level of training and experience. Keeping the group safe, and working within the limits of the core issue and your knowledge, are naturally key.

If you are a coach who works mainly one-to-one, you might find this section of particular interest as it may expand your horizons to work with your clients in a new way. If you are already an experienced group facilitator then you have the advantage of knowing some useful things about how groups function. But you might also find yourself at a disadvantage, because this way of facilitating is rather unlike any other and you may need to unlearn some of your familiar ways of working and interacting with groups.

There are a couple of different ways that this approach can be taken into organizational and business settings within a workshop framework.

Open workshops

These are typically one-day or two-day workshops where a range of individuals who don't have any connection outside of the workshop come together to explore issues, learn something of the methodology, and take part in others' constellations as a representative. An eclectic mix of coaches, consultants, business owners, corporate leaders and senior team leaders gather and are offered exercises and opportunities to experience the approach and gain benefit and clarity around particular issues through facilitated constellations. Often, the bulk of the day is spent working on particular issues brought by the participants, through constellations, using other members of the workshop to represent.

These open workshops offer an excellent opportunity for those who are new to this approach to 'dip a toe in the water' and experience the multiple benefits available. They also provide a useful taster of the approach for those considering a training.

Several constellations are facilitated in these workshops where a member of the group becomes the client and explains the issue to the facilitator. The work is done in full knowledge of the context, the desired resolution, and the role and function of the issue holder. In some cases, however, the client may prefer to work 'blind', where the workshop attendees (some of whom may be about to be chosen as representatives in the constellation) are not told any of the facts; nothing about the situation or context. This is called a blind constellation and only the client and the facilitator know the context and facts connected with the issue, as this is discussed privately before the workshop.

Another way of working is to work double-blind, where the facilitator has no real understanding of the issue or the system either. This is a useful way of working when confidentiality is important, but it can also be applied when the client or issue holder is sceptical about the methodology or is keen to tell the story of how things are. This brief case study was written by a leader two months after a 15 minute double-blind constellation.

Looking for leadership

Coach: John Whittington, London, UK
Client: A change management consultant

My experience of the constellation still feels remarkably fresh – it had a tremendous effect on me and my working relationships. I had prepared my story and so was taken by surprise when you suggested that we do a completely blind constellation. You simply asked me what outcome I wanted and I said I needed to have a conversation with two other people; that was all the data you worked with. I remember thinking 'This isn't going to work', but I was proved very wrong.

You asked me to choose two members of the workshop group to represent my colleagues. What then played out was extraordinary. I had never mentioned 'leadership' but that was what both the representatives in the constellation asked for, demanded of, the representative for me.

The representatives articulated loudly and clearly the exact needs of my real colleagues and demanded that I answer them. In the real world my colleagues ask the same questions but don't demand answers and get very frustrated with me.

As the constellation moved forward I realized what I had been doing that frustrated my colleagues so much. I don't like being told what to do and I assume no one else does either, so in a leadership position I am unclear how to get what I need from people – particularly very experienced people. As both my colleagues are more experienced consultants than I am, I would never assume to tell them what to do – I would see that as demeaning.

After the constellation I shared what had played out with both of my colleagues. I checked with them whether the needs articulated by their representatives were the same as their needs and I got a resounding YES! I checked my assumptions and found that I was wrong. They wanted leadership and clarity. The following week everything changed.

We had just started a large cultural change programme that I was leading. I hired both of them precisely because they are much more experienced than I am and bring the things that I felt I was lacking to the project. However, they told me they needed me to lead the project and tell them what I expected of them, and this is exactly what I started to do. It has had a profound impact on me, on them and of course on the programme, and as a result also on the client.

I shared my experience of the constellation with quite a few other people I work with and colleagues now joke with me about being their 'leader'. This joking serves to legitimize a serious discussion – what type of leadership do we need around here? We now all talk about the leadership question and this is very helpful.

To date I have tended to lead projects and people by bringing something I feel is missing, which I would sum up as a 'creative energy', and somehow hope that others will get caught up in it and follow. This works to some extent, but it's clearly not enough. Now I am much clearer about leadership and more confident about my leadership role and am enjoying providing clear direction to my team.

This has been a massive developmental jump for me and I don't think I would ever have made it had it not been for that constellation.

Introducing the workshop experience

When offering open workshops it will be useful to have a framework that you can share with the group as your range and scope widen. Some of the things that I've found useful to share include:

- In this way of working we are moving from the level of the individual or team to the level of the system.

- You already know what's in your heads – your opinions, biases and beliefs. This approach allows you to find out what's held beyond your head – within your body, your whole being, your gut feel – what your 'other way of knowing' may have to offer. So, let your body speak its mind.

- What we are doing is simply a spatial representation of a system; a kind of map. Once the map is set up you will see it comes alive with information. This is what a constellation offers – fresh information.

- A constellation is a living map of the system dynamics and is held within a boundary. The experience of sitting on the system boundary (the circle of chairs) can be as powerful and illuminating an experience as being chosen to be a representative. The whole system comes to life, including the boundary, and information is available from every part.

- There are several ways to benefit from a workshop like this:
  - bringing an issue for exploration, diagnosis or illumination;
  - being a representative in someone else's constellation;
  - being a part of the holding circle – the boundary to each system we are exploring;
  - asking questions at appropriate points in between the constellations.

- There is a difference between role-play and representation. This work does not encourage or derive any benefit from role-play. It works on the 'empty-vessel' approach and relies on the power of 'representative perception', which seems to work for everybody all the time. Simply by standing in a place in a spatial relationship model, you are able, whoever you are, to pick up information that is of value to the issue holder.

- Remember that feeling nothing is just as important and valuable information to report as having lots of feelings.
- When looking at team or wider organizational issues, it is useful to remember that the natural system hierarchy (who came first, who has most 'weight' in the system, and so on) holds a larger influence over the system dynamics than the imposed organizational hierarchy.

Closed workshops

In a 'closed workshop' a client company invites an experienced systemic facilitator to create a workshop around a particular issue or set of issues that their company is facing. There are two kinds of closed or 'in-house' workshops. The first is when the facilitator is asked to provide the representatives, who know nothing of the client company or its issues. The facilitator works with three or four members of the client senior team who attend the workshop, and explores a number of pressing organizational, structural or other issues that they bring. As a result these workshops provide good opportunities for students of this approach to take part as neutral representatives in a real-world case where the client is present and has a pressing need for clarity and resolution.

The second kind of closed or in-house workshop commission is when a client organization requests a systemic intervention but wants or needs to work only with the people in the organization. This is more common in certain situations. The first of these situations is where there is a very high degree of trust in the team already and they want to look, collectively, at broader organizational or customer issues. The second situation is when there are two or more teams who share an intention to work more closely together and actively want to explore fresh ways of doing so. For a case study in this context see Maggie Rose's on page 205. A third situation is where the issues are so confidential that the organization does not feel able to allow external people to witness or work on the issue.

As we've explored, it's difficult and potentially risky to work with the people who are 'in' the issue when working with teams, as there is a risk of surfacing interpersonal tensions. There is an understandable danger of people either 'acting out' issues that they want to be seen, or the reverse: *not* following their true inner movements for fear of showing something the organization is not ready, in their view, to see. All of these possibilities need to be considered in the workshop design – the exercises and interventions offered – to avoid any danger of exposure of the participants.

Of course, there are lots of situations where this approach is taken into organizations in a workshop format, where a group of in-house leaders, HR and OD specialists look together at generic issues of organizational health.

These workshops, facilitated by an experienced external constellator, are rich and resourcing and will often progress into issue exploration as well. But where the people present are drawn from across the functions and divisions of the organization and the work is kept at the organizational level, there is much less chance of difficulties and interpersonal tensions arising. As we shall see in Chapter 9, there are many ways of working with representatives for abstracts and business elements that can illuminate and clarify many business fundamentals.

However, when you feel able to explore the possibility that behaviours are often expressions of system issues, and/or a sense that you are not dealing with an interpersonal but a systemic issue that has its roots in the organizational system itself – and you sense a strong intention for resolution – you can consider a systems perspective and intervention for an issue-specific constellation.

I got exactly this sense when I was approached by the directors of the European Mentoring and Coaching Council (EMCC) and the International Coaching Federation (ICF) to facilitate a combined workshop with board members from both organizations. The purpose was to illuminate a confusing dynamic that had surfaced in their ongoing talks. Members of both boards had long-established working relationships with good levels of communication and a shared passion for collaboration and professionalism. As a result of their mutual commitment to the relationship, and to resolving the issue and moving forwards, it was agreed to work at the source, with no external representatives; no filter between them and their system issues. As a result, members of both boards gathered in Madrid for this workshop.

Past, present, future

Coach/facilitator: John Whittington, London, UK
Client: The boards of the EMCC and the ICF

The background

Back in 2006, a member of the board of the EMCC, the most influential professional coaching organization in Europe, had reached out to make a connection with the ICF, the global coaching organization. Members of both boards had been meeting on a regular basis since then to discuss and explore closer collaboration and cooperation. There had been good connection and healthy discussion on a wide range of topics.

By 2011, five years after they had started, a level of inertia was emerging around certain aspects of the discussions and both systems were keen to get clarity on the underlying dynamics so they could move forward together again.

It was clear that staying at the level of dialogue – just talking about the various issues – was not enough; something different was required. There was energy for a fresh approach, a release from a sense of stuckness, and a shared commitment to organizational health.

It seemed particularly fitting that the request for this intervention came from the world's leading coaching organizations. To be credible, any professional membership organization must truly live, and be seen to live, their values and demonstrate their commitment to working at the leading edge of their profession with efficacy and integrity.

It was refreshing to see both organizations' search for system health, and the ease with which they were able to understand that their challenge was not at the level of the individual but rested in the wider system dynamics. They already knew that all behaviour makes sense when seen in the context of the system in which it belongs.

Even so, it takes courage for two systems to come together to look, honestly, at their relationship dynamics. This is particularly the case when they are also in the same area of business and, whilst in open collaboration with many shared values and intentions, are also in a kind of competition with each other, for members. To look at their collaborations through the methodology of constellations when the ongoing organizational dialogue is a little stuck takes a willingness to be open to whatever emerges and high levels of personal and professional integrity from every individual present. All of those qualities and more were present in this half-day workshop.

The brief

I was asked to facilitate a session, using the principles that underpin this approach and the constellations methodology, with a view to illuminating any issues in either system that would lead to greater clarity and connection. I was also to see if fresh resources could be found to support a deeper collaboration. So, the brief was simply agreed as follows: 'Clarify the relationship dynamic between the two organizations and resource a deeper collaboration.'

The approach

After facilitating a version of the pairs exercise described on page 231, which allowed everyone present to have an experience of the kind of information available through this approach, I drew the participants' attention to two strips of sticky coloured tape on the floor. I explained that the tapes were there in order to represent a timeline from the origins of each organization right up to the present day, and that we would use these as a framework to explore and illuminate the past, present and possibilities for the future.

We began by looking at the foundations of the ICF, because I believed it had preceded the EMCC. I invited someone to represent the founder and the founding energy of the organization, and an individual stepped forward and stood at the start of the tape, representing the founding energy that emerged in 1995. He began to occupy that founding energy and was soon able to report various feelings, pieces of information and fresh insights.

A little later I invited someone to represent the founding energy of the EMCC, which had, according to the story, started several years later. It gradually became clear, however, that both organizations had their deeper origins in the early 1990s at almost exactly the same time. This simple truth established an equilibrium for the rest of the workshop that allowed each organization to stand fully in the strength of its own identity and foundations. This acknowledgement of the principle of TIME – that both systems originated at the same time – supported a sense of balance and parity over the next several hours.

The timeline, stretching from one end of the room to the other, gradually became populated by representatives for the significant individuals (founders and key contributors) and events (financial and strategic changes) in the history of both organizations between their foundations in the early 1990s and the start of the collaborative talks in 2006. As each representative took their place, they were able to access the information available from that place and report it with clarity and accuracy.

As the process unfolded, two things became clear. Firstly, and of particular interest to the readers of this book, was that people from both organizations felt drawn to represent people and elements from the other system and did so with ease. Speaking from their felt sense of standing in that place, they were able to articulate truths from within the system with a degree of verbal and emotional accuracy that had a powerfully connecting effect on all participants. This mix meant that both as a facilitator and as participants, the conscious connection to each organization became unclear, as if forgotten in the safety of this explorative, diagnostic system constellation. All participants seemed to have equal 'weight' and equal presence, and members of one organization were able to represent key figures and events in the other with neutrality and integrity. This allowed all those present to get in touch with the deeper system truths that quickly surfaced as a result of their trust in what they experienced standing in role. This active representation in each other's system was in and of itself a collaborative, co-creative and resolving process that brought the systems closer together.

The second thing that became clear was that there was a remarkable symmetry in the two organizational systems as they mapped each timeline. Both organizations had very similar dynamics in their history, to do with the organizing principles of systems expressed throughout this book. There were imbalances of EXCHANGE both within and between the systems, loss of PLACE due to exclusion, and other imbalances that had caused stress, confusion and inertia. Acknowledging each of them was a releasing and generative process and a privilege to facilitate and witness.

As the remarkable symmetry of the past unfolded and rolled towards the moment on the timeline that identified the start of the talks, there was much recognition of the similar patterns; recognition through words, movement, tears and laughter. As each step was taken, each insight illuminated, the systems were building a deeper understanding of each other and came closer together. By now they could really see each other.

By the end all the participants were standing in the constellation, representing elements from across 20 years of history all the way to existing member coaches and the 'end-user' coaching clients. To close the constellation I invited everyone to turn back and look at where both organizations had come from with great respect for all those who had contributed, all the events, to see everything just as it was, just as it is. As they looked to the past, back down the timeline, I invited everyone to reflect on this simple truth: 'This is where we come from.' A natural period of silence and reflection followed as everybody stood and looked back into the foundations of both organizations.

The constellation was followed by a 'wisdom circle' in which both the current presidents and presidents-elect were invited to sit in front of a semi-circle of all the other board members present. They then listened to each in turn as they shared their learning, insights and thoughts on next steps.

Summary

By the end of the workshop there was a deep recognition that both had experienced parallel dynamics for similar reasons and that both now wanted to work with a sharper focus on the members, their clients and the wider field of professional coaching. The results of this illumination of the underlying system dynamics resourced a much clearer understanding of the relationship between the two organizations and a deeper collaboration.

Several expressions of the understanding and collaboration were to come as, in the months that followed, leaders of the EMCC met with leaders of the ICF to discuss further opportunities for collaboration in a new spirit of understanding and connection. The workshop acted as a catalyst for a shift in the ongoing dialogue and continued in the years that followed. Soon they had formed the Global Coaching and Mentoring Alliance. Another partner joined this alliance, which continues to evolve as the organizations look to 2020 and beyond.

Multi-team, large-group workshops

In the final case study in this chapter we come back to the UK for a fascinating study of a large workshop intervention facilitated by Maggie Rose, an experienced coach and team facilitator who trained in systemic coaching and constellations with us in 2015 and is graduating as a Practitioner in 2016. She facilitated this workshop, however, after training only to Fundamentals level.

Talk Talk

Workshop facilitator: Maggie Rose, coach and consultant, Southampton, UK
Client: TalkTalk Telecom Group plc, one of the UK's leading broadband, landline, TV and mobile providers

Context

The Technology Division of the TalkTalk business has been seen as something of a fortress, based in the north of England. The commercial operation and leadership of the consumer business is in London. Personnel at the different offices speak of two different cultures when describing each other.

We agreed an initial joint team off-site in the autumn. This was not about forming one team; it was about creating a highly productive partnership focused on results.

The whole notion of systems was a gift in engaging the Technology Leadership team. Systems are their world. Positioning at the outset that we would be thinking of ourselves collectively as a 'system' in service of the customer seemed very logical to them. Also the notion of respecting the separate parts before bringing them closer together seemed very natural to that team.

At the very outset of the day beyond initial introductions by the two leaders, I split the attendees into their two respective teams, inviting them to stand in a circle of their own, self-organizing by 'who came first' in the organization and within each team. I had talked through this activity with both of the leaders prior to the event, so they understood that they might find themselves in different places in the system hierarchy from the organizational hierarchy.

Questions I offered included: How does it feel to be the elder/younger? What are you noticing about your place in the system? How does that feel? Is anyone missing? What else needs to be represented here, if anything? The Tech team expressed that they felt small, to which I responded: 'OK, so adjust that as you need to.' In response to which they then enlarged the physical space their circle was occupying. Spaces were also made for two new recruits that were yet to join.

There was also some feeling of absence from someone who had left the team. 'So what do you need to say to honour them?' With only a little guidance they willingly expressed this by saying: 'Thank you for the part you played in creating this future. You and your contribution will always be remembered.'

The experience of standing in their two different systems provoked a lot of conversation about how people felt given their place. The wisdom and experience in the team was noticed and honoured. The Technology team also set up a spatial representation for the B2B business given their Group responsibility. I chose not to explicitly mark that space as I felt it would have been a distraction to the job in hand. The acknowledgement of the space seemed enough.

So next I took a piece of flip-chart paper representing the customers in the middle of the room between the two teams and asked everyone to organize themselves in relation to that. Everyone slowly organized themselves individually in relation to the customer calibrating distance and orientation in relation to where the customer was positioned and facing. The teams were very intermixed and some individuals positioned themselves very close to one another in acknowledgement of current ways of working. Equally some placed themselves at a distance from colleagues.

I then simply asked everybody in the room to share how it felt given where they found themselves in relation to the customer. A whole range of feelings were expressed which fascinated all members of the group. After they shared what they wanted to, I asked them what would make it better, and to make those adjustments by finding a 'better place' for themselves in the space, in relationship to each other and the flip-chart paper floor-marker representing the customer. In doing so I facilitated a natural process of acknowledgment of others and exchange of requests that gradually resolved discomfort and created a new pattern, a new constellation. This felt resourceful and useful to them, collaboratively aligning with and in service of the customer.

An hour later it had taken a very different shape with the team placing a representative for 'business results' in the constellation. This was initially placed quite separately from 'the customer', as was a representation for 'the competition'.

At the point of resolution, the place for business results and the customer had integrated and everyone's individual place in the system had shifted adjusting either distance and/or orientation towards the customer and each other.

The two teams team then started to focus collaboratively on what they really needed to do at a practical level to take action. A particular initiative was identified that would transform the customer experience, resolving fundamental underlying issues. This single initiative, which emerged towards the end of the constellation, has subsequently informed a key programme of work in the business.

There were also clear indications in talking with the team that there needed to be some further work done to share understanding of work-in-progress to avoid misunderstandings; also to commit to more specific ways of working and holding themselves to account. These two areas of focus became my agenda in working with them in the months that followed.

~

If you were observing the discussion after the constellation exercise, you might describe it as being a typical cognitive discussion of the kind you'd see in working relationships in an organization. What was dramatically different, however, was the ease with which those conversations were able to happen. There was a much deeper feeling of mutual respect in the room. It was very different from the defended, cautious relationship dynamics and style of communication beforehand. The openness and shared intent of the two leaders was also an important part of this.

Benefits

Three months after the event I checked in with the team to understand how they were feeling as a result of my work with them. Here's what they had to say:

Cross functional working continuing beyond the offsite.
Where there's a big issue there has been good collaboration.
High level of collaboration and goal alignment.
It feels more like one team than it ever did before.
No blame, no retribution, going between the two teams.
It's in the consciousness of the teams now.
Loads of day-to-day alignment.
It broke down a number of barriers and some nuggets came out.
Communication is a lot better.
Their agenda is our agenda.
Collaboration has really stepped up.
Much more customer-centric.
Alignment on strategic goal.
Lots of willing behaviours.
Our shared commitment to transform the customer experience remains at the heart of the business.

My learning:

- Simply inviting the client to physically stand in an unspoken pattern provokes a fabulous capacity in the team to surface the unconscious and immediately start acknowledging, exchanging and adjusting with almost no intervention beyond the invitation.

- The lightest of touches can be the most useful for the system.

- The acceptance of working with dynamics within a system landed really easily with technical people. They already have a great appreciation of how systems work.

- Acknowledging separateness as opposed to difference feels really respectful and ultimately embracing of those differences rather than them being a block or a point needing resolution.

- Placing representation of the customer in the room focused them on what they are in service of together at the highest level. This catalysed them to negotiate and re-pattern themselves in relation to that common purpose in a way that naturally released tension from the system.

- I find that the cut through and acceleration of results with systemic coaching is creative and exciting.

This case study elegantly illustrates what can be done with the exercise that we offer as part of the training journey and is also described on page 20 ('TIME: An exercise for use in team coaching'). It captures just how easily senior professionals and technical managers understand this embodied approach without much explanation or demonstration. The idea of standing in your truth is, after all, very simple and we can all make sense of it. Because all systemic exercises and constellations begin with this simple idea – standing in the 'what is' – they are experienced as deeply respectful. This creates, along with your facilitation, a very safe place in which to surface and express unconscious or unspoken patterns or inertia.

This in turn frees the system and the people within it, allowing each and all to occupy their role authority and for respectful generative communications to flow.

~

However you develop and express this approach and methodology in a workshop setting, it's always going to be important to do so on a strong foundation of training and experience. Keeping the group safe and working within the limits of the core issue and your knowledge of systems are naturally key. As well as being prepared for surprises.

Sticky moments

09

Ring the bells that still can ring
Forget your perfect offering
There is a crack in everything
That's how the light gets in.

'ANTHEM' BY LEONARD COHEN

Strategies to release stuckness

Constellations are often used to resolve stuckness and inertia. Your client sets up an image of their difficult issue and embodies the difficulty, the stuckness, in the constellation. That's often a good starting point – acknowledging what's stuck. Standing in the truth of this is of great value, but it can easily be mistaken for a constellation that has become stuck.

The second kind of stuckness is where you as the coach/facilitator feel you are stuck. There is a sense of not knowing what to do next. That's often a message from the system itself and so provides useful information that most often belongs in the system, not in you.

This section provides a selection of suggestions and interventions you can make in either case so that you can resolve stuckness – wherever it belongs – and move forward. These can be applied equally well in one-to-one sessions and in team workshops.

Try different acknowledging sentences

Use sentences to acknowledge the stuckness. Often the most useful sentence is a direct acknowledgement of the prevailing sense of the situation: 'This feels very stuck.' You can also ask this: 'For who in this system are these words true – "this feels very stuck"?' Often the client will then be able to locate the stuckness and move ahead.

Try moving one or more of the representatives

Respectfully test alternative positions based on your own sense of what may be going on. This can be offered like this: 'Could I try moving something here?' You can also ask: 'What would need to move here for this/you to feel less stuck?'

Ask the client to choose something to represent 'the real problem'

Invite your client to choose something to represent the real problem or 'the real issue', and then ask them to find its place in the map. This often brings something hidden in the system to light and an 'aha!' moment.

Ask the client to choose something to represent 'the solution'

Invite your client to choose something to represent the solution or 'the direction in which a solution lies'. This is often equally releasing and creates fresh energy for a movement or change in the system, opening up new directions and possibilities.

Test something else

Try sharing a hypothesis, an intuition or a piece of information that you recall from the conversation earlier. Sharing something, respectfully, that is not quite right will most often act as a catalyst for a sharper focus on what's true for your client.

Check progress

For example, ask: 'How are you doing in relation to your issue or desired outcome?' Or simply: 'What have you got from this already?'

Ask this question:

'Who would be pleased if you can't find a resolution to this issue?' That question will often surface a deeper loyalty to someone or something that prevents the client from moving to resolution and keeps them stuck.

Bring in something to represent a 'resource'

Invite the client to choose something to represent a resource and find a place for it. What they choose and where they place it will provide a lot of new information. The exact nature of the resource will often come into focus after they have placed it.

See if something or somebody has been excluded

Do this by asking: 'If you chose something to represent an element or person that is not seen or has been excluded here, where would you put it?' Invite them to place a representative for the excluded element(s) into the map.

Ask this question:

'What's the best possible question I could ask you now?' This usually leads to a new piece of previously hidden information, which creates fresh material to work with.

Ask: 'So, if this picture is the answer, what's the question?'

This often prompts a deeper connection with the client's issue and surfaces hidden information and nuances under the issue.

Do nothing

On many occasions, as confidence grows in this way of working, the resolution to stuckness comes in the silences between the words and movements. Developing the confidence to simply hold the space for the client's quiet reflections is often a source of insight and resolution. That's often true of coaching in general, but never more so than in this way of working. Leaving your client in quiet contemplation of their map, their constellation, without trying to fix it or them, is often a gift. Just wait and see what emerges, leaving the initiative and energy for change with them, not you.

> Don't underestimate the value of Doing Nothing, of just going along, listening to all the things you can't hear.
>> Pooh's Little Instruction Book, inspired by A A Milne

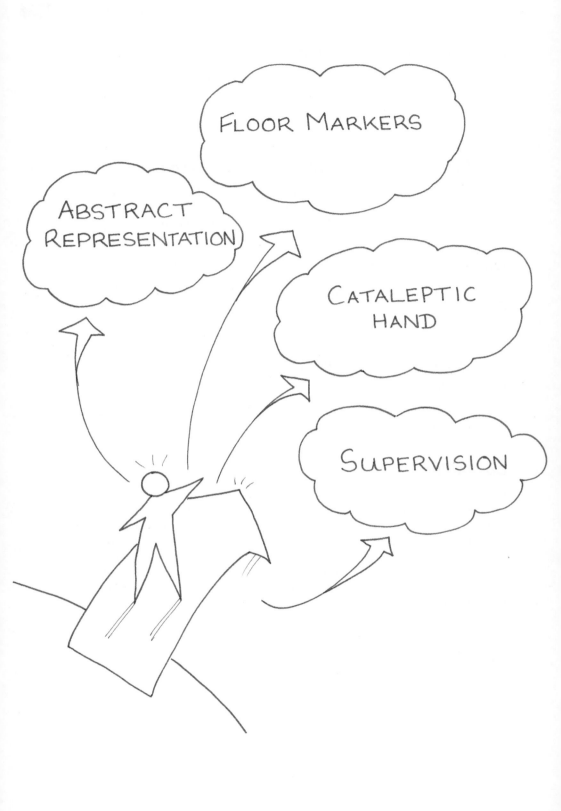

Extending your practice

10

Further practices and applications

> " *Our doubts are traitors and make us lose the good*
> *We oft might win by fearing to attempt.*
>
> **WILLIAM SHAKESPEARE, *MEASURE FOR MEASURE*, ACT 1, SCENE 4**

Once you've combined what you've read here with experience in a workshop or training environment, you may want to develop a wider mix of processes. This chapter explores some of those, as well as taking a brief look at the application of this whole approach in supervision.

Floor markers

In one-to-one coaching it's possible to offer a constellation experience that leaves the tabletop. This involves using floor markers (for example, pieces of card with a directional quality to them) and offering the client the opportunity to step into each of the key places in the constellation. This generates a great deal of useful information, as well as the fresh perspectives you'd expect. With system-orientated facilitation this becomes much more than simply stepping into others' shoes, as the client can experience the representative perception available through this method. Movements can then also be made and sentences offered and spoken from each place.

As well as using floor markers for the client to stand on, it's possible to step in and out of the different places yourself, as the coach. Just be careful not to stay too long and so become inhabited with the energy in each place. With practice it's possible to tap into that energy and get a 'reading' from it, reporting it back to the client or simply reflecting on the information gathered as part of the process. As your range develops you can exchange sentences and movement with the client whilst simultaneously facilitating.

I recall trying this for the first time with an HR director of a large multinational. He was advising the outgoing chairman of the business and supporting him in the succession planning. It was a complex and emotionally fraught transition for the chairman, for him as an advisor and for the organization.

I invited him to set up, using a floor marker, the chairman. He carefully chose one of the pieces of card I had with me and, coming from a collected inner place, placed it slowly on the floor. Something drew me to stand up and stand in that place so, checking for his permission first, I stood on top of the floor marker.

As soon as I did I had an unexpected response. I felt immediately very lonely and frightened, fearful of what lay ahead. We were working on the top floor of a very tall building and I became aware of the view stretching across the city to the horizon on this cold October day. It felt bleak and without any promise of comfort or security. I also felt frozen to the spot, almost unable to move.

I didn't vocalize my response as I didn't want to influence his, but later, after we had done some work exploring the 'best place' for him to be in relationship to the outgoing chairman, I invited him to step into the same spot. As he did so he gasped with surprise and reported the same feelings I had had, including the sense of bleakness and isolation.

This gave him a unique insight into what was going on at a more emotional level for this apparently stoical, sometimes abrupt and perhaps lonely chairman. He was frightened of the blankness, the potential bleakness in his future. This insight, together with others, made a significant difference in the way he worked with the chairman from then on, as he could now see, having experience of it himself, the chairman's fears and insecurities under the bluff exterior. His resistance to the chairman and reluctance to get close to him in a way that could support his healthy exit melted away.

The cataleptic hand

Where possible, especially while you are fairly new to this approach, I would encourage you to start using yourself as a representative in a particular way. Let's imagine you are working one-to-one in a situation where exploring an interpersonal relationship dynamic is relevant and important. You have invited your client to place floor markers down and they are now standing on their own and looking towards the marker they have placed for 'the other'. Rather than standing in the place of the other yourself, you can simply extend your arm with your fingers out flat, briefly touch the marker with your fingertips, and then slowly raise your hand up until your hand is at eye height. This creates a natural focus for the client and brings the 'other' person into the room as if they were standing on the marker.

This is called the cataleptic hand because it allows you to separate your hand from the rest of you and use it to act as a visual focus and also as another way of collecting data. Like many of the things described here it's hard to imagine how this works until you try it, but remarkably straightforward once you do.

The word cataleptic means 'a state resembling trance'. Again, I've never known any coaching client to find this technique odd or distracting in any way; rather they find themselves staring at the palm of your hand, exchanging sentences and moving in relationship to it with remarkable clarity and ease.

Sarah Cornally, a leadership advisor and executive coach living and working in Sydney, Australia, was working with a director in a large professional services firm. This director had asked for some coaching because she had a peer who was also a direct report who refused her authority. This had built up over time, there were several complexities and things were getting so bad that she thought the only realistic option was to leave the company. She certainly wasn't feeling able or ready to have a double coaching session with the peer.

Sarah went in for a first session with a view of creating a coaching plan but, after hearing a little more about the issue, she invited her new client to find a larger room for them to work in together so that she could work with her standing up, using pieces of paper as floor markers and the cataleptic hand technique. Sarah takes up the story and describes what happened in the session.

Finding authority

Coach: Sarah Cornally, executive coach, Sydney, Australia
Client: Anonymous

The initial discussion revealed that there was a pattern in the team of creating roles where the leadership authority was confused and compromised. My client's peer had received a promotion from director to principal around the time of my client's appointment as leader. She as leader was not yet a principal. Her peer, highly respected for her particular expertise, had a history of poor people management and was due to be counselled about this as a serious matter.

The questions my client wanted to have answered were:

- Is there a role/place for me in this team?

- If so, how do I structure the team so it will work effectively?

- How do I deal with my peer who doesn't accept my leadership?

We chose the first question to focus on and I offered to support her as she mapped the current situation out in front of her. A good outcome from her point of view was clarity and a clear path forward. After some discussion the initial elements chosen to be represented were as follows:

- the leader (my client in her role as leader);
- the peer (my client's peer in her role as peer and partner);
- the 'specialist' group;
- the 'corporate' group;
- the operations manager;
- the purpose of the team.

The name of each element was written on a piece of A4 paper, together with an arrowhead to indicate direction/orientation. I asked my client to take the paper, close her eyes and get a 'felt sense' of the inner picture she held of this issue, and then to place the paper on the floor in a position that felt like the 'right' location. Once she identified this, I asked her to stand on the paper and ensure that it 'felt true'. She selected the next representative and used the same process to locate the floor marker. This was done progressively.

As she progressed I used the 'cataleptic hand' to represent each representative. Created by holding my hand where the representative would be located in the field, I've developed the capacity to hold it in a manner where my hand is disassociated from my arm, so it effectively acts as a representative. I can feel sensations in my hand as if it is a representative picking up information from the field. This enables the client to place the representative in their map and interact with it.

The map

The initial image showed that all representatives had their backs to the representative for 'the purpose of the team'. The two peers were also focused in different directions to each other. The leader, my client, was looking towards the representative for the corporate group. The peer was looking outwards, away from the groups. The two groups were not focused on anything and, when she stepped into their places and I used my hand in the other place, my client reported that they were also avoiding eye contact. The operations manager was trying to find eye contact and did, from time to time, with the team leader.

I asked my client to stand on each location and report her felt sense experience from each place marker. Her experiences included fear, anger, conflict, avoidance, separation, powerlessness and confusion.

This first step revealed powerful new insights and fresh distinctions for her. As she reported from each representative position, we examined what changed or did not through speaking and including acknowledging, systemic truths and freeing sentences as they were indicated. All the time I used my hand as the other representative. Using the cataleptic hand throughout this process enabled me to track the impact and adjust each sentence. This significantly helped to minimize any effects of the client's bias.

There was a movement for all of the roles, except the peer, to cluster together facing the opposite direction to the purpose. 'This is what we do to survive.' At this point I introduced a representative for 'the former partners' to provide support.

As we worked together and explored each part of this living map, the representative for the leader looked directly at the peer and said: 'I see and respect the valuable expertise you bring to our work together. It has an important place.' This resulted in the peer making eye contact with the leader, followed by turning towards the purpose and making a good connection with the purpose. All of this was facilitated through the use of the hand.

After this it was possible for each representative to face the purpose and then, through a series of steps, to get each representative into a better place, except the leader and her peer. However, there was still a distance maintained between the other representatives and the peer 'for safety'.

Bringing in a representative for 'the partner in charge' changed the dynamics between the leader and the peer. This part of the process involved acknowledging who was responsible for what. It started with the leader's sentence to the partner in charge, again using the cataleptic hand to help embody this important exchange: 'You are in charge. You have the biggest responsibility for this team.'

I offered a number of other resolving sentences that were exchanged between the triad of the leader, the partner in charge and the peer. These sentences included naming who belonged, everyone's place with special emphasis on responsibility, capability and expertise, and in what ways they needed and respected each other. Introducing the partner in charge became pivotal in finding the path forward to ensure responsibility at the right levels. When they got into contact with their responsibility and purpose, the whole constellation slowly aligned.

When we had finished, I asked the client what outcome had been achieved. She said she was clear about:

- her place and role in the team;
- the steps she needed to take to move things forward constructively;
- what responsibility belonged to whom for what;

- what conversation she needed to have with whom, and how to have them in an authentic, respectful way;

- how to speak about her peer in a way that was accurate and dignified to ensure the real matters were attended to.

It took three months to implement and achieve the desired outcome, which included engaging the partner in charge as a resource, her own promotion to principal, and having the required conversations with her peer in a way that resulted in a more effective working relationship and her authority being respected. She was also able to create the right relationships in the team to enable a higher and more rewarding level of performance.

The advantage of this approach, the use of the cataleptic hand, is that as coach/facilitator you are both 'in' the representative energy and 'out' at the same time. In fact, it embodies the overall stance of this work: both deeply connected into the system energies and apart from them, observing and experiencing at the same time.

A note about representatives

You will have seen by now that when you invite your clients to choose a representative for themselves, it doesn't have to be the whole of them. For example, you can invite them to set up something to represent the role that they occupy, or 'the part of them that occupies the role'. This removes, to some extent, their personal reactivity and allows looking at a more abstract system level. This can be useful for particular clients in particular contexts, especially where there are a number of difficult interpersonal issues or conflicts in the system.

It's also useful to remember that any element within a system can be given a place and represented. The following are offered as just a few examples of the many elements that can be represented.

Groups of people:

- the founders or owners;
- suppliers and partners;
- teams;
- shareholders;
- stakeholders;
- customers/customer groups;
- advisors and consultants;

- employees who have left;
- potential employees.

Other systems:

- parent organization;
- the competitors;
- the government;
- the political system;
- the financial markets;
- the economy;
- national identity systems.

Abstracts:

- the original purpose;
- our current purpose;
- what's excluded by the purpose;
- the current goals/objectives;
- what's excluded by those goals/objectives;
- the culture;
- our shared values/the values excluded;
- resources (named or not identified);
- limitations;
- possibilities;
- what is stuck;
- something that could be the route to solution;
- organizational vitality;
- organizational assets;
- authority;
- leadership;
- the ordering forces of systems.

Personal abstracts:

- my values;
- my resources;
- my behaviour;
- my beliefs;
- my competencies;
- my fears;
- my hopes.

Other abstracts and elements:

- money or the flow of money;
- the winds of change;
- the past as we understand it;
- the past as it really was;
- the emerging future;
- the unknown;
- what could be;
- the next generation.

The following can often be useful 'litmus paper' elements in constellations:

- our existing or future customers;
- those who will be affected by a change;
- future employees;
- something that could be the route to solution.

Application in coaching supervision

Supervision

For most professional coaches, supervision or 'coach mentoring' is an essential, enriching and enjoyable part of their professional work and journey. By providing an objective perspective that improves the quality of the coach's offer, as well as illuminating issues around client/coach relationships and process, supervision has the potential to resolve, clarify and resource.

One of the most effective ways of learning the systemic coaching and constellations approach is to get involved in a learning and supervision group guided by the principles and practices. In fact, any constellations training environment is bound to include a large proportion of supervision, as the group needs a constant supply of pressing issues and questions with which to learn and practise.

Supervision is a central part of the learning journey and a great deal of useful work is done by students of this approach as they bring issues and share their coaching dilemmas. After a day of exploring supervision issues using constellations, a group I was working with spent a while discussing the merits of this approach and methodology in the context of supervision. These were the observations they made, in their own words:

- 'This approach limits the chances of the coach and the supervisor getting entangled in the story, having opinions about what the coach "should" have done...'

- 'Constellations seem to be able to open up a much larger field of possibilities and solutions than a discussion or "ordinary" supervision; it's literally beyond the imagination...'

- 'This creates a safe space in which you can co-create fresh solutions...'

- 'The work itself and the picture of the path to resolution are embodied so go in, and stay in, at a different level. Not just in the head, but felt and retained somewhere deeper. That's so useful when you are about to face a challenging client...'

Constellations in group supervision

A constellation creates a three-dimensional physical map of the inner, unconscious relationship pattern. This map therefore enables 'super-vision' of the relationship system and offers a perspective that quickly reveals dynamics and truths not accessible through discussion or experience alone. A constellation offers a place for the projections, parallel process and stories that keep us stuck as coaches.

The process of constellating accesses the combined embodied knowledge and perception of everyone present, surfacing the field of information that exists in all relationship systems. In group supervision the 'living map', the constellation, is made up of other group members and reveals, just as when using objects one to one, the hidden relationship architecture. However, owing to the phenomenon of representative perception, previously inaccessible information surfaces through the words that are spoken by the representatives. Fresh levels of clarity emerge from the system, which is given a voice.

The approach is somatic and so creates an embodied spatial awareness in which the coach can find the place in the system from where they can be most useful. The capacity to fine-tune this aspect is uniquely powerful in constellations and is often a source of deep insight in supervision. Following facilitated intervention the revised map of the relationship pattern is internalized and embodied, so the coach is left resourced, clear and in their authority and skill.

Systemic supervision changes something in the supervisee and it's this re-aligned inner stance, this sense of 'right place' that, with the fresh understanding and knowledge of system dynamics, resources them.

Jane is an experienced executive coach, mentor and coaching supervisor. She trained with Coaching Constellations in 2014 and started to integrate constellations into her busy coaching supervision practice. In this example of application, the coaches she is working with all work in the same system together and are managers in their own right. It's in these circumstances that finding the inner stance of coaching can be particularly challenging.

They are not only new coaches but also fairly new to constellations, having only experienced the methodology very briefly before in Jane's supervision sessions.

Be useful, not helpful

Coaching supervisor: Jane Cox, Ipswich, UK

Supervisee: Kirsty, an internal coach and senior manager within a local government authority

Client: a group of five internal coaches within a local government authority.

Presenting question: 'Why will my coachee not move on her actions?'

Jane: I asked Kirsty what the issue was for her as the coach and she reframed her question to this:

'How can I help my coachee move forward on her actions?'

Jane: 'What would be different if this was more resolved?'

Kirsty: 'She will have done what she said she would!'

She voiced this in an exasperated tone – and added: 'I would feel like my coaching was actually working.'

Despite the judgement in the question I decided to go with this and see where it went. I was picking up on her exasperation and wondering if this might be a transferred emotion, maybe from somewhere within the system. Kirsty started to launch into the story so I respectfully interrupted her and suggested that we simply map out the elements in their 'what is' state and then see what needed attending to. We agreed that we would create a system boundary with chairs to represent the directorate within which her coachee worked. I then invited Kirsty to choose a representative from amongst the group for her coachee and she did so.

I invited Kirsty to stand behind the woman she had chosen to represent her coachee (C) and, resting her hands lightly on her shoulders, to position her in the space within the circle of chairs, just where it felt true. After a while I asked C what she experienced from this place and she shrugged, looked around and said: 'I'm not really sure what I feel. A bit lost, I think.'

I turned back to Kirsty and asked her if she wanted to say any more about the facts around C and her situation. Kirsty explained that C was a woman in her fifties who still has a young family. She believes that she is overwhelmed, overloaded and can't cope, both at work and apparently in her life as a whole. She said that C has a 'horrible brother' and issues with her mother.

I invited Kirsty to choose people or paper floor markers to represent these elements if they needed to be there.

She placed markers for the mother beside C and brother behind. Both pointing at her. Kirsty then volunteered that her coachee was also doing two jobs. She was transitioning into a new role and had also inherited another role from someone

who had retired. (I sensed that this might be significant, so stored it away for later.)
Jane: 'Do these different roles need to be represented?'

Kirsty put two markers in C's hands, and asked her to hold them over her shoulders, pointing down. The rest of the group gasped in unison at this. 'Wow,' said one of them. 'I wasn't expecting that.' Observing this reaction, I invited C to share what it actually felt like. She said: 'I feel overwhelmed and weighed down.'

Kirsty took another marker and put it by C but then repositioned it under her left foot. 'That's her own job,' she said.
Jane: 'Her own job?'
Kirsty: 'Yes, the job she has been doing for a while... and has been promoted from, but there is no one else to take it on so it's really difficult for her.'

I let that settle for a few moments and then asked if anyone else was in this picture.
Kirsty: 'Well, me, I suppose.'

She chose someone to represent herself (K rep) and moved her into position directly in front of C, facing her.

K rep immediately took a step back and volunteered unprompted that she couldn't see C from that close. She was obscured by all the stuff overwhelming her. Kirsty smiled in recognition and insight. She had got too close.

I asked her if anything else needed to be represented
Kirsty: 'Just her line manager. But he seems really ineffectual.'

I noticed how Kirsty had colluded with the story of the boss but invited her to choose a representative for him (M). She positioned him right on the edge of the system with his back to it. M asked if he could turn around because he couldn't see C. But when he did, he said he wasn't really interested anyway as he still couldn't really see her, only all the stuff around her.. At this, he half turned away and leant on the back of a chair.

I invited Kirsty to walk around and share what she noticed.
Kirsty: 'Well, I realize I can't intervene with the line manager but I want to give him a good shake! I would intervene if I wasn't her coach. I feel really frustrated by them all. No one is helping her.'
Jane: 'This feels important. Shall we represent your frustration?' Kirsty chose a marker.
Jane: 'Where does it belong?'

Before Kirsty could place it, C said, 'It's there!' and pointed to a spot in front of her, in the direction of M and the empty space between them. This was another of the points in the constellation that I noticed Kirsty really take in – she was learning that the frustration was not just hers alone, but also belonged in the system.
Jane: 'Anything else?'

Kirsty: 'Well, my coaching needs representing in some way…'

Jane: 'Say a bit more about that.'

Kirsty: 'It's me being a coach, my professional self, my training,' she said as she placed a floor marker alongside K rep pointing in the direction of C. I suggested to Kirsty that she walk around and look at it from C's perspective, then I offered a sentence inviting her to ask C what she really wanted.

In response to this C replied: 'I want my coach to come over here, beside me.' There was a pause before she burst out: 'Help!'

This set off a spontaneous exchange between the two representatives.

K rep: 'I'm frustrated and angry at your inactivity. You agreed to do things but you haven't.'

C: 'Please help me get out of this mess. I can't find time even to get started.'

On hearing this M volunteered that he had an impulse to take one of the jobs away from C and he removed one of the markers she was holding.

I asked C how she felt as a result and she said: 'Relieved.'

I was moving around with Kirsty now helping her to notice what emerged.

Kirsty: 'Oh. I guess her director needs to be in this. C went to see him to ask if he would help since her manager isn't. And he asked her to produce a task list so he could see what it is she does. He is not a specialist in her area so I guess needs to get a feel for why she is so stressed.'

She asked the only person left to represent the director (D) and it crossed my mind that everyone in the group was now involved. There were no bystanders. Perhaps this in itself was information about the system?

C had a reaction to this: 'I thought that by going round my manager to talk to the director, he would be able to make things happen. But he has just given me one more thing to do – another list. When am I going to get this done? He'll think I'm useless.'

I also noticed aloud the parallel of Kirsty having helped C to create a list of things she wanted to achieve, and the director asking for a task list too.

Kirsty voiced her frustration again, about her own inability to move things forward, and with the organization as a whole.

I offered K rep a sentence to share with C.

K rep said: 'How can I help you? What do you want of me?'

With a slight smile C replied: 'Could you do it for me?'

Kirsty watched this and then said: 'I really want her to get the list together as I feel that if the director knows what's what he will be able to do something. But I shouldn't, should I?' (Earlier in our supervision discussion Kirsty had spoken of how in her manager's role she often sat down with her staff and helped them get started on something, then left them to carry on, with her on hand if needed. She saw this as an effective way of helping them develop.)

Kirsty: 'I am a coach here and that means I have to act differently from when I'm a manager. I need to get her to want to do it herself. I don't see why, if she can make time for our sessions, she doesn't seem able to make time to do what we agree.'

I held this for a moment before saying: 'What if you gave yourself permission to ask her what she wants? Perhaps you might say, "You make time for our sessions, so how could we use our time together to progress your actions?"'

On hearing this K rep turned to C and said: 'What if I help you make a start on your list? You can type it up as we speak. You could use our session to start things moving. And I could even help you rehearse your conversation with the director.'

Jane: 'And what else would be a step towards better here?' I asked of no one in particular.

C: 'Lose some of the work.'

Then I suggested some movement to realign the relationship between coach and coachee by inviting K rep to move alongside C .

Jane: 'What difference does this make? '

C: 'I feel better with you alongside. It's less confrontational.'

Then she said to K rep: 'Please don't keep being so *sympathetic*. Let's get practical, then I won't get so emotional.'

K rep: 'What if I turn away slightly?'

C: 'Yeah, I can still feel you there but that feels better.'

Kirsty frowned slightly then her face relaxed and she smiled with understanding and relief.

Nothing was said for a short while. I let the new relationship pattern settle in Kirsty and then, feeling the moment might now be appropriate, I asked Kirsty about the inherited job and what had happened with the previous role holder.

Kirsty: 'She retired. She was really good at her job. She had built it from nothing. There wasn't really a handover as she went and C just had to sort of pick it up because there was no one else to do it.'

Perhaps this was significant. I offered sentences to invite C to acknowledge the previous job-holder's contribution and let her inhabit the role in the best way she could, given the circumstances. This prompted the representative to say:

C: 'Thank you for doing the job so well. I will do the best I can but I also have another job so I may not do it as well as you. I will do what I can.'

I could see Kirsty was absorbing all this, the larger picture of the system. Then I invited Kirsty to move the marker representing her professional self. She put it under K rep's foot.

I offered K rep sentences to address to C. K rep heard these and then said, in her own words: 'I will help you as a coach. I will bring my whole self to the next session and we can work together on your actions. I can only do my best but I will support you in moving forward.'

There followed an acknowledgement from C that she felt less pessimistic. 'I feel better about this now, less useless. Maybe I will be able to do this if we can just focus on the practical stuff.'

I turned to Kirsty as she started to speak. 'Watching that, I feel able to do whatever I need to for C, whatever she needs me to do. I realize now that being present *for* her (like you kept saying in our coach training) means being myself and not doing what I think a coach *should* do.'

She had released herself from the constraint of what she 'should' do and let go of her assumed responsibility for solving C's problems, let go of trying so hard to get an outcome – albeit with the good intention of helping the coachee achieve her coaching goal.

Jane: 'What if we remove the frustration marker?'

Jane to K rep: 'What occurs to you?'

K rep: 'No, leave it. But put it over there in the space of the organization. That's where it belongs. They have some responsibility for all this. They are asking too much.'

As I was reflecting on the balance of EXCHANGE in this system and the way constellations return responsibility to where it belongs the representative for the director spoke up:

D: 'You're right. And I'm trying to do something about it. But I need to understand the scale of the problem first.'

It seemed that the system was starting to accept its responsibility and offering to rebalance.

Kirsty: 'I sense I could really help her move on by suggesting we use the coaching time to develop an overview of what she has to do and then prepare for her meeting with the director. I see now that he is the key to helping her sort out her workload, not me. That's it. I know how to move forward with the coaching now.'

Jane: 'So, are we done here for now? Is there anything else we need to attend to?'

Kirsty: 'Yes. I think we are done. It's been really revealing. Thank you. I feel much more confident about how to progress this.'

I suggested she gather up the markers and de-role each representative to their seat, thanking them as she did so.

So what did Kirsty, the client of this coaching supervision constellation, learn?

- The constellation allowed her to find her 'right place', literally and metaphorically, with her coachee and so eased the resistance between the two by repositioning them side by side but less intently focused on each other.

This enabled them to redefine their relationship.

- The constellation showed her the source of the frustration that she had been feeling – it belonged in large part within the system itself.

- She recalled that when the manager had seen the pressure on her coachee's shoulders, he had stepped in and removed one of the roles. This felt like important information. Kirsty had been colluding in a generalized judgement of his lack of interest, but that movement gave her cause to reassess this.

- She recognized that she didn't need to intervene directly with the organization but she could be more useful if she supported her coachee to do this for herself.

- Most importantly she really heard the representative for the client say this about being helpful: 'Please don't keep being so *sympathetic*.' It dawned on her that she was not actually being helpful at all, merely intensifying the pressure.

- Kirsty could clearly take this embodied inner sense, this new constellation, of the relationship back into her work.

I received an email from Kirsty some time afterwards in which she told me that she'd followed through on her actions and her coachee had responded well to the different dynamic. She recognized now the parallel of both feeling stuck in the conversation. The more they talked, the more stuck they became, until Kirsty broke the deadlock by doing something different and suggesting they take the next step together.

Kirsty also talked about the constellation and how poweful she felt it was in releasing tensions, showing the hidden dynamics and enabling her to recalibrate herself as a coach.

What did I, Jane the supervisor and facilitator of this constellation, learn?

- This was the fifth supervision constellation I had facilitated and I find it quite wonderful that coaches who have little or no experience of working in this way can enter into it and access the field so fully and authentically, generating fresh information and insight.

- I noticed how much Kirsty jumped in with words and I wonder if I could have stopped her more often – maybe by inviting her to sit down – and checked for what the representative was actually experiencing so we could have got a little more under, or past, the story.

- I didn't revisit the coachee's previous role or indeed her family issues as within this constellation these elements hadn't seemed to demand attention. They seemed to be just more weight that the coachee was carrying, and my sense was that they were not part of this particular system. They might, however, emerge in a future session, in which case we can give them our attention.

- I wondered if I could have swapped Kirsty's representative for Kirsty herself at the end of the constellation so she had an embodied sense of her 'right place' and of being less empathetic, less 'helpful' with her coachee.

- I was glad to be able to find a useful way of acknowledging the previous role-holder as I know that this order of TIME can be so important when supporting leaders to find their authority in role. Especially when they have either left in difficult circumstances or have been very successful and popular, as in this case.

I feel very aware of the challenges and entanglements for those working as coaches within their own organizational system. Indeed, this aspect is a significant part of the training that Kirsty referred to. Constellations are so useful in separating out the systems so that internal coaches have a clearer view of this aspect and can get disentangled. As a result they are proving to be an important part of my supervision practice.

This supervision constellation allowed both the facilitator and the participants an opportunity to experiment with accessing embodied knowledge and the benefits of simply mapping 'what is' to open up other possibilities and paths to resolution. As with many supervision constellations you see in this example how we can often get too close, too entangled with our clients, to be useful. Then we try to be helpful or force action, or take responsibility away from where it belongs in the system.

The attempts to help are often motivated by a mixture of frustration, our own difficulties with similar issues and natural empathy. The impact of helping too much is very often a deepening sense of helplessness and this is clearly articulated by the representative for the one being helped in this constellation: 'Please don't keep being so sympathetic.'

Bert Hellinger said something on this, the difference between being helpful and being useful in service of the whole system. He said: 'Have no intention. Especially to help.'

This learning point and inner recalibration is often cited as one of the most memorable and useful on the learning (and un-learning) journey of systemic coaching. The relief that the coach feels at taking the emphasis off being helpful and instead standing back and seeing the whole, a place from where they can be much more useful, is also felt by the client who then feels free and more able to stand in their own authority and responsibility.

~

Due to the experiential nature of constellations they offer the group supervision process a rich source and methodology for learning for everyone in the group. In Jane's example above everyone in the supervision group is needed by the constellation so each comes away with a direct experience of what it feels like to stand in a field of information, to stand in the ebb and flow of a system.

For constellations that don't require all members of the group to be directly involved there is also a powerful learning experience to be had from watching – or as so very often happens embodying a part of the system that has not been consciously represented in the constellation. This phenomenon is very common and makes it particularly important to allow everyone in the room an opportunity to feedback their experience – even if you think they were only 'observing'.

Information that unlocks something stuck, hidden or forgotten in the system often emerges in these circumstances.

One of the exercises that is used in training is a very simple pairs exercise. This exercise is useful for supervision when as a coach you are preparing for a challenging client. If you are learning about this approach with others then you can try this with a learning partner. However, for the purposes of this book I'll describe it in its application in self-supervision. Self-supervision is something that can be easily and usefully done through this methodology, and it also provides a good opportunity to practise constellating, around a pressing issue, for coaches who are new to this approach and want to practise.

Self-supervision can be done with representative objects or with floor markers. In this context a floor marker is simply a piece of paper with a name on it (your own or that of the client you are thinking of) and an arrow indicating direction of attention. You need to be able to stand on the floor markers.

Coach self-supervision exercise

Clear a space in the room and identify a boundary to that space. Have two large pieces of paper that you can use as representatives of yourself and a client.

Think of a client with whom you struggle to make or keep a productive connection or with whom you are currently experiencing stuckness or another kind of challenging relationship or process issue. Let a sense of the relationship dynamic and coaching process with them occupy you. Take your time and when in touch with your 'felt sense' of your client relationship, select a piece of paper to represent your client.

Standing and then walking slowly in the space with the piece of paper at waist height and held between your two hands, find a place that feels true. Where in this physical space do they belong, and what is the direction of their attention? When you sense that the representative for your client is in a place that feels true (not 'right or wrong', just true), place the piece of paper down on the floor in that place.

Next, slowly find your own place in relationship to them. Do this with a second piece of paper with your name and an arrow indicating direction of attention on it. Forget everything you think you need to know to do this and experiment with different positions. Very slowly, and whilst in touch with your centre, find a place that feels true to 'what is'. If you have done this while in touch with your inner sense of the relationship dynamic, you will find yourself standing in the truth of the difficulty of this relationship that you currently experience with this particular client.

Try saying out loud a short sentence that captures this truth, even just: 'This is how it is'. Simply stand in this place and express, through the processes of constellations you are now familiar with, your experience of this place and of this relationship pattern.

Next, experiment with a small movement that feels like a step closer to an easing of the system. Then try 'exchanging' one or two sentences that resonate with your experience of standing in the particular place. You can find out how each 'lands' by stepping back off your place and standing in the place the client occupies. By doing so, you may well find fresh information from their place that gives you a different perspective on the relationship and/or coaching process. This is an exercise that taps into the information held within systems through your own somatic experience, not a perceptual positions exercise. Turn any sense of fresh information into a sentence, movement or both and notice the impact of doing so.

You already know enough about this approach to take this exercise to a suitable next step or conclusion. You may find yourself with enough fresh information simply through this first stage, mapping what is. You may choose to go further by adding another element or resource.

After this exercise, take some time to note down what you experience and what information you gathered from each place. You may also like to try this small self-facilitated constellation with other issues or questions. For example, you can set up your relationship to coaching, to money, to anything that you are in relationship with.

Self-supervision is an effective way of learning and practising this methodology, as well as illuminating your own relationship patterns.

Outside in

11

> *Problems that arise in organizations are almost always the product of interactions of parts, never the action of a single part.* RUSS ACKOFF

The experience of systemic coaching

Most coaches who learn to coach with the system in mind find that plenty of practical experience of constellating is a resourcing path towards systemic coaching. Standing in the field of invisible information and sensing into the information, system loyalties and entanglements creates a deep understanding of systems. After a while you find that the way you are listening and responding to your clients changes, subtly at first.

It can start in the first briefing, listening to what may be going on in the system as well as at the individual or team level. It can continue in the selection meeting or first session. You realize you are scanning systems as people talk, noticing which systems they belong and are loyal to, noticing their place in relationship to or with each system.

When working as a coach with an individual or a team, you always have a choice: to work at the level of the individual or the wider system. Systemic coaching embraces both and includes insights from the individual's system and the wider organizational systems so that the client is resourced and strengthened. As a systemic coach you begin to see and work with all the relationship systems in front of you and give everything a place and a voice.

The intention of systemic coaching and constellations is to support clarity in the individual or team and coherence in the system around them. For everything 'that is' to be acknowledged and for entanglements within the system to be illuminated and released. To build system-wide health and flow.

When relationship and interconnectedness is central to your thinking as a coach, when you know why goals, emotional intelligence and 'professional development' can be blocks as well as catalysts for progress, when you give everything a place, then all sorts of things become possible, including those in the list that follows. If it feels like a lot, read it again *after* you've facilitated two or three times and you'll be surprised by how many of the qualities you are already embodying, and how many of the insights you have already experienced.

After you've done some experiential training and practice you'll soon feel able to:

- Be useful, rather than helpful, without intention.

- See your clients not just as individuals or separate teams but as part of much larger systems in which there are multiple resources and solutions beyond the coach or coaching.

- Recall the organizing principles of systems and apply them in your thinking, coaching and interventions.

- Work and stay with 'what is' without knowing the answers or even the question.

- Trust the mapping and constellation process to surface system truths.

- Sit back and see and give a place to all the systems to which the client belongs, scanning the organizational system, the team system and the personal systems for patterns, dynamics and entanglements.

- Work without a judgement on what is 'right' or 'wrong' and have an understanding of system conscience, guilt and innocence.

- Support your clients to face into the truth of their difficulty, issue, developmental journey or question; illuminate it, give it its place, and use the understandings as a resource.

- Work with the organizational health and system intelligence in mind.

- Work with minimum information, just the *facts* of what is and not the *story* of what might be, quickly discerning the difference between stories and facts and between primary and secondary emotions.

- Work with the invisible and tacit, alongside the visible and explicit.

- Offer sentences to your clients – as part of a constellation or coaching conversation – that get to the essence of their developmental, leadership, team or personal challenge in a way that supports them to stand fully in the truth and then find resources and resolution.

- Use yourself as an instrument and source of information, but also the client, the representatives and the invisible field held between them all.

- Explore the history, purpose and place of the role, as well as the individual or team.

- Map the systemic hierarchy alongside the organizational hierarchy, and then illuminate the hidden dynamics.

- Develop and offer hypotheses based on your understanding of relationship system dynamics in general and in the particular organizational systems you are working with.

- Encourage the development of system intelligence alongside emotional intelligence.

- Facilitate coaching conversations that are informed by an understanding of what sustains and limits systems. Using the language of systems respectfully, you are able to illuminate the system truths.

- Look at systems grow, change and die without judgement or partiality, and remain in the neutral stance. You do not get entangled with the systems with which you work.

You'll be able to do this because you know:

- That everything has a place. That all people and events have to be included, or the system will attempt to 're-member' them, causing entanglements. Demonstrating the effectiveness of doing so, you model systemic thinking and leadership to your clients.

- That a system's character and dynamics are created by everything that has happened in the past: the founders and founding purpose of the system; all the people that have joined and left it; and all past events.

- That odd, difficult or recurring behaviour may in fact be a message from within the system in which it belongs.

- How to discern individual preferences and behaviours from system dynamics and behaviours, and how to integrate both into your interventions.

- That no one theory or practice can be the answer to all leadership and organizational issues, and that each system finds coherence and dynamic balance in different ways in its attempt to align itself with the organizing forces of all systems.

Once you know, and feel able to do and be all those things, you will also have:

- An understanding of the importance of disentangling clients from system dynamics so that their goals, developmental journeys and objectives can be achieved and endure.

- The ability to use yourself, your client *and* representatives as sources of reliable information.

- The intention and ability to raise system-awareness as well as self-awareness so that another field of information is available to you and your clients.

- A conscious awareness of your own system loyalties and patterns, because you've explored, illuminated and clarified enough of the dynamics in your own family of origin system to know how to manage their influence so that they support and resource your work. You understand your own points of entanglement, as well as the strengths they offer you.

- The ability to see what may be trying to be seen or completed in systems based on the behaviours within them.

You think that because you understand 'One' that you must therefore understand 'Two' because one and one make two. But you forget that you must also understand 'And'.

Sufi Teaching Story

And before long you'll realize that you can see all this and more:

- In teams and organizations you recognize:
  - when and why organizational health is out of balance;
  - exclusion of the founders or founding purpose;
  - exclusion of people and the ejector seat syndrome;
  - exclusion of facts and the entanglements this creates;
  - loss of place;
  - an imbalance of exchange;
  - a violation of the systemic order of time;
  - the impact of joining and leaving systems.
- In individuals you recognize:
  - when leaders are working in service of the purpose and when they are not;
  - leaders who can't occupy their own authority and why that may be from a systems point of view;
  - a leader who is looking to belong;
  - the impact of loyalty to conscience groups;
  - when a leader is carrying something on behalf of the system;
  - the influence of hidden loyalties;
  - hidden leaders and bosses in the system;
  - when leaders are occupying burdened roles.

Beyond constellations

The majority of coaches seem to learn this approach best by first experiencing constellations, then by facilitating constellations, and then by understanding, again, what lies beneath constellations. The exploration should be of experience first (the phenomenological approach) and then the underpinning principles. As a result of that journey, as well as the one along the path, you begin to coach *without* using constellations. Something changes about the language you use and the words you choose as you tune into systems and start to think in three dimensions.

Let me give you an example. As I was writing this book a message popped up on one of the LinkedIn groups we host for students of the trainings. The message was from Chris Dalton (Subject Area Leader for Personal Development at The Henley Business School)

Gifted learning circle?

Hi all,

I wanted to share part of an email I received today from one of my informants in my PhD research. Without going into their back-story, this is what they said:

> 'I just wanted to drop you a line to say thank you for your question you posed to me during your last PhD project session. You asked "Where is your purpose?"
>
> Such a simple question which proved a showstopper at the time and has prompted much reflection and thought since. The use of "where" instead of "what" was and remains very powerful for me. So thank you for that gift.'

There was no mapping or constellating being done, so it shows the power of people's spatial understanding of relationships. I wouldn't have formed that question in that way were it not for the learning circle and this group, so thank you!

Chris.

It's this kind of translation of the principles and practices, articulated as a question, which gives this form of coaching such unexpected and powerful extra 'teeth'. It can reach into spaces, simply with words, that other 'powerful questions' may miss by a hair's breadth. Chris and his client had a powerful experience of that subtle but important difference in language as a result of having learnt how to constellate.

Once you can do that, you can do a lot of effective work without even using representative objects or facilitating workshops. You are working inside out, outside in; you are coaching with the system in mind.

~

Beyond constellations are the kind of systemic questions illustrated above. Beyond those questions comes the ability, with time and experience, of constellating in your mind. In other words, while your client is talking you are listening for the system flags. You are then giving each a place, in your mind, in an imaginary constellation and observing what you notice.

As you facilitate a systemically-orientated conversation, you also facilitate the constellation in your mind, moving elements around and testing different positions. Sentences will come to you as a result of this process and you will notice how they impact different parts of the system. This is a good way of exploring options and illuminating possibilities. Be prepared to let them all go but don't be surprised if they turn out to be accurate and useful to your client.

It may be that you consider offering your client your inner picture; the constellation in your mind. You will know when the time is right.

We tend to blame each other or outside circumstances for our problems. But it is poorly designed systems, not incompetent or unmotivated individuals, that cause most organizational problems. Systems thinking shows us that there is no outside – it shows that you and the cause of your problems are part of a single system.

Peter Senge

FAQs (B): More answers to frequently asked questions

The questions here were asked as written, in workshops and trainings. The answers are based on those given at the time, then expanded or clarified for this book.

Say something more about 'place'. There seem to be a number of different ways you use the word.

Yes, the word 'place' is used in several ways here. It's a powerful and evocative word that can have several meanings. Here's the way I understand and use it.

- PLACE as in one of the organizing principles in systems:
  - Everything that has contributed to the system has a place and, if excluded without acknowledgement of the contribution made, will create an additional bond. Everyone and everything needs to have a unique and equally respected place in the system for it to thrive. When people, facts, products or services are denied their place, are excluded by force or deliberately not talked about, then they will be 're-membered' by the system.
  - When everything is acknowledged and given a place, the system will let go of those that have left, and the past can be integrated into the present and be useful in the future. This leaves the system and the leaders and others within it free to bring their individual and collective experience and skills to bear.

- Place as in finding your place in relationship to your client and their issues – your inner stance:
  - If you can maintain a place that enables you to scan all of the system to which the client belongs and listen for system flags, then you will be able to add significant value with systemic observations and interventions.
  - Staying in the neutral, 'useful rather than helpful' place is central to systemic coaching and constellations.
- Place as in knowing when you are in the right relationship or place to someone or something else:
  - Standing in a constellation, in a particular place, is an opportunity to have an embodied sense of an inner relationship structure and dynamic. The place where you find yourself standing in a constellation as a representative allows you to 'know' certain things you didn't have access to before.
  - Representatives have powerful embodied experiences and can report with great accuracy whether they are standing in the 'right' place or the 'wrong' place in relationship to the rest of the system. This same experience is felt by your client when they stand in the 'right' place in their own constellation and later their own system.
- Place as in everything in a system needing a safe and respected place in order to support organizational health:
  - Remember that it's not just people but also roles and purposes that need a respected place in the system. Roles must be created as a result of business purpose and needs, not around individuals. Each role must be recognized as equally valuable by the leaders and be given an appropriate and reliable place in the system. People who try to occupy a role that has not been given its right place, or who are asked to create a role around themselves, will usually burn out trying.
  - The purpose needs its place. Organizational systems can thrive when the purpose is acknowledged, shared and understood. When people establish a self-serving business connected to an unspoken personal purpose, the business will struggle to thrive and survive.
  - Money needs its place. Businesses don't survive without a constant supply of money and it is the job of the leaders to ensure that the people working within the system have a regard for the importance of money and its place in the system. This is especially true for non-profit organizations where money is often not given its place.

How can systemic coaching and constellations help align the coaching and the coachee with the overall business objectives or purpose?

- This can be done in both the contracting and the actual coaching:
  - When contracting it is useful to talk about 'working in service of the wider business system', rather than only the individual or team. This usually settles something in the coachee or team and allows them to expand their horizons and settle into their developmental journey.
  - When constellating, whether in a one-to-one or a workshop setting, put something in to represent the business objectives or purpose. It can also be useful to include a place for the customers. These are all good litmus tests of a 'good resolution' and help ensure that the wider system is included.
  - If the coaching is not working in service of and aligning with the organizational purpose, then you are working in service of the individual, not the system.

How can working with an individual affect the company-wide organizational health?

- It's true that if the coach simply *thinks* about the system, that alone may make little difference to how the client interacts with it and so affects it. However, this way of working requires something more than simply bearing the system in mind.
- To affect organizational health a systemic coach will need to challenge for the truth of the system. They will need to support their client to stand fully in their own responsibility (and where appropriate their own guilt) and think about how their actions and behaviours align with the organizing principles of systems and the purpose of this system.
- Supporting the coachee to see their own systems, the conscience groups they are loyal to and the entanglements they bring with them into the organizational system, changes the way they are as leaders.
- In this way the leadership community gradually learns about how systems are sustained and can grow, take full responsibly for their own individual actions but also for the wider system, and develop themselves in the context of the whole.
- As knowledge about what sustains systems increases, a kind of system homeostasis is created across the organizational system.

- Once this knowledge exists in the system, organizational health begins to flow and build. It becomes much harder for leaders to violate the natural organizing principles once they and those around them are aware of them. Something shifts in the individuals and the connections between them.

How would I introduce this work with a client?

- Ask if it is OK to 'look from another perspective'. There is no need to talk about 'constellations'. It's a way of thinking and working, an inner stance, not a tool that you need to name.
- You could call it mapping or 'creating a living map'. Most people are comfortable with that idea and will be willing to explore further.
- Ask: 'Would you like to see the issue rather than just talk about it?'
- Just start, respectfully and small, working within your experience. Know when and how to respectfully stop.
- Rather than talking about 'constellations', talk about working in the service of organizational health or working with 'the wider system in mind'.

In what ways is acknowledgement useful for leaders?

- Leaders who truly acknowledge and face into their difficulties build trust, loyalty and respect, because staff and customers alike know they can trust what the company says and their place in that system.
- Leaders who openly share the history, particularly the nature of the founding idea, and include all the difficult things that happened and the people who contributed along the way, alongside the success stories, create calm and productive systems.
- Whatever is excluded will hold a powerful energy that will distract until it is included. So acknowledge and give a place to everything (where you've come from) and everybody (who contributed to get you here) that has been excluded. Let it all back in, in order to let it all go with respect for its contribution.
- Leaders need to acknowledge and face into the truth of the system. That truth will be different for every organization and is often hard to discern.

How do I use this when working as an in-house coach?

- The hardest place to bring the insights and practices to life is when you are part of the system in which you are coaching or consulting. This is because you will inevitably have your own loyalties and entanglements within the system, and because you will have a different level of permission when working with others within the same system. As with any coaching, it will always be important to pay attention to contracting and psychological safety, and never more so than when in-house. When you are in-house, you are part of the system as well as a facilitator of it.

- There is, however, a great deal that can be done through the application of the stance that supports this way of working. When an internal consultant can find and establish a truly neutral stance, in service of the system in which they work, then they can add a great deal of value.
- Facilitating constellations with and for others in the same system can be a very effective way of separating out from the system and seeing it with fresh eyes. This can be done, after training, on a one-to-one basis and also in a workshop context for certain kinds of organizational issues.
- This privileged position requires a good grounding in system awareness so you can work within the system and yet stay free of it. Supervision will be particularly important in this context for this reason.

Tell me more about the principle of exchange in business systems.

In all interactions there needs to be a good balance of exchange. All systems will attempt to redress an imbalance of exchange – you can see this time and again in global politics and war, as well as in financial systems and at the personal level.

- A system is made up of a continuous series of exchanges that creates a dynamic balance. One part of the system gives, another takes. The taking is returned by giving and the giving is balanced by taking, each movement initiating a reciprocal movement.
- Too much giving (in terms of salary, recognition and reward, for example) weakens belonging and motivation just as much as too little giving does.

Sometimes I describe this organizing principle to clients in this way:

1st level of exchange (visible and conscious)

- What experience do your clients, suppliers and partners have of your business – are they getting what they want from the business and do they feel that they pay a fair price for it?
- This is the first level of exchange and it is relatively easy to see, to measure and to calibrate. It's vital to do so or your clients, partners and suppliers may feel that you don't value what you are offering or don't ask enough, or too much, for it in exchange.

2nd level of exchange (private)

- The second level of exchange is harder to see and exists between those who have given most, often the founders, and the business. Balancing the level of risk and responsibility they have taken is challenging but necessary.

- When this is not attended to, those that gave the most may begin to feel resentful and withdraw their energy and commitment, looking elsewhere for the right level of exchange. Founders often think they want to leave at this point. However, it is common for the motivation to fully return when the imbalance in exchange is really attended to.

3rd level of exchange (invisible and unconscious)

- When people join a business they do so under a formal contract of some kind – even those who are temporary know the level of pay they can expect in return. That's at the conscious and visible level of exchange.

- The other contract that's made when people join a business system is of course the psychological one. This is invisible, unwritten, unspoken and much harder to influence. It governs what someone is willing to offer a business and what they expect in return.

- Employees have their own set of unspoken expectations and will move their attention elsewhere if these are not met. This level of exchange is set entirely by the employee, and the employer may be completely unaware of it. Even the employee will not be fully aware of their own expectation – only discovering its importance after it has not been met or the unconscious contract has not been honoured.

- When looking for this kind of imbalance of exchange it can be useful to remember that underneath every complaint is a request. There are many unspoken or disguised requests that are informed by the unwritten expectations for exchange.

How can I use this work when exploring my 'personality type'?

- If your coachee (or your peers in a professional development context) is familiar with MBTI (or other similar models) then you can experiment with setting up the elements and see what you notice.

- For example, set up your 'dominant mental function' and then the other functions in relation to that.

- If you are doing this with peers, invite them to move, very slowly, in response to any feeling or inner movement they have.

- This will provide you with fresh information and open a window for a better inner alignment of your innate preferences.

- Then try to set up a current challenge or issue adjacent to this first map and see what impact one has on the other.

You can experiment – particularly when working with a coach/peers – with bringing your 'Belbin' or other reported type, 'influencing style', 'conflict style' or 'trait' into the constellations. These experiments always provide useful learning experiences and fresh insights.

How can I use this work when meeting a potential coachee or person who commissions coaches for the first time?

- Sharing insights from the perspective of the system can have a very positive effect at first meetings, as the simple truths of system thinking connect the potential coachee with their material, deeply. Organizations and coachees are looking for outstanding coaches with fresh insights and an ability to challenge the individualistic way of much coaching.
- You can do all this by asking system-relevant questions: about the past, the history of the role, the overall purpose of the company, who has contributed and left, how leadership and authority is expressed, and so on.
- You may also want to consider, for example, inviting the potential client (whether direct client or commissioner) to set up a simple map of 'what is' using found objects.

For example, you could say something like:

'OK, so if I've understood you correctly, you are saying that this leader is finding it challenging to find their place in the team with appropriate authority? To help us both get an even clearer picture of what might be going on, would you just choose something here – it could be your phone, that bottle of water or whatever – to represent the leader. Now, let's say that this piece of paper/area of the table is the team and the whole table is the company... where would each belong, just as they really are, not how you'd like it to be...?'

- Simply mapping the current situation will always reveal fresh information and insights. Then simply ask: 'What do you notice here?' This approach often reveals what the system is trying to show and the. underlying dynamics.

What other questions that respectfully open up the client's system could I ask when starting to use this approach?

- When hearing of an individual, team or organizational stuckness, ask: 'To whom (or to what) is this an act of loyalty, staying stuck like this?' (or 'Who would be pleased to see it like this?')

- When hearing of a difficulty in role (individual or team), ask: 'What happened to the previous person/team/role holder(s)?'
- When hearing of leadership difficulties with no apparent source, ask: 'Who has left this system in the past (and not been acknowledged for their contribution)?'
- 'To whom in the wider system around you/this does your question really belong?' (or 'Who else would recognize this pattern; this map of relationships?')
- Who was here before you?
- 'For what question is this the answer?' (or 'When you look at this pattern what first comes to mind?')
- 'What has been excluded here?' (or 'Is there anything/anybody else to be included here?')

These are just a few examples of the kind of questions that you can ask, in service of the system. If you contract with your clients by saying that you are 'working in service of the whole organizational system', then more questions and insights will begin to emerge naturally, for them and you.

Can I use this approach without having to physically 'map' or 'constellate'?

- Yes, very much so. The principles and practices can inform the way you listen, the way you respond and the way you coach. More important than actually constellating is the inner stance of the coach and the application of systemic insights through questions, observations on potential systemic dynamics and solutions.
- Start by asking systemically-orientated questions.
- There are several ways of carrying out 'systemic coaching' without using the processes of constellations. All of these depend on an understanding of the organizing forces that influence and sustain systems and the ability to voice system dynamics.
- However, the best way to learn how to do all this is to learn how to facilitate constellations first. Without that aspect you've only got one way of knowing: in your head.

Are constellation workshops always emotional?

- Because this approach evolved out of workshops exploring relationships in family systems, it developed a reputation for strong and intense emotional experiences. However, the issues in family constellation workshops are often to do with trans-generational trauma, loss, or a damaged or difficult connection between a parent and a child. Naturally these are emotional issues and the emotions expressed are often those of a child to its parents. Appropriate and healing levels of grief for loss and other emotions are therefore sometimes expressed.

- Family systems are by their very nature vast and almost timeless. Organizational systems are only ever temporary in the scale of things. For this and other reasons, overpowering emotions are not often a part of a workshop that's exploring coaching, leadership and organizational issues.

- When strong emotions are experienced it's a reflection of the strength of the bond or the depth of the trauma. If the bond is very strong in an organizational system, it often indicates a confusion or projection involving a family system issue or loyalty. If a personal issue emerges in a workshop setting it is respected and boundaried, and only explored with the explicit permission of the issue holder. In an organizational context, even a business issue with emotional intensity, resolutions can often be found with a light touch.

- The exception to this is constellations that include endemic bullying or organizational trauma, where there are likely to be strong emotions that rightly belong in the organizational system.

Can you use this approach as a catalyst for system-wide behavioural change?

- Yes. Remember that all behaviour makes sense in the context of the system in which it belongs. This is why system constellations are particularly useful in this context, as you can access the system and find out what is driving the organizational behaviours, and what the system requires in order to change them.

- This is a large and fascinating subject in itself and one of several topics within the wider subject of organizational health.

Can you describe some of the organizational applications of constellation workshops?

There are a wide variety of applications for this approach. Some are in development while others are tried and tested. They include the kind of organizational issue resolution we have been looking at here – exploring issues in a constellation workshop or one-to-one setting where neutral representatives, other members of the workshop are used to explore apparently intractable challenges, leadership questions, and team or abstract issues. However, it's also possible to use this approach for strategy development, where alternative strategies for the whole business, or teams within the business, can be explored through the use of constellations in workshop settings.

Any change in organizational structure creates significant systemic changes and associated dynamics. For example, in mergers and acquisitions, leaders and their coaches can gain fresh insights into how the restructuring can be best achieved. They can see what conditions are required for successful merger or growth through a workshop designed to illuminate the dynamics and best potential outcomes through constellations.

There are also a number of ways of gaining fresh consumer and other stakeholder insights using constellations. For example, a number of alternative products or hierarchies of different products can be tested. This kind of work is also often done in a workshop setting where there are plenty of available and 'neutral' human representatives.

There is also a significant amount of work being done around brand development with 'branding constellations'. Branding constellations offer brand owners opportunities to test brands and brand developments.

~

Please explore the Appendix at the end of this book for links to other expressions of the work and further resources.

"THIS IS WHERE I COME FROM"

The F word
Familiar patterns

12

It begins with your family,
soon it comes around to your soul.

'SISTERS OF MERCY' BY LEONARD COHEN

Exploring the resource available in the family-of-origin

This approach originated and was first applied in the context of family systems. Applying it in coaching does not require that you train as a therapist or in the application of family system constellations. Some experience, however, as a representative in another's constellation, and exploring your own issues, is useful. Many coaches training in this approach attend family constellation workshops to experience and benefit from the application of this approach in that context. Any training in systemic coaching and constellations for coaches will generally include a module that addresses family systems and the family system of the coach.

In this chapter I want to give just a flavour of what's possible in terms of resourcing yourself and then, if and when appropriate, in one-to-one coaching, your clients. We will come back to that in a moment, but for now let's start with us; with ourselves as coaches.

We all come from systems, the first of which has the most influence over our life and work: our family system. Many people, coaches included, try to move away from this simple truth in an attempt to distance themselves from their origins, in an attempt to become free.

Fill your own cup first

Most coaches are interested, by definition, in personal and professional development. Not all are lucky enough to experience their family-of-origin as a resource or strength. Some are deeply entangled in complex, often painful, family dynamics. After all, no one escapes some difficulty and confusion in their young life, and many people who offer support and guidance to others are looking for something similar themselves.

> When we struggle to internalize our source, our parents, we struggle to internalize our value and success and we may find ourselves feeling under-resourced in life and work.

This area – exploring the impact of where we come from and receiving what was available from there – is important. The clearer we are about who we are and where and how we belong, the more resourced we will be as coaches. Attending to this area allows us to support our clients in a particular way. When we can access the resource in our family system we can develop and embody a sustainable capacity to live, work and lead.

The dynamics that are alive in us as a result of our relationship with our parents as a child, and how we hold them in our hearts and minds as adults, play out, of course, in our work as coaches. Coaches, just like every other human being, will often repeat, in life and at work, the very same dynamics that they are blind to in their origins. This can lead to frustration, a sense of stuckness, and even exhaustion from supporting others' journeys.

Bert Hellinger originally identified what he called 'orders of love' as a way of describing the organizing forces he kept seeing at work in families through family constellations. These are orders that sustain systems and are designed to keep them coherent. These ordering forces serve love in families, the flow of love and the passing on of life. They are invisible forces that only manifest when they are aligned or violated.

When our family-of-origin systems are out of alignment with one or more of these natural ordering forces, the effects will be experienced by us but also, in subtle ways, by our clients, in the way we work. Simplifying a large subject for the purposes of this very brief summary and in the context of coaching, we may feel under-resourced as coaches in particular ways. Becoming entangled with our clients and their issues in ways that confuse and cost us, and may also weaken them, is one of many ways that the sense of not being resourced by our origins may manifest.

It's important to acknowledge that people who have a particular wounding, in this example a difficulty finding a secure place to rest back into, often make extremely effective coaches and consultants, particularly for clients or whole companies with the same dynamic. Similarly, coaches who have had an individual excluded from their family system or endured an imbalance of exchange in their family system can become very skilful in seeing the same patterns in their clients and organizational systems.

> Our wounding is a source of insight and clarity so it is very often the source of our core strength, particularly when it's conscious and the coach is illuminating it and opening up to it with compassion and understanding for its source.

The concept of 'the wounded helper' is well understood, after all. However, if coaching with your wounding or pattern in your unconscious, you may be drawn in to 'help' clients and you will pay a price for that through feelings of isolation and exhaustion. You will also risk making clients helpless, attached to you and weaker. As we've already touched on earlier, the purpose of systemic coaching and constellations is to support strength and freedom in our clients.

If you choose to explore any of the challenges and dynamics you face in this area, you could of course do so in a family systems environment (one-to-one or workshop-based) using constellations. This provides the double benefit of learning more about the methodology, underpinning principles and processes, while also illuminating and perhaps beginning to resolve your own wounding.

There are so many dynamics in families and so many possible combinations that, in this book, I'm going to focus our thinking right down into one area. How to access the resources in our family-of-origin system, especially when we don't feel that there are many available.

As a first step you may like to read the brief meditative exercise that follows. It is designed to be a first step towards finding your place in your family-of-origin and accessing the resources that are available, no matter what your circumstances are. This is not a 'family constellation', though the language will be familiar to those who attend family constellation workshops, rather it is a reflective process where you are invited to imagine your family-of-origin in a way which resources you.

The meditation allows two inner movements. The first in connection with your family-of-origin and the second with your coaching clients. Give yourself time and don't go further than you feel comfortable with.

This exercise is designed to resource you and so its focus is on receiving what is available from behind you and uses the system orientated sentences that you are by now familiar with. So, when looking back into your origins this is not an invitation to express pain, blame or hurt, nor to offer forgiveness, but rather an opportunity to go deeper, beyond those judgements, opinions and stories and into something else. Deeper into the resources that are available. That is not to say that difficult memories and emotions may emerge but if they do then offer this kind of sentence that allows you to acknowledge what is and then continue with the meditation. 'I realize that what's between us is not yet resolved. I will hold my part respectfully and when the time is right, return.'

Exercise: Receiving what's available

Note: You may like to record yourself reading this and then listen to it with your eyes closed as a kind of meditation.

Part One

Imagine yourself standing in the centre of a large circular and warmly lit space. You feel safe and comfortable.

Now, slowly turn and face the other way. When you feel ready allow an image of your parents, just as they are or were, to emerge in front of you. They are standing at just the right distance from you, a distance that feels safe and comfortable. Allow the story of who and what they were to soften and see them just as two people who, together, created you.

As you stand and look, they begin to look back. Acknowledging the principle of PLACE, say something that states 'what is', the simple truth of your life. Perhaps it will be something like this:

- 'This is where I come from.'

- 'As my parents you stand behind me and as your child I stand in front of you.'

Notice the impact of these words on you and on them.

Take a moment to reflect on the principles again and acknowledge the simple truths of TIME. Like this perhaps:

- 'As my parents you came first and as your child I came later.'

- 'Together you created me, you gave me life.'

Notice the impact of these words on you and on them.

If you'd like to, imagine your mother's parents standing behind her, then your father's parents behind him. Your grandparents, just as they are or were. Passing life on. Their parents behind them, your ancestors. Each has their PLACE in this family system. Imagine saying to your parents:

- 'You came from your parents and they came from theirs, together connecting us back to the mystery of the source of life.'

- 'If it wasn't for all of you I would never have been here.'

Notice the impact of these words on you and on them.

Next, you may like to reflect on what you are able to receive with gratitude from your parents as well as what can be left with them with respect for the source of the difficulty. Try and offer sentences to embody these aspects, pending context and appropriateness, using suggestions from this structure.

Acknowledging what has been received:

- 'My life came through you. Thank you.'

- 'Thank you for what you passed on to me. My life.'

Acknowledging what is being kept:

- 'What I take from you, and keep with thanks, is... '(eg strengths, qualities, looks, intelligence, values, attitudes etc).

Notice the impact of these words on you and on them.

Acknowledging what is being respectfully left with them:

- 'What I leave with you, with great respect, is...' (issues you have been carrying or trying to resolve for them, or behaviours that you learnt from them that you'd like to soften or change). *Note* that 'with respect' in this context means with respect for where these difficult issues or behaviours came from, from behind them, from a trauma or entanglement that happened in the system around them.

In these cases you may perhaps also like to add:

- 'I was trying to help, but I'm just the child. I will leave you to stand in your own difficulties. And to stand in your own strength.'

Notice the impact of these words on you and on them.

Acknowledging what is being done with the gift of life they have given you and the opportunities you now have:

- 'What you gave me, my life, is enough.
  I will do the rest myself. Thank you.'

- 'I will make good use of the gifts you have given me.'

- 'I have opportunities that were not available to you. Please smile on me as I take them and enjoy living my life fully, in a way that may not have been possible for you.'

Notice the impact of these words on you and on them.

Look at your parents, your grandparents, and if you choose to, all they come from behind them then notice who smiles on you, who is available as a resource for you, who gave you even more than life but something else as well. Breathe it all in, just as it is.

When it feels appropriate to do so imagine yourself turning back, with your family-of-origin behind you and facing forwards again. Feel the resources behind you.

Part Two

If you'd like to go a little further, imagine all your teachers, your personal and professional guides standing each side of you in an order that feels resourcing for you. All those who have been of significance on your journey to here, to your work as a coach. Imagine that each of them holds a gift for you – the gift of what they shared with you when you knew them. Take a moment to look to your left and right and thank them with a nod of your head as they give you their gifts in a way which resources and strengthens you. Notice who smiles on you, who is offering which resources and breathe in all that is offered to you.

As you look over your shoulder and to each side of you say 'Thank you'.

Notice the impact of these words on you and on them all.

Your clients have now emerged into the space in the other half of the room. They are at a distance that enables you to see them all. Get a sense of the resources behind you, look over your shoulder again if you'd like to, look to each side and then bring your attention back to your clients.

Look into their eyes, stay a while with those with whom you have a difficult or challenging relationship. Feel the resources available around you and look again.

If you feel able to, say something like this:

'Because of what I have behind and around me I am deeply resourced.'

Notice the impact of these words on you and on them.

If you do try this exercise for yourself, either simply in your 'mind's eye' or using floor markers, give yourself time because you are looking at one of the most important connections a person has in this map of your family system.

> Understanding the impact of your own family system, the hidden dynamics, loyalties and entanglements within it, is one of the most effective ways of understanding this approach and what you bring and can offer as a coach.

That short meditation is designed to start to illuminate the relevance of the systemic principles of TIME, PLACE and EXCHANGE in your family system. It's important to note that in family systems the organizing principle of EXCHANGE works differently to that in the workplace. In families, for life and love to flow it needs to travel in one direction. Parents give and children receive. This however is not always the case. Here are some further notes about this important dynamic.

Difficulties with the balance of EXCHANGE

- Some children feel that they didn't get enough from their parents. A sense of being owed something persists throughout their lives and creeps into their work as a coach.
- A child who grows into a professional coach may need to attend to this dynamic or face feelings of resentment and being owed by their clients. They may feel that whatever they can pay them, in financial and feedback terms, is never enough.
- These coaches may burn out trying to establish a balance of giving and receiving. They may set themselves up to be too available, too used, and become exhausted. They give their clients and their relationships too much with the hope that their needs will be met.
- Some coaches may find themselves parenting their clients. Perhaps the nurturing they needed to receive as children wasn't there because the parent had a greater need. So instead of receiving from their parents, they give and give.
- When we can take from our parents what we need and leave the rest with them, with respect, we can become full enough from what came before to pass forward what is needed in front of us.
- If you notice yourself giving your clients too much, you may find that your clients know that they cannot balance for what you have given.

"THANK YOU"

In these cases they may become distant or inaccessible or may leave the coaching process. You become too big (like a parent) and they become too little (like a child).

- Such coaches may also risk becoming lonely. They become 'big' and everybody depends on them to sort things out, but they also become unreachable and may burn out trying to help, fix or befriend everybody.

This chapter, the many other books available on the 'family system constellations' approach and the workshops and trainings offered worldwide provide a resource for those who are interested in exploring and illuminating these important issues more deeply. They offer the opportunity to start a different journey into a way of receiving what's available, from the source and far beyond.

> *For each one of us, the source is, first of all, our parents. If we are connected to our parents, we are connected to our source. A person who is separated from his or her parents is separated from his or her source. Whoever the parents are, however they behaved, they are the source of life for us. So the main thing is that we connect to them in such a way that what comes from them can flow freely to us and through us to those who follow.*
> Bert Hellinger, a workshop in New York, June 2011

Your client's family system

An important aspect of systemic leadership is recognizing the impact that your family-of-origin, the family you were born into, has on your leadership style. This is a large subject and one that is under-represented in organizational development and leadership. We all had our first experience of systems in our family of origin and that has a significant impact on how we operate in business systems. After all, the family system is the key pattern maker for the rest of our lives and work, and all patterns repeat themselves until the source is illuminated.

I would just say that it is always useful and leads to significantly higher levels of self-awareness and emotionally intelligent leadership if leaders have done *some* work in looking at their place in their family-of-origin. This work could explore how they experienced their place in their family, and how that maps over their current role and performance, particularly how it affects their leadership style.

It's especially important, for example, for a leader to be able to tolerate a slightly different level of 'belonging' than others in the system. Leaders need to be able to tolerate the loneliness of system leadership. Those who come from secure and rooted families may find this easier than others who hold onto their position or place in an organization as part of their security and identity; as a way of belonging.

> *As long as we reject, exclude or devalue parents or other members of our family, we are forced, whenever we enter other social fields, to repeat, to continue and to re-enact our struggle.*
>
> Albrecht Mahr

When people get confused about the difference between family systems and business systems, as they often do, it causes difficulties for employer and employee alike. Inappropriate expectations are placed on the business system, which it can't possibly meet. Understanding this is important for people in business because, unlike in families, membership of the business system is, by definition, temporary.

So how do we as coaches offer support to clients and assist them in identifying their family-of-origin as a resource without 'doing therapy'? What I've found useful to share with clients, if and when the context and permission are present, are two simple truths:

- All you need from your parents is life. They've already given you that.
- If you can't receive life from your parents, you will have difficulty resourcing yourself to lead others. You will not be connected to your primary source.

Resourcing clients through their family-of-origin

I realize that a number of coaches sense that any work in the family or personal arena is somehow 'out of bounds' and that it requires a therapeutic training. This is a view I've consistently resisted as I think it excludes a vast depth of resource that can be the catalyst for breakthrough coaching. Nothing in this book or in this example requires training as a therapist, but a strong and growing awareness in the coach of their own family system dynamics, and sensitivity to the whole system and what's important to the client. Using the family system as a resource isn't therapy; it's resourcing. It simply requires an understanding that unless we honour each person who has contributed to our existence, we will struggle to find the lasting resource we need in life, in coaching or in leadership.

As a subtle distinction, and I hope a useful starting point, there's often a need for connection with our same-sex parent that requires particular attention. Put simply, men who are not resourced by their father, who are in deep conflict with him or refuse to take from him, will struggle in certain ways in life and work. Similarly, women who are not in 'good contact' with their mothers may find areas of their life and work where they experience stuckness, anger or pain. Above all, both will find it hard to know what to 'lean back into' when searching for strength or fresh resource.

While it's true that to flourish a child needs to trust and feel able to resource themselves from both parents in order to feel their own strength and sense of identity, as we grow into adults a different kind of taking in, to address and resource leadership, can become necessary. There is a sense of drawing strength by 'leaning back into' our same-sex parent. Using objects or floor markers in one-to-one coaching, it's possible to open up to this possibility. What follows are two examples of this, firstly for a male and then for a female client.

David Presswell wrote this next case study when he was Head of Coaching at YSC, a talent assessment and development consultancy working with a large number of FTSE 100 and Fortune 500 companies. He maintains a systems-orientated stance throughout his work and regularly employs constellation techniques in his one-to-one coaching. In this example, David describes using floor markers to work with a talkative client whose search is for a more grounded authority in their role. Despite the story of how things are, the client's family-of-origin proves to be a surprising and enduring source of strength and resource.

A line of men

Coach: David Presswell, executive coach and team facilitator
Client: Michael

Michael placed the floor marker for himself opposite the marker for his team. He took time to step into and tune into his felt sense in both positions.

'This isn't working for them,' he said. 'They can see what I'm asking for, but they feel observed and judged – as though I could do it better than any of them.'

'How about you move your marker behind them – in support, leading them from behind?'

He took this position, but soon started swaying uneasily, losing his sense of physical balance and inner authority. 'It feels too uncomfortable,' he said. 'Right for them, but somehow too much for me.'

We were three sessions into an executive coaching intervention aimed at supporting Michael to find his feet following a very significant promotion. Still in his mid-thirties, he was a 'high-flier' whose technical skills were not in doubt, but whose ability to find and hold his leadership authority was subject to constant, inner misgivings.

Much of the coaching conversation had focused on his insistence on putting other people's needs ahead of his own. In the previous session I found myself asking him for ways in which he was similar to or connected with his father. The question brought him to a quieter, reflective place and he said that he simply had no idea. He told me how his father would go into depressive cycles, mainly triggered by alcohol, and that Michael had spent much of his childhood trying to talk him out of bars and pubs – trying to rescue, save and fix him.

I heard about his grandfather, a missionary in Africa who he described as a 'hard man'. His grandfather had sent his son – Michael's father – to boarding school, aged nine, on a one-way ticket. I also heard about Michael's wife, a woman from a very different culture, and the many ways in which he tried to fit in with her family's customs.

When I asked him what *his* needs were, again there was silence. He simply couldn't tell me. I suggested he might talk to others who knew him and see if they recognized this theme of 'self-sufficiency' in him. He came back really surprised at just how much his wife and his mother saw him as someone who invariably put other people's needs first.

A pattern was emerging. From a systemic point of view there was an imbalance, a difficulty with exchange – the balance of 'giving and receiving'. It seemed that the father had not received what he needed, emotionally, from the grandfather, and may have been using alcohol to numb the longing to connect. Meanwhile, Michael was also blocking this exchange through his refusal to receive and therefore, perhaps, struggling to find the inner resources to fully occupy his role in leading his team.

I encouraged Michael to work on 'actions' to help shift this. As a result, and after some time, he asked his younger brother to join him in the support of their father, and was amazed by how touched his brother was to do so. Then he wrote to his father telling him how, with the imminent arrival of his first child, he had to place his own family first, but also of the gratitude he genuinely felt for the start his father had given him in life. His father responded with one of the most emotionally open conversations they had ever had – he was both relieved and delighted. He felt their relationship had dramatically shifted.

But, back in the room, Michael was struggling. 'It's too much,' he repeated, still swaying with uncertainty.

I could see he needed resourcing, but it felt like a risk to do what I was tempted to do and bring his 'weak' father in to support. In my coaching work I had not previously grafted a personal and organizational constellation together so overtly.

'I'd like you to notice,' I said, 'what happens when I place behind you a marker representing your male line – first your father and then your grandfather. They came first, before you, and you followed. These are the men behind you. This is where you come from.'

The swaying steadied, and then stopped. For a while he drank in this new sensation, the experience of simply standing in the truth of what is, without judgement. 'Yes, I can feel them there, for me. Supporting me.' He turned to them and, without prompting, bowed in respect and gratitude. After some more reflection he slowly turned back. He was standing noticeably taller and stronger.

After a while I invited him to notice the floor markers representing his team. 'How is that for your team?'

In his mind's eye, he said, he could see their experience and diversity and feel himself enjoying that, trusting it. He could see himself encouraging them to be the best *they* could be: sometimes he was guiding, sometimes coaching, sometimes directing. He could feel the connection from behind him and he could imagine leading with a more settled, enabling authority.

Flow was coming back into his system, his *whole* system. A couple of months later, as we concluded the sessions, the shift in both his leadership and his relationships with the team remained.

When I invited David to contribute a case study for this book, he contacted his former client to request permission and to check for accuracy, as these sessions were held two years before this book was published. What he discovered was that not only had Michael continued to occupy his authority as a grounded and rounded senior team leader, but that his father had completely stopped drinking since the reconnection and big conversation with his son.

In connecting with his father in a new way, as his son, and allowing him to stand in his authority as a father, his own authority had emerged and endured. He had also given in return a great gift to his brother and father, his family system. He, his father, and his team leadership were flourishing.

Although the benefits of this approach, brought to life through this example, may be experienced and described as 'therapeutic', David is not a therapist and was not attempting to 'do therapy'. He is an executive coach with a range of perspectives and approaches at his disposal. His intervention was simply to resource his client in the simplest, most essential of ways. It required no more than the understanding that until we can take in life from where it naturally comes, just as it is, we will struggle to resource ourselves in life, work and leadership.

~

In this next case study, involving a writer who'd been experiencing a sense of inertia, it gradually became clear, over a number of sessions, that this particular same-sex resourcing might be at the root of a fuller resolution. This case study was written by the client herself, a professional writer. Please see the final image in the block of photographs in this book that was taken during the coaching session.

The heart of the matter

Coach: John Whittington, London, UK
Client: A writer

I've always known where I come from: a warm, loving family with parents whose lives revolved largely around their children, and siblings who loved each other growing up, and still do. My father was a large, warm man, expressive, clear, intelligent, enquiring. Everything in our lives happened around him. He was the central figure of my childhood. My mother was always to my child's eye somewhat eclipsed by him, despite her gentle lasting presence underpinning him and our home.

As children we were governed by an ethic of loving kindness, of endeavour, of thinking, of doing, and especially of doing one's best. It was a home that thought about itself, reflected on its past, with my father tirelessly capturing in scrapbooks, recollections, journals, letters, the tiny histories that make up a family's identity. If ever there was a disruption in our house, it was only ever ultimately about the management of love.

Despite having carried this knowledge of my family throughout my adult life, I arrived in my late forties stranded from myself. I was successful in my chosen career, and although without children of my own, I was in a good relationship, with children in it. My parents had both passed on in my thirties, several years apart, my father first. The grief of their loss revisited me silently every day. I had not found the modern alchemy to turn the pain into acceptance, or been able to find the healing elements meant to be contained within the passing of time. For grief is love robbed of its object, love without its resting place.

My first (slightly self-conscious) encounter of working with constellations helped me to take a look again at my nuclear family. Once I got over the oddness of seeing them through the constellation process, I was surprisingly quickly able to integrate my girlhood with the woman I had become, in part by re-acknowledging my place as the youngest in the family, and recognizing the safety, protection and strength this gave me.

This prompted important discoveries outside the coaching process. I found a letter my father had written to me when I was a young woman, exhorting me to turn my life to writing. To dedicate myself to it. 'Do what you are good at,' he said. The letter of almost 30 years ago was a study in benign paternal guidance, unwittingly itself a poem of sorts.

Reading the letter again now I wondered why I had not taken his advice. His permission had always been so important to me. And so I put my toe in the water.

I wrote a little. It came like black gold. From nowhere. Unbidden. Satisfying. Like an act of love.

Other people liked my writing and told me to get on with it. It was obvious to them that this is what I should be doing.

But I could not sustain it. I side-lined it. I put other tedious career matters before it. Despite my father's explicit permission, I could not justify it to myself as a proper way to occupy myself. Writing, surely, was a life for artists and fools. The sense of paralysis, indecision, incompleteness stayed with me.

Further one-to-one coaching constellations brought me back to the family. And this time I saw her. My mother stepped forward, or rather emerged from behind everyone else. There was nothing in the space between me and her. I saw her revealed. Her individuality. I remembered her.

I recalled the beauty of her in old age. The curves and turns of her body in the late summer of her frailty. The delicacy of her feminine lines. The same body that had held mine within it and let me go. My genesis. My source. I felt an unexpressed pain that I had not loved her enough, could not make something unnamed up to her, slip and lose its grip on me. I saw myself through her eyes, satisfied with me, not because of anything I had done or achieved, but because I had once been her baby, and was, for eternity, her youngest daughter.

I saw that there was a type of love that could only ever flow one way, from her to me. That I was helpless before her love. And that this love still flows. Here, today, through an unbreakable umbilical, stronger than life, stronger than death. I saw her peacefulness with me as her child. Everything else in her life belonged to her, her own loves, griefs, successes, disappointments. But I was her daughter. My job was done, and had been the day I was born.

The constellation grew. Behind my mother, her mother appeared, and in turn the line of women behind her extended. Generations of them. Each one of them a part of me, and me an un-mined fragment of them. I moved slowly, respectfully, up the line of women, showing each of them my writing, my book. I heard them say 'We've been waiting for you. We knew you were coming.' And I said to them 'I know your stories.' And they said 'Take up your place in this line. You belong in this line, you are part of it. Now live, and then pass it on, like we have done before you.'

Today I consciously carry things of my mother's that I love and cherish: behind my bright exterior, I have her seriousness. Beyond my wayward feelings, which carry me this way and that, I have her dispassionate eye. Underneath my paralysing desire to conform, her often irreverent heart still beats with mine, that longing to blow a gun-powdered hole in the midnight sky. And contained within my acute need to belong, her preference for separateness endures in me.

I still come from that loving family with my remarkable father, my loving mother and my caring siblings. They are the same people, and the truth of my family has not changed. But my understanding of where I belong in it has shifted. I understand my place in it. And I see my mother standing in her own light. Most powerful has been to see the eternal, unbreakable, undamaged connection to my mother, which in turn connects me profoundly to myself and my own true abilities. The writing flows.

In the final case study of this book we get a first glimpse of what's possible when you facilitate a constellation, at the request of your client, which goes beyond resourcing by same-sex parent. In this example leadership development coach Wendy, who works with senior leaders in large corporate organizations, finds herself with a client who asks for more personal work. Wendy has completed only the first two modules of the training journey and has no therapeutic training or desire to be a therapist.

In letting the client's permission-giving guide her, and trusting that she can hold a safe place, she facilitates a remarkable and very effective piece of work in this one-to-one setting. Using movements initiated by the client and sentences emerging from the system she steps through a process that leaves her client less entangled from a complex family system dynamic.

This case study is written in the format of the template we provide for students who are applying to complete their systemic coach training on the Practitioner journey. As with all the case studies in this book the client's name has been changed and they have agreed to publication.

The flow of love

Coach: Wendy Bedborough, London, UK
Client: Anna

Context

I had worked with Anna three years previously and she had asked to come back for some personal coaching. She had outlined her objectives for the coaching, which highlighted four areas where she wanted to make progress and was feeling stuck. Against each of these she had identified how she would evidence her progress.

What I noticed

Only one of the areas was related to her work. The other three were more personal. One that jumped off the page at me was 'to find love/let love find me' – and she had noted the following four points as how it would be evident to her:

- I am open to the possibility (of love);
- I allow myself to be vulnerable and strong;
- I feel safe;
- I will heal my 14-year-old self.

From my previous contact with her I was aware that her parents had divorced around the time she started secondary education, and that she had divided loyalties to many members of her family. I sensed that Anna was not going to make lasting progress on her objectives until she had better integrated her past. I felt that she needed to get more of a sense of place in her family, and re-align the balance of EXCHANGE – what she had given and what she had received.

How I offered

We had a telephone conversation to discuss her coaching objectives, and I told her that I thought she might benefit from working from a systemic perspective. I chose to explain this as 'invisible forces' that impact us that we are often unaware of and used the analogy of a magnet and its invisible force field, which moves iron filings. She was open to trying 'something new', and we agreed to meet for a face-to-face session.

What I did

At the start of the session we talked about her coaching objectives, and I shared with her what had struck me when I read them. I had highlighted the sheet – and asked her what she noticed when she looked at the page. Her reaction was to say: 'What an emotional wreck I am.' I asked again if she was willing to work in a different way, and whether she would be open to looking at her relationship system. She agreed, and I talked first about all the people in her history, what was behind her, and how these people might have an impact on how she is today.

Anna spoke of her connection to her grandmother, and how she had fairly cool relationships with her parents and her sister, and hardly any relationship with her half-brother from her father's second marriage.

I talked briefly about the principle of TIME and she drew a 'family line' (the order of her grandparents, parents and siblings) and then I asked if she would like to make a physical representation, a map of her family relationships. We used Lego people and even a Lego building plate to provide the boundary.

FIGURE 1

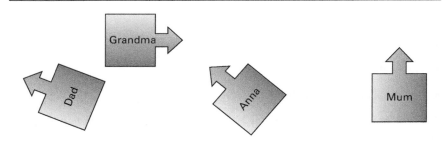

I asked Anna to identify who she thought was important to work with; initially she identified her parents and paternal grandmother. I asked her to place the figures in a place that felt right for her, along with a representative of herself (Figure 1).

FIGURE 2

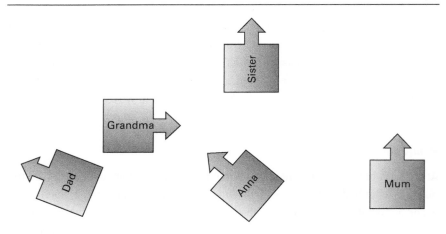

When she had done this I asked her whether anyone else was important and she added her sister – who she placed lying down and facing away (Figure 2). I asked: 'What do you notice as you look at this?' She was silent for a while before saying: 'Two things. I am stuck in the middle of this, and my sister and my mum need to move!'

After some reflection time I invited her to slowly and mindfully move them to a place that felt real for her. She did so, turning them more towards each other (Figure 3). Her sister was still lying down. Again I asked: 'What do you notice?' She said: 'How angry I feel!' I remained silent and held the space for her.

FIGURE 3

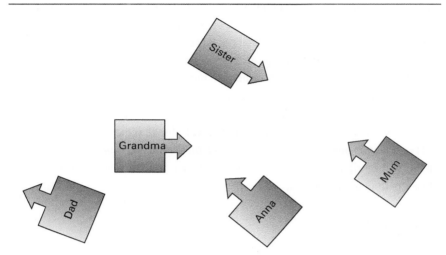

She continued: 'My mum really supports my sister as she constantly plays the victim, and she is always asking me to support her too, and my sister expects this from both of us. That's why she is lying down – she is incapable of standing on her own two feet! I support Grandma, and my sister never does! Dad does a bit, but not enough – he expects me to do it too. I feel like I am supporting everyone and no one is there for me.' I remained silent as she kept looking at the figures. 'Grandma used to be there for me when I was younger and I do want to be there for her – but I don't think it should just be me'.

I asked Anna if she knew when she had taken on this supporting role and she started to cry. It was a while before she could say it was about the time of her parents' divorce. I asked if she would like to try some 'special sentences'. We tried one or two until we found the ones that resonated. To each parent individually she said: 'I've taken on the role of parenting when it didn't belong to me. Now I am ready to give it back to you and be your adult child.' After saying this, there was a noticeable change in her physiology – she sat up straighter, and her breathing seemed both deeper and lower.

I asked if there anything else she needed to say, and she said 'Lots' and laughed. I waited to see what would emerge and she said: 'Dad, I will always love my grandma, and I will always care for her – but it is not right for you to expect me to take responsibility for her.' She paused for a moment before saying to me: 'I feel better already, but I need to say something to my sister.' I waited while she looked at the constellation. Then she said: 'For too long I have tried to be both mother and father to you, and I realize that's not fair to you or me – you are an adult who can make her own decisions and I'm not here to be used as your escape.' Her shape 'shifted' again and I was aware of the changing tensions in her body – I asked if there was anything else that needed to be said and she began to cry. She said she was so angry with all of them and she felt very foolish that she had allowed herself to be so entangled for so long. I sensed the tears were healing her 14-year-old self.

I asked: 'Is it possible that the representative of you on the table is the young girl who was caught up in the drama of her parents' divorce?' She nodded. I suggested that she try the following sentence: 'I've stayed here too long, and now it's time for me to move forward into the strong, independent woman I am.' (See my reflections and learning points below.) She said that saying that would feel like she was abandoning them and she didn't want to do that, so I asked what would feel the right thing to say or move to make. For a while we sat in silence while she thought about it all.

FIGURE 4

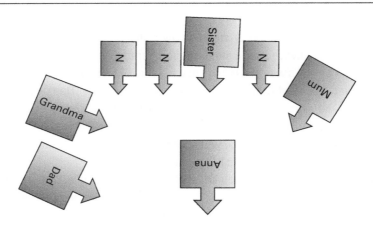

She then said she had forgotten to include her nieces and nephew and they should be there too (Figure 4).

After this everyone was moved: her father closer to his mother, and her mother closer to her sister and her grandchildren. She stood her sister up between her children, and then moved herself so that she was looking away from them, and at a distance. I asked what she noticed as she did this – and she became very still.

She said: 'This might sound really weird, but I feel a huge sense of relief – as though a heavy weight has been lifted from my shoulders. I know that they will all be OK and that I don't have to be there for them all of the time. It is bizarre but it is as though something has released me – I don't quite know how to articulate it.'

FIGURE 5

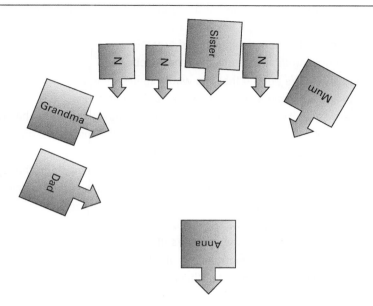

I asked her to just notice what she noticed, and feel what she felt, while considering if any other changes needed to be made. She just looked at the constellation for a while, and then she slowly moved the representative for herself, putting a little more distance between herself and the others (Figure 5). I asked, 'What's happening?' She said that she was ready to move forward, and she just knew that they would all be encouraging her to do that. She was smiling widely. I asked her if there was a sentence that felt appropriate for her to say.

After some quiet reflection she said: 'I allowed myself to be caught up in the tangle of your divorce, and I took on too much. We are all adults now and I am ready to move forward in a different way.' I suggested that she also say: 'I will take responsibility for me and leave your responsibilities to you.' She did this and then added: 'Know that I still love you all.'

For a while she was still and silent, and then she said: 'That feels so different, I feel lighter.' I asked her if she felt she had done enough, and she said she had. I encouraged her to take the constellation apart in a way that she felt was right for her, and she very carefully removed every representative and placed them back in the box they had come from.

Benefits, observations and integration

After the constellation, we moved away from the table and Anna reported feeling much more relaxed and 'somehow lighter'. I asked her what else she noticed, if anything, and she said she was excited about what might happen in the future. She said she was a little 'scared' of being on her own, and yet she had a new sense of strength and courage.

I had observed her body language and breathing as she shifted her 'shape' – she was not holding as much tension in her upper body and her breathing was slower and lower. We agreed that she would spend some time reflecting on the experience and take time to notice what was different for her.

As a practitioner it was comforting to notice how receptive my coachee was to trying something new and the relative ease in which the 'sentences' came to her and also to me. I felt no attachment to my sentences, and was happy when she changed them to what felt just right for her. The entanglements in this system seemed obvious to me, although I am sure there was an element of luck involved and I was delighted by the ease of using this systemic approach.

I learned that by observing the client I could interpret whether or not a shift had taken place – and sometimes the shift was obvious and sometimes more subtle. I sense that as I have the opportunity to practise my systemic work I will gain confidence and be able to develop further.

My learning

I was reflecting on this session later and in particular when I had offered the sentence *I have stayed here far too long, and now it is time for me to move forward into the strong independent woman I am.* This movement forward was clearly too soon for the client, and she rejected the sentence. Perhaps if I had stayed with 'what is' (the pain of the divorce) I could have offered a sentence something more like: *When you separated it hurt me and I didn't know who to be loyal to* – allowing her to voice her truth and simply stay alongside her as she processed it.

I also noticed how I was working beyond the explicit goal and how the softening of the underlying family system issue was likely to free up her emotional energy to make a connection with a loving partner when the time was right.

Follow-up

At our next coaching session Anna reported that she had been in contact with both her parents and it had been 'easy' for her in a way that it had not been before. She commented that she felt much less anxiety in relationship to her grandmother, and that her sister had called her out of the blue which was a big surprise. This conversation with her sister in particular had amazed her as she had offered to do things for her mum and grandmother for the first time Anna could recall. In summarizing the impact of the constellations she said the whole session had a 'touch of magic about it' and that she couldn't fully articulate just how much positive impact it had.

Anna has since reported that the relationships with her family have changed positively, especially with her father, who she feels is now providing appropriate parental support to her. She requested more systemic coaching, as she finds that it enables her to 'get out of her head', to 'stop analysing and thinking so much' and to focus on what she is feeling. She also commented that this way of working enables her to explore her issues and problems with the safety of knowing that she can move the representatives and 'try out' different relationship patterns, sensing which feels possible and what inner shift is required, before making commitments or taking actions.

~

The simplest and deepest ways of acting are in the family, from the father to the mother in relation to the children, and from the children in relation to their parents. These are the greatest and deepest actions, and are the basis for all others.

A person who is in harmony with his fatherhood, or her motherhood, or partnership, childhood, brotherhood or sisterhood, and simply takes on the tasks that emerge from this, is one who brings his or her self to completion. It is in these simple acts that an individual can be fulfilled. In such acts, there is a sense of being in quiet harmony with something great. There's no propaganda, no dogma, and no moral demands – those are all meaningless in this context.

From an interview with Bert Hellinger in the book
Acknowledging What Is

An invitation

This is an invitation to self-facilitate a second part of your own constellation, as a 'bookend' to the opening exercise.

Return to or recreate the map you made in the first part of this self-facilitated exercise (see page 91). Take a moment to just look at it and let the impact of the pattern you see settle in you again.

If and when you feel ready, reflect on all you've learnt by reading this book and by exploring and practising with others, and facilitate a movement or sentence that turns the heat up on the underlying dynamic. Just see what impact that has on the other places by making physical contact with the representative for yourself, and then for the other elements you have in the constellation. Work with what emerges.

Now consider what resources you may require to start to move this situation to a better place; towards a resolution. Find a place for them. Facilitate your own system with all that you have learnt – movement, sentences, perhaps even a ritual if you are working with floor markers. Find the best possible relationship between each element, giving each its place.

Now, having identified the resources available within your family-of-origin system choose and place a representative for them, in relationship to your own representative, in a place that feels resourcing. Notice what impact this has; the influence it has on your working relationships and your work as a coach.

Conclude in a way that's appropriate, perhaps with a sentence, spoken out loud, that captures the essence of the final picture. A sentence of resolution, or of action if that's more appropriate. A sentence that settles, realigns and provides energy and clarity to the system and so to you.

APPENDIX
Resources and further reading

Online

By the author

- For trainings that bring the stance, principles and practices described in this book to life, facilitated by the author and his colleagues together with resources for systemic coaching, please explore: **www.coachingconstellations.com**

- Constellation workshops for leaders, designed to support the flow of leadership and organizational health, facilitated by the author: **www.businessconstellations.com**

- For coaches considering buying the wooden figures shown on one of the photographs in this book and created by the Coaching Constellations team please explore here: **www.coachingconstellations.com/resources**

- To better understand limiting dynamics that may be influencing challenges in your life, in intimate relationships and work you are welcome to visit this site by the author: **www.lifeloveleadership.com**

By others

- For information and workshops by Bert Hellinger: **www.hellinger.com**

- For coaches considering buying the grey blocks or Playmobil figures seen in some of the photographs in this book, along with many other books on systemic themes, please explore the website of German publisher Carl Auer. Click on the graphic titled 'Aufstellungsfiguren' for the figures: **www.carl-auer.de**

- A resource and information site in four languages with links to many other international practitioners worldwide. Explore under 'Links/ Countries' on this page: **www.talentmanager.pt**

- For in-depth reading on the principles and applications of this approach in multiple contexts subscribe to the quarterly systemic magazine *The Knowing Field* through this site: **www.theknowingfield.co.uk**

Offline

Because this work is best learnt through experience, the most effective way to learn more about it is to experience and practise it. Building your understanding of the natural forces that underpin systems whilst experiencing them in action is a combination that leads to insight and understanding.

The following mix of learning styles and environments is offered as a suggested starting point.

Workshop attendance

Consider attending a number of workshops facilitated by a range of facilitators to build your understanding and experience as many ways of working with constellations as possible. The experience of being a representative and of processing your own issues is one of the most effective ways of learning.

Training

Consider attending a training in the Essentials of Systemic Coaching and Constellations. In combination with this book and practice with your clients, this is the most effective way to learn how to apply this method in one-to-one and team coaching and organizational development.
www.coachingconstellations.com

Systemic supervision

Consider attending a systemic coaching supervision group or getting one-to-one supervision with an experienced systemic coach, mentor and experienced constellations facilitator. Alongside reading and training this is an effective way to learn and grow your embodied understanding of systems.

Recommended reading

There are a growing number of books that explain and explore the principles and practices underpinning this work. The following are suggested as useful reading material that will both broaden and deepen your understanding of systems and systemic constellations. I recommend the books that are *not* about the application in coaching just as strongly as those that are. This work originated in family systems and an understanding of its origins in that context has proven to be of great use to the many students of this approach who coach in contemporary organizations.

Books about organizational and business systems

Praxis der Organisationsaufstellungen
Gunthard Weber's fully revised book on organizational constellations and systemic coaching, available in German and as an e-book in English. This book includes contributions from Claude Rosselet, Judith Hemming, Albrecht Mahr and many other international facilitators and teachers, offering a breadth of practical examples across many contexts.

Invisible Dynamics
By Klaus P Horn and Regine Brick, Carl-Auer Publishing
This book was one of the first available in the early days of this approach and it contains much wisdom and many useful case studies. Written with leaders of industry, government, health and education in mind, it's a great reference point and includes a useful reminder that all behaviour makes sense when seen in context of the system in which it belongs.

Fields of Connection
By Jan Jacob Stam, The Northern Light Publishing
This book, written by one of the first generation of international organizational practitioners and teachers, describes many examples drawn from Jan Jacob's experience in organizations across the world. He describes the underpinning principles and brings their application to life in his typically insightful and creative way. Jan Jacob and his wife Bibi established and lead the Bert Hellinger Institute of The Netherlands.

Miracle, Solution and System
By Insa Sparrer, Solution Books
This book provides a comprehensive description of 'structural constellations' and 'solutions-focused therapy'. Insa Sparrer and her partner Matthias Varga von Kibéd have pioneered a great deal of work in this area, becoming experts in this particular development of constellations in multiple systems.

Unraveling Branding Systems
By Wim Jurg, The Northern Light Publishing
This focuses on the perceived usefulness of branding constellations. A comprehensive and in-depth review of this specialist area as developed by Wim Jurg is provided.

Books about family systems and personal issues

Acknowledging What Is
By Bert Hellinger and Gabriele ten Hövel, Zeig, Tucker & Co. Inc
I recommend this book to all students of this work because it expresses with real clarity many of Hellinger's key insights, as well as the methodology itself. The book is a lively interview with Hellinger in which Gabriele challenges him, with her journalistic scepticism, on the fundamentals of this approach. His answers are as challenging and insightful as they are refreshing and illuminating.

I Carry Your Heart in My Heart
Dan Booth Cohen, Carl-Auer Publishing
This book is about the application of this work in prisons in Boston. The 'clients' that Dan works with are serving life sentences. The compelling descriptions of their lives, and family systems they come from and the interventions offered are powerful and evocative. The second part of this book describes the constellation process and provides a rich resource on the evolution of this approach.

In the Presence of Many
By Vivian Broughton, Green Balloon Publishing
This useful book includes descriptions of the underlying principles and practices, many of which are directly relevant to application in personal and executive coaching. If you want to get a good understanding of the application and development of this approach in a personal setting, then this book will serve you well.

Family Constellations
By Joy Manne, North Atlantic Books
This short but skilfully expressed little book describes the approach to family system therapy through Joy's own practice as a therapist and her educational experiences with Hellinger. When not working in her Swiss home base, Joy teaches internationally in family constellations and relational intelligence.

Trauma, Bonding and Family Constellations
By Franz Rupert, Green Balloon Publishing
A comprehensive and very readable book, which covers this huge subject with great skill. This is another of the family system books that I encourage coaches to read, as it describes so many of the underlying principles and practices that underpin this approach.

POSTSCRIPT
Outside in inside out

Over the last few years I've become fascinated with what we can do as coaches to create the conditions for organizational health to emerge. Of course systemic coaching and constellations can make a very significant contribution in this area. But that is still an intervention, done by others, coaches and facilitators. Outside in.

Shouldn't health emerge from within?

My sense is that it's the organizational leaders, those within the system, that should hold the knowledge of how systems work. Take that idea a step further and I think that one of our aims as coaches should be to put ourselves out of a job. That would be the natural result of a successful shift from outside knowledge and intervention to inside knowledge and systemic leadership. Inside out.

This would require leaders, not just coaches, to adopt a systemic stance, to understand the impact of belonging, hidden dynamics and their family-of-origin. It would require leaders to recruit, manage and lead change with the system in mind, to take responsibility for the whole. This will only happen when there is a general wider interest in the hidden drivers of organizational health.

The shift from the hero leader to a collective sense of responsibility for the system has only just begun, despite protestations about progress. People still try and impose values, when they must know that values emerge as a result of the leadership behaviours and relationship-system dynamics. People still believe that their intelligence and authority are greater than the system and so lead from their ego. And they still recruit and dismiss people as though this has no impact on them or those that remain.

It seems to me there is a great deal of support for rational, linear and intellectual ways of looking and knowing in the field of leadership and indeed whole organizational development. There is less support for working in ways that harness our 'other ways' of knowing, beyond the rational, beyond the head and the ego.

While hundreds, possibly thousands of coaches are now facilitating constellations in individual coaching and team workshops it's only a beginning. Constellations are useful, really useful, and we need to find more and better ways of allowing their benefits to be experienced within the systems we work with. But we need to do more, to find other ways of educating executive leaders and young managers about the foundations of systemic organizational health, to support them in seeing and working with the systemic perspective, stance and methodologies.

If outside in really could become inside out it would transform organizational life and positively impact millions of people in and around them. The knowledge could then pass into the family systems of employees acting as a catalyst for flow in those systems as well.

This way of working is now evolving and my focus is moving with it, looking at and working with systems in a more proactive way. In other words rather than only using systemic constellations to illuminate and resolve stuckness, release entanglements and dissolve hidden limiting dynamics, how can we harness their profound power to design the future? How can we support the creation of new healthy organizational systems and to catalyse the emergence of enduring health in existing systems? And do this in a way that leaves the insights and knowledge in the system, so they can take care of themselves.

If I write another book that is what it will attempt to do, to introduce this way of thinking, this way of being and the methodology of constellations into the day-to-day lives of managers and leaders. So that organizational health emerges as a result of an understanding, acceptance and integration of the organizing forces of systems.

It will be quite a journey. Perhaps you will join me?

Meanwhile I wish you very well on yours.

John Whittington, 2016

www.businessconstellations.com
Constellation workshops for leaders

www.coachingconstellations.com
Constellations training for coaches